An End to al-Qaeda

An End to
al-Qaeda

*Destroying bin Laden's Jihad and
Restoring America's Honor*

MALCOLM
NANCE

St. Martin's Press
NEW YORK

Design by Fritz Metsch

ISBN 978-0-312-59249-3

Dedicated to:
"The Young Jedi"
Mohammad Salman Hamadani

Contents

PART IV
COUP LANCÉ: ENDING AL-QAEDA

Introduction

ANY GIVEN TUESDAY in Iraq would be a good day to put an end to al-Qaeda. I thought this to myself as I sweated in a backseat of a white Mitsubishi Gallant sedan. It was a thought interspersed with wondering if today would be the day I would die. Working in Baghdad in 2004 with the American-led coalition was listed under the dictionary headings of "insane" and "lethal." Being exposed on Baghdad's streets required skill, alacrity, and an unshakable belief in a higher power—in my case that was the M-4 carbine and fragmentation grenades. Weaving through the raindrops of chaos of Baghdad was like playing dice with the angel of death. Unfortunately, they were his dice.

Exiting a safe house in the Mansour district meant accepting that you quite possibly were heading to your doom. Questions abounded before one ever considered starting one of these high-speed trips through the Mesopotamian Hades. Would we run into an insurgent checkpoint and be forced to gun it out with my eight-man Iraqi security team? This thought made me double-check my weapon. It would be ready to fire fully automatically if needed. I hefted the assault rifle to my shoulder and practiced a quick snap shot through its illuminated optics.

Would we turn into a blocked street and run into an American Bradley Infantry Fighting Vehicle? Knowing the soldiers, if they saw or suspected one weapon on board they would mistake us for terrorists and vaporize us in a pink mist of 25 mm cannon shells. Hundreds of Iraqi civilians had died this way, and Central Command was indifferent to the results unless an American Bradley was lost. I checked the infrared Day-Glo pink "Don't shoot" placard on the passenger's visor. It was emblazoned with the American flag and our call sign, "KNIFE-01." Another question posed itself: were we already under surveillance and would we drive right into an al-Qaeda or criminal kidnapper ambush outside of our gates? Anyone could perform that job. Al-Qaeda in Iraq; the Sunnah insurgents; the Shiite death squads, real or fake; the Iraqi Ministry of the Interior police commando; or even our own Shahwanis, the CIA-backed Iraqi Intelligence Service and Special Forces. It didn't matter; anyone who attempted to stop us without a Bradley would be shot first, quickly, and with accurate sustained fire until we were safely away or dead. The luxury of determining friend or foe was not one that we could ever afford.

I asked my three Iraqi operatives to do a quick contact drill before we left the driveway. On the shout of *"Contact left"* the driver would look for an escape route and the left rear gunner would spray his clunky squad automatic weapon across a wide arc of the left side of the vehicle as I and the rear passenger would disembark and engage over the hood and trunk. It took a few seconds and it pushed the adrenaline up. We were ready to leave the front house.

It was my tenth month in Iraq and moving any distance over a quarter mile required using our armored BMW or Chevy Suburban. Today we were going low profile. We drove an unarmored Mitsubishi with a BMW 750 chase car. We were trying to look like normal Iraqis. My black leather coat was typical for an Iraqi winter. We wore them two sizes larger to hide the heavy Level IV body armor. The massive bulge made by two rows of ammunition for my M-4 assault rifle and the bulk of night vision goggles, trauma kit, dual multichannel radios, and four fragmentation grenades was arrayed along my waist. My carbine lay flat across my lap, out of sight. My tan gloves had my name stitched in. I took the habit of labeling my body parts with my name so if my body was blown apart by a suicide bomber I could be repieced by matching the name on the gloves, helmet, clothes, and boots. It might give my wife some comfort to know I was almost in one piece. A helmet was set between my feet and my right and left thighs carried a pistol, a folding knife, red and purple smoke grenades, and extra rifle ammunition. From the neck up, I looked like just another dark Zubayri, a southern Iraqi of African descent, riding around with his Shiite friends in West Baghdad. From the neck down I bristled like a lethal porcupine. I was committed to not be the next al-Qaeda beheading video star.

On this trip to the relatively safe Karradah district of Baghdad I pondered a series of questions the intelligence community were informally kicking back and forth in Iraq: How do you remove the base of support from a group that prides itself on fanatical Islamic piety and love of death?

How does one remove the underlying religious buy-in? Can it be purchased? No, that wasn't working for anyone. Iraqi Ba'athists can be bought; al-Qaeda jihadists cannot.

Yet this war for the hearts and minds of the Muslim world was not a street battle where a single bullet could decide the matter. It was clear that the campaign to short-circuit al-Qaeda had to be a strategic battle where their very ideas had to be contested in public. Yet how do we show the truth about a terrorist organization in the middle of our years-long effort to destroy the historic Islamic capital of Caliph Haroun al-Rashid? This was the city of Islamic science, literature, and literally, the heart of the Islamic classic *A Thousand and One Arabian Nights*. America was setting any chance of retribution for the perpetrators of 9/11 back a decade by coming to Iraq. AQ capitalized on this folly and tried to kill me in the bargain.

I love Islam and the Islamic world. Many times had I wondered if I believed enough to take the Shahada, or Witness, into my heart. As I had been raised as a Christian it would not be a great leap in faith, since adherents to both religions, as well as Judaism, are considered Abraham's children. That moment never came, but like Sir Richard Burton, the great British Arabist, I came to understand Islam as being a logical and spiritually satisfying religion. Half of my siblings are Muslims and proud Americans.

I had worked in the Islamic world for so long and was treated like a brother so many times that I feared for it as soon as I saw the 9/11 attacks. Now I was hunting men who were, as far as my understanding of Islam went were no longer Muslims. The word to describe them is obvious . . . al-Qaeda were outsiders, Khawarij—just like the seventh-century murderous cultists. AQ is a cult.

I mentioned the concept to my best friend, sitting in the rear passenger seat, Ali Hassan. Ali was a Shiite and agreed that AQ was a different type of Sunnah. He laughed and said, "Mr. Malcolm, maybe they are worshiping Shaytan in them's sleep?" We laughed. No? He then volunteered, "Chief, perhaps they are having sexes with them jinn!? You know them Wahab ones, man. *They are crazy!*" We laughed harder and let it go. The mission had to start.

One English word, "Rolling," was spoken on the radio and convoy mission 117, call sign SINDBAD-06, shot out of the front gates, turned into traffic, and blended into the dusty streets. We got exactly five hundred meters away before the suicide car bomb blew up down the block. *Contact front!* All cars tried to reverse at high speed and circled at a safe intersection. Debris started to fall on us, striking the hoods of our cars. Everyone dismounted and awaited a small-arms attack, weapons up—ready to counter-assault and take lives. Ali Farhan, our Iraqi Brad Pitt and well-known soccer star, arced the Squad Automatic Weapon back and forth seeking targets—no man was ready to kill like the nineteen-year-old Ali Farhan. The attack was over—no follow-up was expected and we moved out of the street. We cautiously moved forward toward the burning wreckage of six cars and a demolished house. We could see from the twisted burning metal that no one in it or nearby had survived. The target was one of my neighbors, Iraqi Prime Minister Ayad Allawi. The Prime Minister's Green Zone–bound convoy had been missed by the bomber, but eight other neighbors were killed. Their families saw our group was armed and associated with the Americans. First they begged us to check one body and then the next and to give aid to the wounded. We did this without question. Then, in panic, they screamed at us the way only a person in mortal terror and pain can. The wails were unbearable . . . the dead were recovered, so we left. But AQ was not finished. As if they wanted to send me a token of their commitment, I found the discolored torso and spine of the bomber at my feet.

It was long before 2003 that the flaws in the ideological basis of what was being called militant Islam were being argued. My introduction to radical religious extremism came in high school. The 1979 Iranian revolution, which I watched unfold on television, had just ended. When I looked at this, combined with the European terrorists of the 1970s such as the Irish Republican Army, the Red Army Faction, Action Direct, and the Combative Communist Cells and the Palestinian Liberation Organization's Munich Olympic murderers, I was desperate to understand why men behaved this way. This gave me an early and deep historical interest in terrorism and the history of counterterrorism and counter-insurgency. I then entered military service and joined Naval Intelligence. I completed nearly two years of education in Arabic and training in collection operations in time to take part in one of the first major underestimations of America's response to terrorism. When I arrived in the field in early 1983, I saw how information immediately impacted Middle East policy. As an intelligence operator I could watch how information went straight to the heart of foreign policy decision makers and could be used or ignored. Documents or reports we generated or advice from our lips could result in aircraft being shot down, ships being sunk, oil platforms set afire, and nations relentlessly savaged.

I learned firsthand that intelligence is power and all powers have an ideology that guides them. Good intelligence with the wrong ideological world-view is dangerous. My first tour of duty was in early 1983. I arrived in Beirut, Lebanon, with the U.S. Marine Expeditionary Force a few months after graduating from the Defense Language Institute. I was just in time to experience America's first lessons in suicide terrorism. Within a week of my arrival the American embassy was destroyed by a suicide car bomber, or, as it is now called, a Suicide Vehicle Borne Improvised Explosive Device (SVBIED). The attack not only struck at America's presence in Lebanon, but it also killed virtually all of the intelligence community's field officers. For months all local intelligence collection fell on the navy and marine units. With only five of us who could speak Levantine Arabic, the local dialect, collection became a daunting task. Our knowledge of Lebanon's confessional extremism was adequate, but the phenomenon of Islamic fanaticism using suicide tactics was new and few of us had even a clue as to how truly motivated the terrorists were. Incredibly, the first suicide bomb attack did not prepare us for a second. In October of that year the Iranian-backed Shiite militia, Hezbollah, attacked using their Islamic Jihad Organization terrorist arm. They blew up the U.S. Marines barracks at the airport with a massive suicide truck bomb. Two hundred and forty-three marines and sailors would die that day along with fifty-eight French paratroopers when their headquarters was struck as well. Horribly, this was just the beginning of my education in the school of political violence by suicide bomber. I spent most of my time in the field; I was on ships, submarines, or land. I traveled to almost every Muslim country and half of sub-Saharan Africa hunting and targeting information on terrorist organizations, their operations, and their state sponsors. My destiny was to witness a litany of human cruelty, from skyjacked passengers being shot in the head and dumped on cold tarmacs to the beheaded bodies of hostages being delivered to families who could not pay ransoms or meet impossible demands. All supposedly in the name of a select God or from a peculiar political bent.

It was in 1993 that I had my first encounter with what would soon be known as Tanzim al-Qaeda. While working in the Balkans during the Bosnian war the militants from Saudi Arabia, Algeria, Egypt, and Pakistan were popping up where they were not expected, particularly in Albania, Macedonia, and Bosnia. After the first World Trade Center attack the pace of militant cross-pollination picked up and it became clear we had a burgeoning global religious extremist terror problem. Algeria descended into religious civil war, where fundamentalist militants slit the throats of more than one hundred thousand civilians. The First Chechnya War, which began in 1994, gave an operational battlefield even more of these extremists, who started to propagate their "courage" though video disks with grisly throat slittings and beheadings of captured Russian soldiers. This form of organized militancy was on the rise, coordinating worldwide and operating well above the radar. In rapid succession there would be suicide and truck bomb attacks on the Saudi National Guard headquarters and the U.S. Air Force barracks at Khobar Towers. Though all of this activity was from a wide variety of groups in wide-ranging geographic regions, it was inspired ideologically by the man who would become their de facto leader, Osama bin Laden.

Many have said that the first Clinton administration had little interest in al-Qaeda immediately after bin Laden declared war on the United States in a public statement. That is patently false. Within a month of his declaration of war on America, I was at the U.S. Navy Survival, Evasion, Resistance and Escape (SERE) School in Coronado, California. We prepared Special Forces soldiers for operations at close proximity to AQ's Islamic extremist terrorists. We created the Advanced Terrorism, Abduction and Hostage Survival School (ATAHS), where Special Forces soldiers, Navy SEAL, and students from other government agencies were taught to survive work at close quarters with al-Qaeda. There I began leading a simulated al-Qaeda terror cell. These covert operators would be taught AQ's strategy, tactics, and ideology so that they knew it better than the terrorists themselves. The first ATAHS class formed on the same day as the 1998 Kenyan and Tanzanian bombings, and within days our students graduated and headed straight out to what writer Steve Coll called the Ghost War.

During this program the staff detailed the strategic vision of bin Laden's variant of Islam. It was clear from the start that his beliefs about Islam were wildly at odds with those practiced for centuries. The AQ's claims to validation and justifications for murder were directly in conflict with the words of the Prophet Mohammed.

It was the morning of September 11, 2001, when my ultimate lesson in how AQ corrupted Islam was revealed. I had just witnessed the New York attacks and drove right into the Pentagon attack. I had left Capitol Hill and was sitting in my car on Independence Avenue next to the Lincoln Memorial when I eyewitnessed American Airlines Flight 77 flying in from the west, passing by the Sheraton next to Arlington Cemetery, and gliding directly into the side of the Pentagon. I realized we were under a nationwide attack. I frantically drove to the site and assisted hundreds of others in the rescue effort in the burning halls of the E-ring and at the helicopter pad. While I worked I was well aware of who had performed this attack and why. This was revenge from al-Qaeda for the 1998 cruise missile attack on their terrorist training center at Zawar Kili al-Badr. They took an airliner and turned it into a human-filled cruise missile. At the end of that day I was sure that there was one man in Afghanistan who, in a bankrupt corruption of Islam, had ordered nineteen young men to commit suicide—an act expressly forbidden in Islam—and burn alive three thousand innocent men, women, and children. In the following eight years his attack would lead to the deaths of over one hundred thousand others, 97 percent of them fellow Muslims.

The Islamic world is not a homogenous society. Political opinions and cultural practices vary wildly from one country to the next, one city to the next, and one neighborhood to the next. The bond that is consistent throughout the Muslim world, known in Arabic as the Ummah, is the proper practice of Islam and a belief in monotheism and devotion to God (Allah).

Religion aside, the world Muslim community was as normal as any American small town. They only wanted to have an opportunity to prosper, live in peace, worship freely, and, most of all, see their children grow up to have a better life. The Muslim dream is the American dream. This dream needs to be nurtured.

An End to al-Qaeda

ISLAM HAS BEEN in a constant struggle for equality and respect since its inception. In a single day, Osama bin Laden unraveled nearly all tolerance for the Muslim world gained over fourteen centuries. They are a community largely innocent of complicity in the acts of one or a few terrorists who happen to be Muslim. As the Indian Muslim journalist and scholar M. J. Akbar famously said, "You cannot hold Islam accountable for the bad acts of a few Muslims, just as we cannot hold all of Christianity responsible for Hitler, who was a Christian, and the Holocaust."

Since the death of the Prophet Mohammed, Islam has been met with suspicion and hostility, particularly from Christianity and more recently since the formation of the nation of Israel. Bin Laden feeds on these suspicions. He relies on them to meet his goals. Today, in justifying the mass murder of Muslims, Jews, and Christians, he claims fourteen centuries of Islamic tradition as null and void. He claims genocide is beautiful to the eyes of God. Bin Laden even bizarrely alleges that the Qur'an allows him to carry out God's judgments by his own hand. He asserts that he and his lieutenants have the power to elevate murder and suicide into deaths that please God. How could they possibly know? These two examples should be reason enough to call them what they are: heretics.

In Islam only God can make the ultimate judgment about the final disposition of OBL and his terrorist allies. Bin Laden and his believers, for all of their claimed scholarship, apparently cannot distinguish the true meaning of Islam from the direct commands of Satan.

Is there a terrestrial way to put Islam back on its natural orbit and to reject the hatred of a man and his blind legions? Yes. The West, working directly with the Islamic world, can come to a new understanding about who and what the threat really is all about. Using simple counter-ideological tools of compassion and debate I believe al-Qaeda can be damaged to the point of complete incapacitation in less than twenty-four months.

Is another debate really necessary? We have debated whether Islam is evil and whether bin Laden is evil. The real debate is whether this new confession, which many experts call bin Ladenism, is a misguided Islam based on love of God or just a cult based on a single man's desire to create his own earthly nation. That debate itself could cripple the organization, because the one thing AQ detests is having to justify or argue the validity of their actions. How will ending al-Qaeda work? Well, it will take more than guns, bombs, and helicopter rides. It will take a global strategic counter-ideology and counter-terrorism campaign that is executed with commitment, coordination, and lethality. AQ's bin Ladenism must be attacked with the intent to abolish his ideas. For those who are Muslims the realization that bin Ladenism is an extremely bizarre heresy to Islamic practice must come through.

The demise of the world's most prolific terrorist group has been denied for over twenty years, and the attempt to destroy them with arms has been nearly a decade-long failure. If we take the steps proposed in this book, the death of al-Qaeda could come so unexpectedly it would stun those long used to hearing the name.

Why will it work this time? First, the myriad of American military, intelligence, and legal methods for dealing with al-Qaeda are no longer in the hands of incompetent ideologues who favored putting thoughtless amounts of bullets downrange over carefully guiding a counter-terror plan to deny the enemy a base of support. That error has cost us the lives of more than fifty-five hundred American soldiers and tens of thousands of civilians. It was an unnecessary loss. Second, al-Qaeda is in fact already bankrupt both morally and ideologically. The missing component is the broad-scale discussion of the truth of al-Qaeda and fostering a public rejection within Islam. Members of AQ have a loving and forgiving community, but that community is not aware of al-Qaeda's true goals. This book will help the global community come to terms with a massive potential heresy that could dissolve the last strands of sympathy for Osama bin Laden and his followers.

The fortunes of most terrorist groups have waxed and waned depending on the intensity of counter-insurgency and political or religious counter-ideological warfare, yet they all fail miserably when they lose public support. For example, al-Qaeda in Iraq, which received the bulk of global attention as the central enemy in the Bush War on Terrorism, is now critically damaged. This devolution occurred in less than one year because their sponsors, the Sunnah insurgents, suddenly saw them as a greater threat than the U.S. Army. Al-Qaeda forced marriages into Sunnah families and attempted to impose Sharia law and their extremist interpretation of Islam and to carve out a piece of their community as the Islamic Emirate of Iraq. It was too much for the former regime loyalists-turned-insurgents to endure, and they turned on al-Qaeda, first with their own weapons and then by inviting the Americans to help kill AQ. By early 2009 AQI was all but completely destroyed, principally at the hands of other Muslims.

Post 9/11, AQ central commanders reconstituted in the sanctuary of western Pakistan. Aligned with the Pakistani Taliban, AQ is gaining political allies in hopes of destabilizing that nation and working with its allies to secure nuclear weapons. Our emphasis on the killing portion of the game is simple but cannot effect a victory without defeat of the ideology that buoys the terrorist's motivation for combat. To paraphrase Mao, as every potential terrorist is like a fish in the ocean, the ideological buy-in of a religious justification for bin Laden's jihad by the Islamic world is their water. In this instance where the ocean cannot be drained of water, we can certainly introduce a virus to kill this specific species' habitat.

The leadership of AQ is not unaware of their vulnerabilities. Al-Qaeda terrorists themselves have contributed directly to the debate about how to destroy their own base of support. In 2007 Abu Yahya al-Libi, an al-Qaeda commander and Islamic scholar, was so sure of American failure in countering al-Qaeda's ideological dominance that he delineated six key steps to break the link between his group and Islam. Those steps, which have been explored by scholars and counter-terrorism practitioners alike, have been detailed in this book. For nearly two years the deputy of bin Laden, Dr. Ayman al-Zawahiri, has been locked in a very fractious, raucous public debate with the main theologian of his Egyptian Islamic Jihad organization, Sayyid Imam abd-al-Aziz al-Sharif. Mr. Imam has sparked an ideological war of such ferocity that al-Zawahiri has had to release several audiotapes or letters to counter the charges that al-Qaeda is a cultlike corruption of Islam. No matter the source, it is apparent that the same conclusion about the group's vulnerability is being reached—if we break AQ's spiritual link to the Muslim community they will be quickly defeated.

I concur with Mr. Imam and Mr. al-Libi. Breaking the link to Islam is the principal goal to defeat al-Qaedaism from spreading and flourishing. The dismantling and isolation of AQ needs to start with a globally organized campaign for a massive counter-ideology movement.

Circuit Breaker

IN THIS BOOK I have consolidated such a strategy into a campaign called CIR-CUIT BREAKER. The CIRCUIT BREAKER strategy relies on inciting an ideological backlash against al-Qaeda and other religious militant groups acting throughout the Muslim world. The greatest weakness of AQ's religious militant ideology is vulnerability to any deep analytical dissection of their religious motives.

In addition, any successful strategy must identify the core organizations and personalities that have corrupted Islam and ask whether they are sanctioned or are illegitimate cults and cultists with traits such as al-Qaeda exhibits.

CIRCUIT BREAKER can provide the platform to spread the message that a new era for reconciliation and cooperation with the Muslim street has arrived: the United States and its values are no threat to Islam or to their culture. Our enemy is the cult of al-Qaeda and their spiritual followers. President Obama has already taken those first steps of the campaign. This is a message the world needs to hear daily, loudly, and clearly. In the war of ideas, al-Qaeda and their viral messengers need to be shouted down.

America needs to reengage al-Qaeda using a strategy such as this as its principal weapon. With AQ ideologically under attack we can strengthen our intelligence and military ability to hunt and neutralize this group, once and for all.

In addition, I will stress that America and the world need to surrender their unfounded fears of the ubiquitous terrorist bogeyman. The reach and effects of terrorism have been blown out of proportion since 9/11. With the Obama administration taking charge of a newly energized foreign policy,

America and the world have a second chance to eliminate al-Qaeda. If we lose it, there may not be another. The ideology and movement of "bin Laden-ism" is at a crossroads and if left unchecked could become widespread in the Middle East. With a decade of blundering as its catalyst, its strength must be sapped at once.

This book was the result of an intensive effort to collect and analyze unclassified public information related to al-Qaeda and the global counterterrorism effort. No classified information has been used or sourced in this book. Every attempt has been made to use open-source, independently collected data and corroborate it with public individuals or materials. Much of this work is based on official reports from the United States government, foreign governments, academic studies, news media transcripts, attributed works of independent journalists, and analysis of al-Qaeda documents, videos, magazines, and communiqués. This book was literally written over the past four years on the streets of Washington, London, Cairo, Casablanca, Lahore, Abu Dhabi, Peshawar, Dubai, Baghdad, Basra, Mumbai, and Hudson, New York. In the course of its conceptualization a half-dozen friends and associates, both Muslim and Christian, lost their lives either as victims of AQ attacks or combatants in the two wars against them. Most of these friends and associates were direct contributors to this book. I pray that God gives them solace. I also pray that they will be among those who can sit in Paradise and look down upon the members of al-Qaeda who reside in Hell.

How many tens of thousands of others have to suffer and die at the hands of a cult and its leader before the world stands up to actively end their desire to control the destiny of a billion and a half others? We must start the debate within Islam. We must identify al-Qaeda as a cult of death and corrupters of the faithful. We must resolve that they must be stopped—now.

Part I

———

En garde:
A New Mind-set of Terror

1.

From Tragedy to Triumph

We ought not fight them at all, unless we determine
to fight them forever.
—JOHN ADAMS[1]

A Stop for Coffee

ALL I WANTED was a cup of hot coffee. A café latte was being brewed for me at the Cosi coffee shop at the corner of 3rd and Pennsylvania Avenue in Washington, D.C. A few blocks from the U.S. Capitol, I had arrived early to take my newest employee, Beverly, to the offices of the House of Representatives and Senate intelligence committees. It was a clear, warm morning and Beverly was excited to be working for a small anti-terrorism firm in its secretive offices in a Georgetown neighborhood. We had arrived early and had planned to discuss her duties as chief of staff for the small office with its ten employees and interns. The Special Readiness Services International really had one mission and one contract: to analyze and educate the Special Operations Forces in the tactics, techniques, and procedures of the al-Qaeda organization.

It was 8:30 A.M. when the cashier handed me my change and two cups of coffee. The television on a wall near the counter was tuned to CNN that morning. The café had added it for the congressional staffers to watch the votes in the House and the Senate on C-SPAN. Above the din I heard the quiet murmuring of the anchorman, but something was wrong with the words as they reached my ears: ". . . no one knows what kind of aircraft it was that hit the building . . ." These words were all wrong for TV news. I looked at the TV on my right and saw the smoking tower of the World Trade Center complex. The air was clear in New York City—a bright sunny morning with fantastic visibility. How could a small airplane hit that building? Was it a sightseeing helicopter or a light airplane? From the ground view it was hard to know how bad the fire atop the building was.

I said to Beverly, "You know a B-25 hit the Empire State Building in 1945?" We watched for a few minutes and listened to the news announcers speculate on the crash. It seemed like a small disaster until I heard the words "the FAA is reporting an aircraft has been hijacked." That piqued my attention. Just a few months earlier I was a subject matter expert on terrorist hijacking of aircraft. At my last military posting we ran hijacking and terrorism survival courses and simulations as the shadowy terrorist group in Afghanistan, al-Qaeda. It was difficult to hijack an aircraft in the United States, I thought. A moment later I would be proven wrong.

The aircraft came in from the right of the screen and struck the building. That instant I could not speak. I knew who was flying this. My first conscious thought was, *You did it . . . you said you would take it down and you've done it.* I instinctively made one calculated gesture . . . I struck the "5" speed-dial key on my cell phone and called navy Petty Officer Brad Michaels, my former deputy at the SERE's Advanced Terrorism, Abduction and Hostage Survival School in Coronado. Brad was in bed and, after having received excited calls about terrorist attacks from me over the years, he had learned to put the phone on answering machine. The year before it was the USS *Cole* attack at 3:00 A.M. He never forgave me for waking his wife and son. The answering machine came on as the fireball at the WTC tower billowed outward, raining sparkles of flame, debris, and the remains of humanity. I let the machine beep and then screamed into the phone for him to get up. He snatched the phone and asked what was wrong. . . . I could not tell him. I was stunned. All I could do was shout, "CNN! CNN! CNN!"

He held on and a second later shouted back into the phone, "What the hell is happening!"

I told him what I knew the instant the airplane appeared: "It's al-Qaeda . . . it's a restrike of the WTC!"

He hung up and went to his office at the North Island Naval Air Station, where we would call each other in coordination. One of the first things to know about a terrorist attack is that one needs a line of communications, a lifeline far from the incident to maintain perspective and collect intelligence.

Dozens of us stood transfixed at the café watching the macabre spectacle. Minutes later cell phones and beepers went off all around us. The Capitol staffs were simultaneously being recalled to the Hill by the sergeant of arms. The staff members quickly started flowing out of the shop and back up Pennsylvania to the congressional office buildings like great swarms of geese. I told Beverly we needed to move. "Where?" she said. I replied, "New York City, of course. This is the greatest act of terrorism in history and we are going to help."

We drove rapidly down past the Washington Monument. Most of the world had not responded to the attack and tourists were still strolling on the beautiful morning. I put on National Public Radio. They were reporting on the response to the attack in New York City and the reports of hijacked aircraft. I stopped at the intersection of Independence Avenue next to the Lincoln Memorial. As I listened I saw a silver airplane coming from the west over the Sheraton at the Navy Annex. It was descending in a smooth glide path as it passed south of Arlington Cemetery. I casually told Beverly it looked like they were rerouting airplanes away from the Potomac and over northern Virginia. Then the aircraft descended in a line down past the rim of the Pentagon and exploded. As it did, I thought of a navy expression I remembered from a battle I once experienced with an Iranian patrol boat: "Cruise Missile Inbound." The aircraft was a human-guided weapon, and once the flames rolled over the top of the building it created a huge black cloud. Beverly saw it but did not recognize what had happened. "What's that?" she asked calmly.

"We are under attack! A nationwide attack! That's the Pentagon! It just got hit!"

I shot the car forward and spiraled onto Memorial Bridge; within sixty seconds we rolled to a stop in front of a police car a few hundred yards away from the furiously burning Pentagon crash site. I gave Beverly the keys and told her to go back to Georgetown and call me every thirty minutes. She drove off and I ran into the fray, checking victims as they emerged. I ended up following the orders of a feisty army combat nurse who had survived the attack and accidentally found herself thrust into command of the medical evacuation effort at the crash site. Until the northern Virginia fire departments and disaster teams arrived and organized themselves, the few hundred civilians, servicemen and -women, and first responders in a lone ambulance were the rescue party at what we dubbed the Battle of the Pentagon. I spent hours in and out of the building, moving the provisional field hospital we set up and prepared for more victims. Once the fire had consumed the building to the point where a section collapsed, even the fire department had difficulty entering. We then organized the stretcher teams to evacuate the numerous bodies we expected to be found. I received calls from all around the world while working; my former SERE school commanding officer called and wanted a status report for the U.S. Commander of the Naval Fleet in San Diego;

Beverly called to tell me that the WTC complex had collapsed, but I refused to believe it; and Brad called to give me a count of the hijacked aircraft. We were missing one, but a few minutes later we would be informed it had crashed. All the while as I danced with chaos it was clear to me who had perpetrated these attacks. This airplane-turned-suicide-cruise-missile was specific revenge for the 1998 cruise missile attack on a terrorist camp in the Afghanistan-Pakistan mountains, Zawar Kili—the famous al-Badr camp that had been built during the Afghanistan war against the Soviets for the Arab mujahideen. The group running the al-Badr terrorist center was called al-Qaeda and its leader was a radical Saudi Arabian dissident named Osama bin Laden.

Thus begins the story of the vector of an ideological plague. This plague was violently injected into the bloodstream of America by nineteen men who hijacked four airliners and struck deep into the American psyche. Their mission had consumed the hearts of the men who did it and was calculated to consume all of America and poison the well of the 1.5 billion innocent Muslims. I ended that day of days feeling the burning pain in my heart. My family had spent nearly a century defending America, and the massive failure made the pain insufferable. My nation had been attacked. Thousands of innocent civilians were dead. Hundreds of rescuers were engulfed in flame and steel. Now the reckoning must come. The men who had planned this mission had only one option left for them no matter how long it would take. This battle was a blood fight to the death. Bin Laden would die at our hands and quickly. Or so we all thought.

Al-Qaeda's Ideology of Terror Unleashed

BY 2002 AQ's operational terrorist forces in Europe, Africa, the Middle East, and Asia were executing a post-9/11 strategy to keep the pressure on the West and to incite a pan-Islamic jihad. A mania of revenge and fear was permeating America and Europe, and AQ bet that it was as good a time as ever to keep feeding the beast that lashed out wildly at Muslims. Around the world the AQ and their ideological affiliates started to strike regularly in a series of suicide attacks at major cities and tourist destinations. First terrorists in Bali, Indonesia, struck Western tourists and left 202 dead; then the Madrid subway system was devastated, with 191 dead; then attacks in Tunisia, Morocco, Egypt, Saudi Arabia, London, Russia, Mumbai, and Algeria left almost a thousand more littered in their wake. Numerous attempts at suicide bombings were foiled or unsuccessful, including the attempted bombing of an airliner when the AQ convert Richard Reid attempted to detonate explosives in his shoe; attacks on churches in Strasbourg, France, and Paris; and a foiled chemical attack in England. OBL's philosophy of training and inspiring smaller, unaffiliated groups of "self-starting" jihadists was taking root in Europe.

Most surprisingly, in the midst of these pressure tactics the United States was slacking up in its pursuit of the AQ leadership and the Taliban. By August 2002 the Bush administration was preparing an invasion of Iraq, which by the close of 2003 was proving a disaster. While Iraq burned, other resources were being expended in areas that seemed of little value other than to bring more AQ recruits out to fight America worldwide. In 2006 the United States engineered the invasion of Somalia with an Ethiopian Christian army. Because a few members of the coalition government had ties to al-Qaeda, America unwisely and quickly toppled the Islamic Courts Union regime that had brought a measure of calm and stability to the country for the first time in thirteen years. This unleashed the Shabaab terror group. There was also much strong language about attacking the Shiite Muslim regime in Iran. The administration pressed Israel into a disastrous onslaught in Lebanon that killed over one hundred Israeli soldiers and a thousand civilians and destroyed Lebanon's fledgling economy. The loss gave the terrorists sponsoring Hezbollah increased prestige. All of these actions, supported or encouraged by President George W. Bush, created what OBL thought was an ideological backlash that could only support his goals.

Bin Laden was a happy man. He had reason to be. For more than eight years OBL and his Taliban allies were left virtually alone in their sanctuary. The American method of operations was becoming clear on the Afghan-Pakistan border. Where the Americans met Taliban combat forces in the field they pinned them down and then pommeled them with air strikes, but this method inflicted grievous casualties and alienated the very people needed to defeat the guerillas. The Americans were also adopting the Israeli method of selective assassination of key leadership using Predator and Reaper drones and the occasional air strike inside the Federally Administered Tribal Areas (FATA) of Pakistan. On occasion, the Pakistanis would swarm in with a new general in charge, get slaughtered, and cut deals in order to have a chance to lick their wounds.

Afghanistan suffered from a passionate neglect by the Bush administration. Every effort was going into breaking the four wings of the Iraqi insurgency. Afghanistan was left to the North Atlantic Treaty Organization. These forces were relatively small and did not appear to operate well or share intelligence. They appeared to be marking time until America won in Iraq and then could turn its full attention on Afghanistan. This was strategic folly. It gave AQ over seven years to regroup and return to executing its strategic vision to destabilize the nearby enemies of Pakistan and the Middle Eastern nations while striking and punishing the distant enemies of America, Europe, and their allies.

OBL has defied all odds. He has created a physical sanctuary in Pakistan that appears impregnable. More important, he has created a viral new ideology. Some call it al-Qaedaism; I call it bin Ladenism, which, like all good social diseases, spreads fastest by direct contact. The host itself is an invisible carrier and loyal missionary. While the physical war goes on, the war for the hearts of millions of new recruits is being waged on the battlefield of the mind. It is here OBL has held the advantage, and it is here we need to take it away from him.

The safe haven given to al-Qaeda on the Pakistan-Afghanistan border was not what bin Laden expected, but after the rapid disintegration of the Taliban it was just what he needed. OBL had envisaged a rampantly angry American force descending by parachute as they had done in Qandahar early in October 2001. He had spent years preparing his fighting force in the "Islamic Emirate of Afghanistan" to fight the Americans in a ground war similar to that of the Soviets. Bin Laden saw his men in Afghanistan standing up and fighting in the face of the Americans with his Afghan Taliban brothers. AQ had run Taliban training camps, developed terrorist and land warfare curricula, manned anti-aircraft guns, and supported hijackings of an Indian airliner as practice for their mission against America.

The Americans would come, OBL knew. His attack in New York City would ensure it. He did not calculate that he would be pushed into Pakistan so fast, but it did not matter so long as he had his base of support building in the Pakistan FATA. Since 1980 AQ had been cooperating, enriching, and sharing their ideals and ideology with the poor Pakistani tribesmen of the FATA. OBL's men had blood ties, as their local wives were from the provinces; they had wed sisters of foreign fighters to the tribesmen in exchange. It was a model in miniature of what AQ believed was a spiritually based Islamic community made up of *muhajiroun*, emigres, or those who believed that spiritual excellence required them to emigrate away from "unclean" lands and live in one where the laws and people of Islam are unspoiled. In this case that was Afghanistan, until the "Crusaders" came and displaced them into the FATA region of Pakistan.

The most misunderstood portion of the war against AQ is: what does OBL fight for? The answer comes in many forms, most ignorant of both the man and his actions. For seven years I lectured hundreds of diplomats, intelligence officers, special operations soldiers, and common citizens on one simple fact that was lost after 9/11: bin Laden does not want to take over the world, topple America, or impose Islam on non-believers. Even he knows that it is his idealistic vision that could continue to inspire his followers centuries after his death. He has another goal worth fighting for. He wants to re-establish a New Islamic Caliphate (NIC). The last Islamic Caliphate, stewarded by the Ottoman Empire, was ended in 1924 by Mustafa Kemal Atatürk. It was a crushing blow to contemporary Muslim extremists, one of whose goals has always been to revive this pan-Muslim state. OBL relishes the challenge to resurrect the Caliphate. Iraq, until it fell to the traitorous ex-Ba'athist tribes, had given al-Qaida a central emirate from which to spread jihad—that gone, a new nation was being reborn in not just Afghanistan but also a militant Pakistan. For him, the ultimate goal is to fight for and create a New Islamic Caliphate—this one centered in Afghanistan and Pakistan . . . and in possession of nuclear weapons.

A future NIC with Pakistan's atomic weapons at hand could dramatically speed up the process of creating the bin Laden version of a new Islam. For those who cannot join him, the Internet allows them to fight and inspire recruits in all Muslim countries until they can meet up from border to border to border.

By 2006, with the newly motivated Pakistani Taliban at his hand, OBL realized the plan was unfolding altogether differently. Despite the setbacks in Iraq and, more recently, in Pakistan, bin Laden sees the birth of the NIC spreading not from Baghdad, but from his sanctuary, into both Afghanistan to the west and Pakistan to the east.

A Most Dangerous Game: The High Stakes of Failure

AFTER NEARLY A decade of combat in the Middle East, America is confused, exhausted, and losing focus on the stakes of not decisively defeating AQ. There are two sides to the debates. Senior Fellow at the Center for a New American Security Steve Clemons once asked: What is the strategic rationale for continued combat operations in the War on Terror and Afghanistan in particular? Does America's security require it to embark on a multidecade nation-building exercise in this specific nation? Granted, AQ needs to be brought to justice, but at what cost?

In 2007 conservative theorist Frederick W. Kagan claimed that the United States should spend "whatever it takes" on the War on Terrorism. He also felt that the fact that terrorists are regenerating at our expense was inconsequential and would not change their rhetoric. Kagan wrote:

But honestly, the presence of American forces in any numbers in a Muslim land can serve as a recruiting tool. It doesn't matter to the terrorists if there are 160,000 Americans in Iraq or 160—the propaganda about "United States occupation" will be just the same. It does matter if they can claim to have defeated us again.[2]

The boast of defeating America may sound true, except that one can clearly argue that the strategy under people like Kagan has yielded nothing short of increasing terrorism by an order of magnitude.

The tragicomic attitude of the political right was best and most accurately described by a Marine Corps lieutenant colonel turned comic, Rob Riggle. He accurately described the American dilemma in Afghanistan and summarized the Kagan war policy on *The Daily Show*, where he mused:

In 2001, there was a memo—Bin Laden determined to attack United States from a safe haven in Afghanistan . . . Now, seven years and seven hundred billion dollars later, we get a new memo saying bin Laden determined to attack United States from a safe haven somewhere around Afghanistan . . . We are right back where we started. We could have gotten here by doing nothing.[3]

What are the dangers of leaving Afghanistan or the region as a failed state, weak and at the hands of the militants? It is not that we seek a position from which to dominate Central Asia, as AQ contends, or to topple an Islamic regime and impose Western decadence, as the Taliban asserts, or even to control the crossroad of the trans-Afghanistan gas and oil pipeline. We entered this engagement in the pursuit of a criminal mass murderer and the followers of his philosophy. Period. Although we have not conducted ourselves in a way that has honored our grievance and demand for justice, that does not invalidate the true reason we have had to inject ourselves into South Asia and the rest of the Islamic world. In fact, the injustices and errors give us a window of opportunity to offer discussion and redress to those transgressions. All humor aside, the stakes for continued stagnation or inaction are dire. But American treasure could be far better spent reworking the frame in an arena AQ most fear, the war of ideas.

The Challenge

SINCE THE MISSION of countering the perverted ideology of AQ was largely ignored, the spread of its message has permeated a larger portion of the Muslim world in a way that could never have been imagined—particularly since the ill-starred invasion of Iraq. Now America is attempting to contain a fire that is spreading outside of all controls. The stakes of a spread of bin Ladenism are serious and could include:

Potential loss of mainstream political control in Pakistan: The extremists in the FATA/NWFP (North-West Frontier Province) and Baluchistan of Pakistan are generating and exploiting political instability within the nation. The assassination of Benazir Bhutto, a dramatic use of suicide bombings, direct combat with the army, and seizure of whole provinces by armed militants have shown a remarkable downtrend to keeping Pakistan from devolving into a partial failed state. It is this point of instability that the extremists seek in order to propose their method of restoring order as an alternative. In as early as 2006 the Fund for Peace and *Foreign Policy* magazine listed Pakistan as number 9 of the top 10 nations on the Failed States Index. It had a precipitous drop from number 34 in just one year. This poll of 146 nations lists from worst to best for continued viability; regrettably, Afghanistan was number 11.[4]

Destabilization and resurrection of the Taliban in Afghanistan: The sole result that the irreconcilable extremists will accept is the return of the Taliban to absolute religious rule in Afghanistan. The continued armed attacks and suicide bombings are designed to ensure that the government of Afghanistan and NATO cannot offer the security that existed under the Taliban. This contrast in images of the "American-provoked" destabilizing peace and the "Islamic Taliban–style peace" is the entire basis of the message that is offered to the Afghans. In this frame Muslim terrorists are an attractive alternative for the common citizen, especially when compared to the American peace casualties suffered by aerial attacks and no real change on the ground in development or commerce.

Dramatic inroads to mainstream AQ ideology in Islam: Despite the rejection of the tactics of terrorists by the majority of the Muslim world, AQ's ideology of radicalism has been offered as an alternative to regimes that support American policy actions in the Muslim world. The mainstreaming of the Takfiri doctrine (the practice of labeling Muslims as nonbelievers) could never dilute its militancy, as bin Ladenism rejects all moderation in religion. Despite this doctrine's being ruled as heresy by the Muslim religious leaders, OBL seeks to make it a mainstream component of acceptable practice in Islam.

Destabilization of the Kingdom of Saudi Arabia: The arrival of al-Qaeda in the Arabian Peninsula (AQAP) and dramatic terror incidents starting in 2005 in the Kingdom of Saudi Arabia have led to a period of destabilization. However, by 2006 this trend was reversed by a massive Saudi counter-ideology campaign. The results are still out, but the campaign, along with a brutal counter-terrorism campaign, did appear to break the main force behind AQAP and force them to merge with al-Qaeda in Yemen (AQY) in 2009. Should these groups gain power of influence due to a political crisis, such as the Israeli attack on Iran, the radicalization within the Kingdom could become overwhelming for the monarchy.

Political control of the Kingdom of Saudi Arabia and the two holy shrines in Mecca and Medina: The ultimate goal of AQ is political and religious control over the Kingdom. Though it is an extremely remote possibility, if this was achieved they would have religious control over the spiritual destiny of over a billion and a half people. The entire movement of AQ is based on establishing a new Caliphate in which a new era of purity would reign over their variant of Islam. No goal, apart from acquiring the weapons to achieve this, is more important to OBL. It is assumed that this will be a multigenerational effort that will continue well past the death of bin Laden.

Access to a nuclear arsenal: In an effort to gain power, prestige, and influence to intimidate and cause the Kingdom of Saudi Arabia to cede power, the terrorists ultimately need access to the Pakistani nuclear materials. They will work through subterfuge, direct attack, political seizure, or total destabilization and collapse of the state to achieve this goal. Pakistan, which exploded its first nuclear weapon in 1998, is said to have between thirty and fifty bombs of an explosive yield between one and fifteen kilotons.[5] The fathers of the Pakistani nuclear program are alleged to have met with members of the AQ leadership and discussed the construction of nuclear weapons. In Pakistan the infiltration of the military and national security apparatus through religious beliefs is a more serious threat than a direct seizure of the weapons.

Pushback

WITHOUT QUESTION, THE fight against AQ in South Asia and the Middle East is a critical part of American national security. But, no less august person than Gen. David Petraeus, U.S. commander of the Central Command, has noted that

> Afghanistan has, over the years, been known as the graveyard of empires. It is, after all, a country that has never taken kindly to outsiders bent on conquering it. We cannot take that history lightly.[6]

In this vein, American combat-centric operations throughout the Middle East, particularly in Iraq and Afghanistan, have had the unfortunate effect of giving AQ energy, attention, and focus that they desperately need in order to feed off of the anger of the Muslim world.

In 2008 then-senator Barack Obama outlined a five-point strategy to defeat the threat of AQ's terrorism. He said:

> When I am President, we will wage the war that has to be won, with a comprehensive strategy with five elements: getting out of Iraq and on to the right battlefield in Afghanistan and Pakistan; developing the capabilities and partnerships we need to take out the terrorists and the world's most deadly weapons; engaging the world to dry up support for terror and extremism; restoring our values; and securing a more resilient homeland.[7]

It is an ambitious plan that also addresses the reality that a military solution is not always the first, best choice.

I agree that neither military victory nor political stability will come quickly or with costs we can endure unless we adopt a more radical stratagem, only part of which was touched upon by the President's speech. We must execute a civil-military strategy to short-circuit the al-Qaeda ideology and remove their base of support.

I propose in this book a hybrid, asymmetric counter-ideology campaign that will help fulfill the core tenet of the President's five-point plan: "engaging the world to dry up support for terror and extremism." To do this we must learn to accurately define the extremists we seek to disenfranchise and redraw our ideological battle lines and retool in order to defeat our opponents.

This emphasis on removing the base of support, in comparison with continued years-long armed combat, can be achieved relatively simply and inexpensively. Another aspect is that it can also start a dialogue that will benefit America politically, economically, and culturally, if approached with honesty and mutual respect.

Takfiri Hiraba, or terror insurgency on society, the basis of AQ's existence, seeks to destabilize, wear down, and then capitalize on our patience and expenditure of capital. OBL calls it the Long War. This is how OBL sees his insurgency: as a multidecade war. There is no reason for this to be so. The counter-ideology war against AQ need not be so long. There is no utility in playing to bin Laden's time line.

Within the bubble of AQ strategic communications every event in the world can be attributed to the street-level terrorist actions of his followers or directly to their love of God. The Israeli armed incursion in Gaza can be directly avenged by suicide bombers in Afghanistan or Iraq. Anywhere that the link between America and what AQ calls their Zionist enemies can be exploited and turned into a communiqué or video clip furthers their message. I will explore in greater detail how the level of success that OBL seems to enjoy in terms of claiming a direct impact on the U.S. economy was directly enabled for several years by statements from George W. Bush and Dick Cheney. An example is the 2008 economic downturn related to the global housing crisis. Bin Laden takes credit for the meltdown. An attack on the American economy may have been envisioned by OBL as bleeding the West dry, but the 9/11 attacks actually played only a bit part in the retreating American economy. However, to hear AQ describe it they "are continuing this policy in bleeding America to the point of bankruptcy."[8]

Any crisis that is related financially or politically to the Muslim world gives AQ an opportunity to claim their attacks forced America to foolishly expend its capital. Our own propaganda messaging about the impact of 9/11 appears to constantly validate OBL's theories about the weakness of the West to asymmetric attacks. AQ's claims may be dismissed in Western media but they play well in the streets of Peshawar and has a wide following in much of the Muslim world as well. AQ's continuing ability to generate an alternative vision of America must be predicted and countered.

Winning Muslim Hearts and Minds?
Total Mission Failure

THE CORE OF a counter-ideology is the field of strategic communications. Strategic communications are defined as the "processes and efforts to understand and engage key audiences to create, strengthen or preserve conditions favorable to advance national interests and objectives."[9] Strategic communications use a fusion of coordinated information, themes, plans, programs, and actions to project a nation's message and image. Done correctly, strategic communications should be a key component within the nation's soft and hard power structures to defeat opposing ideologies.

Alarmingly, it is this factor, the overt and covert strategic communications strategy of our adversary, that has been nothing short of excellent. Radical extremists have communicated their missions, goals, and clear, easy-to-understand examples of sacrifice and stories of romance to their local and international constituency. Bin Laden realized the vision of creating a radical community of militants and knew how his predecessors such as Hassan al-Banna; Sayyid Qutb; Mohammed Qutb, Sayyid's brother; and Ayman al-Zawahiri had dramatically influenced many young men in the Muslim world. The hearts of these individuals had been infuriated by the political policies and culture of the West. Bin Laden set about using street-level communications popular in Islamic missionary work such as university lectures, public speeches, and cassette tape recordings of speeches and readings. In the mid-1990s, when the Internet was new, many audio clips and voice-over videotaped recordings were converted to digital files and posted publically on Web sites in English, Arabic, and Urdu. Some were extremely popular with international students and adventurers who desired the romantic life of the hard, grizzled Afghan resistance fighter, such as the al-Muhajiroun and Azzam Brigades Web sites.

In contrast, the American strategic communication effort since 9/11 has been an unmitigated failure at nearly every level. Despite the speeches of President Bush and the thousands of TV commentators and retired generals about our success in rolling back al-Qaeda, the missteps started almost immediately and continue to this day. The lack of knowledge about al-Qaeda and their religious-based ideological strategy led President Bush to declare the "War on Terrorism" a new Crusade. The Muslim world was shocked and suspicious of America's true intention, which was clear (to kill bin Laden), but was being couched in terms of dominance over the Muslim world. The Islamic world heard: "Crusaders will kill Muslims." The only one to benefit from this characterization was Osama bin Laden himself. It also became clear early on that the American news media were happy to be the President's mouthpiece for the case against al-Qaeda. In an effort to keep the twenty-four-hour news cycle fed, many accepted the frame of the clash against al-Qaeda being a war on the Muslims. Many pundits and politicians, particularly from the right wing, gave voice to a swelling of anti-Islamic paranoia in the West and started to describe the "war" against AQ as a culture war against Islam. The media often became cheerleaders for the activities of the Bush administration. This gave the global audience a clear impression that what-ever information would emerge from the American media would target the American population with propaganda, not inform the world about facts. This, too, would come to aid bin Laden's efforts.

Why did the Americans' communications effort fail? Because the Bush stra-tegic communications policy was focused like a laser on the American public, who had no problem understanding the gravity of 9/11. But getting the Amer-ican people to understand terror was not the goal. The push behind the poli-cies to influence the nation's message was designed to target changing American laws to benefit the conservative agenda in America, not counter the ideology of bin Laden. By choosing to spend billions on influence operations to change the internal dynamics of American life with the objective of what presidential political advisor Karl Rove called working toward "a permanent Republican majority," the Bush administration effectively surrendered the war of influence in the Muslim world to bin Laden.

Looking at Iraq, a highly unpopular war from the start, virtually all Amer-ican strategic communications efforts were oriented to putting a face of suc-cess on a dramatically failing counter-insurgency. Instead of communicating to the local population a consistent message of localized operations, the De-partment of Defense actually paid out hundreds of millions of dollars to Amer-ican marketing companies to pass that money on to Iraqi journalists for writing articles on American "successes" to be published in their newspapers. To the average Iraqi citizen, these amounted to nothing more than a good laugh at the foolishness of the Americans to believe that an article on a new Halliburton-built schoolhouse opening in Basra would mask the ill will gen-erated by the deaths of dozens or hundreds daily.

The Iraqi public, under fantastic amounts of criminality, bombardment, or murder or racked with sectarian tension, were apparently judged and treated as fools. As far as American policy makers who funded these efforts were concerned, the Iraqis did not seem to know what was good for them. It would take much loss of American blood for the policy makers to realize that effective operations of influence were going to have to start at the street level and with guidance from the White House.

On a positive note, in 2006 the Pentagon expanded and capitalized on the new counter-insurgency doctrine developed by the staff of Gen. David Petraeus. Military Provisional Reconstruction Teams, armed with cash and the ability to make projects happen; army Civil Affairs Teams, working at the street level with tribal leaders; and the Special Operations Psychological Operations Teams with linguistic skills and media distribution systems attempted to fill the distance for the Bush administration between what was being said and what was being done (known as the "Say-Do gap"). It would take a full five years after the war's start before reasonable strategic communications could be judged even marginally effective in Iraq.

Another major error in American influence operations was the way the American army rejected the Vietnam-era concept of "winning the hearts and minds" of the local populations where they were fighting. The Vietnam-era doctrines that could explain what was happening in Iraq and Afghanistan were thrown by the wayside on September 12, 2001. Many people I knew in the military viewed the role of the post-9/11 army as an army of revenge—against not only AQ but the Muslim world in general. Though this can be disputed, it is indisputable that some form of institutional indifference to "collateral damage" contributed to over one hundred thousand dead noncombatants in both Iraq and Afghanistan. Officers coming to Iraq or Afghanistan after 9/11 were tacitly expected to kill "terrorists," not win hearts and minds.

Another often misused term, "Shock and Awe," was informally taken as marching orders in how to behave toward the insurgent supporting population. The massive loss of civilian life through the liberal use of artillery and airpower often brought this effect about at harrowing loss to the locals, who would then be forced to decide between al-Qaeda and America. Combat in Baghdad and Fallujah and a half-dozen air strikes alone in Afghanistan killed hundreds of civilians per event. By 2008, this, too, was wrestled into control by General Petraeus.

"Winning the hearts and minds" of the Muslim world and AQ has been a difficult nut to crack. AQ could always talk about "Crusader savagery," but the evidence was lacking . . . until the offensives on the Iraqi city of Fallujah in 2004. From that point onward the Americans essentially performed AQ's propaganda campaign for them. During the Fallujah offensives the American media snapped up and broadcast triumphant press conferences by beaming American generals who gave highly detailed briefings for the world on their handiwork in destroying homes and mosques and denying any collateral killings of civilians in the face of hundreds of dead bodies of women and children being shown twenty-four hours a day on Al Jazeera. Brutality was one thing, but this brutality wrapped in hypocrisy was another. From November 2004 on, America's own officers showcased a phenomenally huge Say-Do gap when bragging of their ability to kill terrorists, while almost completely ignoring civilian casualties. These press conferences, wholly indifferent to the world's dismay at American effects on local people, did the recruitment work a thousand AQ Internet video clips could not.

In May 2009 alone over 140 men, women, and children were killed in a single Afghan village. These errors give the distinct impression to the Afghan people that American soldiers give lip service to "precautions" against collateral damage. In almost every instance AQ manages to document and distribute more accurate accounts to the local populace. What these actions did better was work to the enemy's message with inadvertent brilliance: America is here to kill you.

In the modern insurgency, it takes just one IED attack, one successful suicide bomber, or even finding weapons in a village that was assumed friendly for a single soldier to perpetrate an act that can destroy the entire image of an army or a nation. Unfortunately, the combat arms aspect of our messaging has been wildly successful. It can be said that once our soldiers have set their minds to killing someone they will bring down enough firepower to make it happen.

It took ten years of bloodletting in Vietnam to realize precisely what was being done wrong. It took five years to implement a rudimentary strategy to reverse losses in Iraq. Only after General Petraeus took over as the U.S. commander of the Central Command did the concept of fighting to help, not to hurt, take root at the level of the foot soldier. However, for the average soldier, there is still great resistance to tolerance and acceptance of other peoples and their cultures. For the soldier on the street the populations of Iraq and Afghanistan are difficult to separate mentally from AQ, just as the soldier in Vietnam had difficulty seeing the difference between the Vietnamese civilians and the Vietcong.

In 2005 the White House saw that even the most basic efforts at strategic communications were failing in attempts to put lipstick on the proverbial pig. The neoconservatives had convinced themselves of the infallibility of their policies. As with all of their actions, they believed that the reason their message of victory, righteousness, and triumph was not propagating must have been a question of loyalty, personality, and technique. President Bush deployed his personal media specialist, Karen Hughes, to the U.S. Department of State, and she became the Under Secretary of State for Public Diplomacy and Public Affairs. Mrs. Hughes was given the unenviable task of explaining why the years of incompetence and neglect were good for a world that was insulted, rejected, and in some cases brutalized by her superiors. The basic awareness of the dictum that foreign policy, not public diplomacy, determines how a nation is viewed was entirely missed during her tenure. This image of America's policies as being entirely the reason the country was distrusted was confirmed by a 2007 Pew poll of the Middle East.[10] For example, American favorable rating among Muslim allies ranked from as low as 13 percent in Turkey to the highest, 31 percent, in Egypt. These are dismal statistics by any measure.

Battlefield of the Soul

AMERICA'S OVERALL FAILURE in influencing the Islamic world should bring to mind a singular question: how can the goal of defusing al-Qaeda's militant ideology be achieved in such a way that it short-circuits the entire base of support for AQ's global insurgency?

On occasion, this question was discussed and addressed by academics and pundits; it has made only small forays into the arena of policy, inevitably lost in the pressing political and military decisions about how many men, women, and bombs must be expended on achieving an acceptable outcome in the fractious series of actions against al-Qaeda around the world.

After the massive expenditures of treasure, blood, and values even the most jaded observer can agree that destroying AQ is not going to be a question of always killing them on the battlefield. We must remove their raison d'être. We must shift our focus to the battlefield of the mind and make them question what will happen to their souls if they continue in armed resistance. This may be achieved by invalidating the link between the armed religious extremists and support from the civilian community. They must be shamed and argued out of existence. The Americans' failure to understand their enemy and isolate them from their recruiting and support base will affect the world for decades to come unless the system of belief in the AQ militant ideology is debated aloud in their own villages. The world needs to hear from within Islam what is and is not acceptable in Islam and it must be heard with American assistance, not resistance.

This a regional crisis that threatens to respawn and, if left unchecked, break out into the rest of the Muslim world. The clash of states and the mission of supporting the governments of Iraq, Afghanistan, and Pakistan must not be allowed to remain within the Muslim world as a one-dimensional military engagement. That is precisely what AQ desires most: the military clash.

Should We Engage the Muslim World Using American Ideology or Discuss al-Qaeda's Ideology in Islam?

IF WE ARE to win the hearts and minds of the Muslim world or facilitate the Muslim world to change its perspective toward AQ, there is at least one key question: should counter-terrorism incorporate any discussion of Islam into the ideological and information warfare sphere?

Dr. Assaf Moghadam of the West Point Combating Terrorism Center believes that the debate of AQ's ideology should not be fought on the grounds of Islam. Writing in the counter-terrorism journal the *CTC Sentinel*, he says:

> Therefore, a counter-terrorism approach that highlights the corruption of Salafi-jihadist ideology not on religious, but on secular, grounds is more likely to have the desired effect of weakening that ideology's appeal. Rather than highlighting the doctrinal and theological inconsistencies among Salafi-jihadists, the United States and its allies should grasp every opportunity to highlight the disastrous consequences that Salafi-jihadist violence has wrought on the everyday lives not only of Westerners, but first and foremost on Muslims themselves.[11]

Dr. Moghadam is correct that the accurate labeling can have grave implications on policy, but limiting the ideological discussion to strictly secular motivations could also hobble a policy maker's knowledge of the basis of the terrorist's ideological center of gravity and depth of commitment of the militant extremists. On a national level the Department of Homeland Security and the National Counterterrorism Center advocated that U.S. government agencies should avoid the usage of Islamic words and debating in terms of religion. These, too, are good recommendations, but it is a fact that for over eight years the United States fielded few representatives in the Middle East media or coordinated a massive national strategic communications strategy to support its message with the assistance of its allies in the Muslim world.

The constituency that OBL seeks and recruits from is multinational, multilingual, multicultural, multiracial, and multitalented. He seeks to unite them under the corrupt ideological banner of one man. AQ's only link to the rest of the Muslim world is their professed love of the same God. They seek to swim invisibly in a sea of people who worship and love God the same way. This belief in a bond of religious understanding gives terrorists tacit leave to act in manners and ways that bring shame and sorrow down upon the Islamic world. That ideological link can be broken. It is high time that we assist the Muslim world in bringing shame and disgrace upon the terrorists and show that the root of Islam is in peace and that Muslims are truly merciful and compassionate people. AQ are men who have gone astray in the path of a murderous criminal who seeks to destroy the youth of the Muslim world one at a time and in ways that are a disgrace to the true meaning of the Qur'an.

Defining al-Qaeda's Terms of Murder and Love of Death

WHEN DISCUSSING THE AQ philosophy it is important to know that words mean a lot more than they appear to mean. The rhetorical words and phrases bandied about in the struggle against radicals and extremists take on great meaning for the combatants. It is very important that we do not validate the words used by AQ and their adherents, because for them that is a small victory and it frames the debate on their terms. Let us look at how they see themselves.

In the global insurgency of extremists and religious radicals of OBL they fly not their nations' flags—those of Egypt, Algeria, Morocco, Lebanon, Libya, Saudi Arabia, Uzbekistan, Qatar, Kazakhstan, China, the UAE, Yemen, Kuwait, Ukraine, Iraq, Kyrgyzstan, Russia, Bosnia, the United States, or Britain—but the flag of al-Qaeda with the Arabic words from the Shahada, or Witness, that read: "There is no God but God and Mohammed is His Messenger." It is the unifying message of all Islam and the same words as on the green flag of Saudi Arabia but written on the black banner, a copy from the era of Prophet Mohammed himself.

The AQ terrorists are unified by four things: First is their often passion-ately professed love of God and equally passionate hatred of all who do not love or believe in God as they love and believe in Him. This is a confession called al-Wala' Wa al-Bara'.

Second, al-Qaeda members are unified by an almost equally ardent and devoted love of their prince of religious warriors (Emir al Mujahideen), Osama bin Laden. In their minds he has shown the clearest and most ac ceptable way to demonstrate love of God and defy God's enemies.

Third, Al-Qaeda members are unified by their status as warriors of God, chosen specifically to effect their murderous deeds. They fervently believe dying while performing God's duty of religious war (jihad) will be bountifully rewarded if they die in the hands of the enemy as a martyr (*shaheed*). They seek the most acceptable and preferred method of *shaheed*—direct face-to-face com-bat with a perceived enemy. They believe it is a guarantee of an express ticket to heaven, Paradise. They desire this death above all things. They are judged by their peers on the basis of their desire to meet God this way.

Fourth and finally, they are unified by unrelenting hatred of all things non-Islamic and make profligate use of declaring all who do not believe as they believe *kufir*, or non-believers. This title they apply with great passion to Muslims who do not follow OBL's path and non-Muslims born into other re-ligions or cultures alike. For this reason, they are not considered true jihadists. They do not fight in a legitimate jihad; therefore, referring to them as jihadists only empowers their corruption of the word. So I will not refer to them as such.

AQ members and followers believe they are empowered to execute a form of declaratory excommunication against Muslims by simply declaring those who do not believe as they believe *kufir*. If you are a non-Muslim, they insist, it is completely acceptable to kill you. If you are a Muslim, it is also completely acceptable to kill you as you have become a non-Muslim simply because their members said so. This ideology of instant excommunication is called Takfir. For the sake of conciseness, I will simply refer to AQ terrorists and supporters of the bin Ladenist ideology as Takfiris or Takfiri terrorists.

The members, ideology, and leadership of AQ and all of their followers and supporters of bin Ladenism are actually outlaws in Islam principally be-cause they practice a deviant form of policies that are referred to as Bid'ah, or "heretical innovation." Bid'ah in Islam is forbidden and Muslims were warned against it by the Prophet Mohammed himself. In that respect, AQ and other bin Ladenist organizations are fighting outside of the laws of Islam as they embrace Bid'ah. For example, within Islamic law there are two classes of illegal combat: Baghy (insurrection/insurgency) and Hiraba (terrorism or war on society). Al-Qaeda and their allies choose to use both in their combat operations. Dr. Abdal Hakim Murad, an Islamic scholar, notes that the AQ insurgents when fighting within Muslim countries and issuing illegal religious rulings called fatwas are committing Baghy, or armed militancy:

> Had the authors of such fatwas followed the norms of their religion, they would have had to acknowledge that no school of traditional Islam allows the targeting of civilians. An insurrectionist who kills non-combatants is guilty of baghy, "armed transgression," a capital offence in Islamic law. A jihad can be proclaimed only by a properly constituted state; anything else is pure vigilantism.[12]

"Vigilantism" is a mild term for the acts of al-Qaeda, and it is for this reason that "jihad" is not an accurate term that should be applied to their actions. Learned Muslims and Islamic scholars do not define bin Laden's jihad as a jihad at all; they call it deviance. Using Hiraba as their principal weapon AQ conducts Baghy. "Hiraba" is defined as "violence carried out by individuals or groups that has the effect of spreading fear, by preventing people from taking any safekeeping measures against physical or property damage."[13]

The best way to break the link between the Muslim world and al-Qaeda is to confront the messaging of the militants' corrupt Hiraba by speaking it aloud: "War for war's sake, death for death's sake, killing for the love of killing, is un-Islamic and the work of Satan, not God." This is the message that the Muslim world needs to incorporate and transmit when discussing the global Takfiri insurgency. Many young men who join the Takfiri insurgency claim that they are coming "for the protection of Islam and the Muslims." We cannot challenge their philosophy by political tactics such as "divide and conqueror." We must adopt a more culturally attuned strategy of "Debate, Translate, Rehabilitate to Eliminate." This strategy is one where the ideology is called out into the public realm, and debated vigorously as to its corruption, allows the Muslim world to translate the true meaning of the Qur'an and rehabilitate those former militants who return to the community.

How Do We Wish to Be Seen

IN A SPEECH by then-senator, now president Barack Obama, he noted that the potential recruits for bin Laden and his allies come from many nations in Asia,

Africa, Europe, and the Middle East. He pointed out that our servicemen and -women, diplomats, aid workers, and visiting citizens see their world often from the back of a helicopter, and asked, ". . . it makes you stop and wonder: when those faces look up at an American helicopter, do they feel hope, or do they feel hate?"

We have within our means the ability to stop the rhetorical hate that many in the world feel emanating from this corruption of a mainstream global religion. Instead of allowing them to spread their virus by glorifying rape, execution, and false words of God, a full airing of how ignorant and dangerous their words are to the true meaning of Islam must be played out on an international stage and they must be called back into the fold or face elimination. This campaign must come from the mouths and efforts of the Muslim mothers, fathers, brothers, sisters, spiritual leaders, and community. The West must seek a leading role in helping re-interpret AQ's terror and offer to help empower the Islamic world to combat it. We must look to defuse the hatred, break the dark grip of the cultlike ideology, and allow a natural rejection of the poison from a man who kills or causes the death of more Muslims than all of his enemies.

2.

Crushed in the Shadows

In the absence of this popular support, the Islamic
mujahed movement would be crushed in the shadows.
—DR. AYMAN AL-ZAWAHIRI

Mass Murder to Please God

THE WOMAN AND the boy were not particularly noticeable at first. The woman had a weather-worn face that carried her forty years well. With her eyes closed she looked almost serene. Afghan women can be unexpectedly attractive behind the burqa, but in this case there was nothing to gauge it by. Her black hair was asunder and clearly not used to being exposed to the air in public. She held no grimace, no look of disapproval except for the small gap in her mouth where the muscles had gone slack after her body bled out. Death gave her a slightly astonished look. She had a right to be astonished. The night before, the armed boys from the Taliban had entered the Afghan village of Dast Mastan in Helmand Province. This lot of young uneducated toughs had Kalashnikov rifles and the walk of men who did not care. Though they could barely read the Qur'an, they held in disdain anyone of less fortune than they.

They forced their way into the woman's house and brought her outside before another armed man they called a *qadi*, or judge of Sharia law. This man was a *qadi* because he was told he was. With this power, passed down from Mullah Omar, the leader of the insurgency, the *qadi* could apply judgment to anyone in his area. The foreign brother, Sheikh bin Laden, had men who assisted in choosing those to exercise their law in this Emirate. The *qadi* was devoid of any scholarship, except what he gleaned from being told by his commanders or how he interpreted among his friends or misread in the Peshawar extremist seminary. Most of the time he learned from what he saw and

heard being performed in front of him. This man was now the human embodiment of Sharia in this few-kilometer area of Helmand Province. He had
been told to identify spies by the foreign members of his unit; Uzbeks, some
Saudi, others Kuwaiti, or, on occasion, British or American—they all knew
how to find spies. A spy was anyone who had a cell phone, money, or relatives
who worked in the government. The foreign mujahideen who came to his
sector had crossed the mountainous region of the Pakistan Afghanistan border
to help him perform jihad against the Americans. They all fought to establish a
new Islamic Emirate on both sides of the border.

The woman was dragged out of her home. The boys rifled though the
small mud house and returned with an old cell phone. The mobile phone was
presented to the armed *qadi*. He looked at it, did not recognize the model, and
declared it a satellite telephone used only by American spies. The cell phone
was like any other, but in the region of the new Islamic Emirate of Afghanistan anything that was not clearly identifiable as useful to the locals was prob-
ably used for spying. The *qadi* came off the hood of the car and proclaimed
that in God's name he declared her an enemy of Islam, a *kufir*, or unbeliever.
Because she was now a *kufir* she must be put to death—immediately. He then
sat back on the hood to watch the ritual that they were performing at a rate of
one a day in his sector. Of course, she screamed for her son's life and God's
mercy.

A young boy walked up to her, leveled the Kalashnikov rifle, and fired a
burst of three bullets into her chest. She fell to the dirt with an astonished
look on her face. The boys turned and then dragged her thirteen-year-old son
behind them, hung a rope over the tree in their front yard, lashed it quickly
over the child's head, and pulled him into the air, strangling. He kicked out
at them and gurgled as his throat shut. In his last moments of life, he was not
given a chance to pray, or call to God for his past transgressions or even ask
God to forgive the men who had just murdered his mother. The child had to
ask himself as the boys laughed and went about their task of pulling his neck
apart, *Were these men* ifrist . . . *demons? Were they* Iblis . . . *the devil? Were they*
jinnis? No answer would be known. Life soon left him and his soul went to
God, exactly six minutes later. The boys with the AK-47s went away, the
blood on their hands drying, and the *qadi* told them that they had just done
something beautiful in God's eyes.

To Osama bin Laden, mass murder to please God was to be a necessary
part of his new order for purifying Islam. According to his interpretation,
yes, it might be Bid'ah (a heretical innovation in Islam), but it was being

done by mujahideen, or men of jihad, warriors in a struggle for the community, and so it would be forgiven by God. It was ruled that anything or anyone *ferengi*, or foreign, except for the Arabs and Central Asians who fought with the Taliban, could be seen as part of the Western conspiracy to destroy Islam. However, there would be different standards for the terrorists and the common folk: al-Qaeda cell phones were blessed by Mullah Omar and Osama bin Laden as a way for warriors to communicate, but a poor widow's using an old cell phone to call relatives made her a spy. Al-Qaeda's men were honored as holy and blessed students of Islam even if they raped, murdered, or decapitated Muslims. This poor woman's Islam, practiced in a dirty corner of the mud mosque behind the women's partition, was not good enough for them, and hence she was not Muslim enough for God. As the acclaimed Urdu writer Qurat-ul-Ain Hyder said of all the mortifying events and murders since 9/11, "Death is not even considered a tragedy anymore!"[1]

There have been many long trials in the friction between religious groups throughout the history of Islam. These have led to wars, secret sects, and violent political murders. The Prophet Mohammed himself stated, "Whoever among you lives after I die will see many differences. I urge you to adhere to my Sunnah and way of the rightly-guided caliphs."[2] However, throughout its entire 1,430-year history, rarely has anyone in Islam made the argument that mass murder was a religious duty and that each murder of a Muslim was a pleasing sight in the eyes of God.

Another, more salient example of the sharp contrast between mainstream traditional Islam and the cultlike fringe that is al-Qaeda was on display in March 2009. In a small courtroom at the U.S. naval prison at Guantánamo Bay, Cuba, five men were brought before the military tribunal to hear their case in participating in the 9/11 attacks. The leader and master planner of the attack, Khalid Sheik Mohammed; Ramzi bin al-Shibh; Walid bin Attash; Ali Abdul Aziz Ali; and Mustafa al-Hawsawi issued a statement from what they termed the "9/11 Shura Council" (*Shura* being Arabic for a religious advisory council). The surprising statement read that the five confessed to their crimes and gladly accepted the title of terrorists. They asserted that they would continue "killing you and fighting you, destroying you and terrorizing you . . . all considered to be great legitimate duties in our religion." In a twist, they chose to declare that the 9/11 attacks were an act of worship: "These actions are our offering to God."[3]

Islam Is Not Militant—al-Qaeda Is

THE LABELING OF Islam as militant, radical, or extremist is a popular foil for those looking to equate al-Qaeda to the entirety of the religion. It is ignorant of not only Islam but also the history of Christianity and warfare. Attributing offensive warfare for the purpose of conversion as the core tenant of Islam has long been a method of disparaging a religion that many in the West simply do not understand. Al-Qaeda's use of religious war rhetoric has spawned an entire cottage industry in the West that exudes bigotry, racism, and a deliberate misunderstanding that has led to a poorly served American public. TV pundits, scholars, and armchair experts erroneously insist that Islam equals war and, by immediate connection to OBL's professed faith, often assert that Islam equals terrorism.

There has always been war and conflict in the Islamic world, just as there has been in Christianity. Islam flourished in a period of clashing empires, struggles for control of trade routes, and men seeking political gain from Europe to China. Few were the Western and Eastern religious leaders, political masters, or trade moguls who were not involved in the business of murder, resistance, or war for capital, convenience, or influence. This trait of human acrimony was applied with greater or lesser equality in the homelands of all of the major religions, including Islam, Judaism, and Christianity. One of the greatest myths extant is that Islam was "spread by the sword." In truth, the image of a militaristic, unyielding, and merciless Islam was propagated by the very first vanquished empires that it came into contact with.

Indeed, Islam was born through tribal skirmish, just as Christianity was born through Christ's public execution. In 632 the Prophet Mohammed fought to win recognition against the pagan tribes of Mecca. This was a localized series of skirmishes, not uncommon in most tribal cultures at the time. The difference is this one had a unifying religious concept flying under its banner. It also encompassed key beliefs from both Christianity and Judaism. Islam initially started as a threat to trade and commerce in Mecca and a direct threat to localized pagan beliefs. However, in context of the seventh-century western Arabian desert its introduction by armed resistance and the winning of battles was clearly not the operating principle of the religion itself. That is wholly a Western manifestation.

As recently as 2006, Pope Benedict XVI, the leader of the Roman Catholic Church, chose to point out some of the inaccurate historical comments related to this misperception when he quoted Emperor Manuel II Paleologus of the Byzantine Empire, who said of Islam:

Show me just what Muhammad brought that was new, and there you
will find things only evil and inhuman, such as his command to spread
by the sword the faith he preached.[4]

Manuel II's belief is spoken aloud daily in the West and considered a
ground truth. What is missing from commentary like this is the original
context that seems to equate the religion with warfare. In the age of empires,
as it is today, it was politically expedient to characterize one's enemies in a
propagandistic way. Emperor Manuel II was at the time presiding over the
end of a millennium-long reign of the Byzantine Empire, and under great
pressure from a Muslim force bent on ending their rule. Writing in 1391,
Manuel II was having discourse with a Turkish listener just before the capital, Constantinople, would come under a seven-year siege by Sultan Bayezid
I. Put succinctly, the Byzantine Empire was teetering on the cusp of dissolv-
ing into history. Despite the fact that Christians were and remain a protected
people in Islam, the rapid loss of Manuel II's Christian empire to a Muslim
one, under the sword of the typical military campaign, could have influenced his words. Still, the modern media machine and bigots of all stripes
perpetuate his words.

Notably absent from this discussion are the forced conversions by Christian swords and conquests that ranged from the Roman Empire's forced
conversions of pagans under Theodosius to the forced conversion of Jews and
Muslims during the Iberian Reconquista of Spain in the fifteenth century
and the imposition of Christianity on African slaves in the Americas. The
most overlooked example of forced conversion is that the entirety of the
Western Hemisphere was brought to Christianity by armed Spanish, Portu-
guese, and French religious and military missions that conducted mass conversions of Native Americans. Those societies who did not submit were
generally killed in wars of submission or ethnically cleansed. This is the very
reason that Latin America is the Christian bastion it is today. Yet somehow
popular perceptions in the West have not equated Christianity with conversion by the sword on an equal level as it does Islam. In fact, the greatest period of expansion in Islam came not in the early Muslim conquests but in the
early twentieth century during a period of absolute peace.

Many today use misplaced historical pieces of propaganda to justify how
Christians should view al-Qaeda interactions with the Western world. It is,
in effect, as if the words of Manuel II and the political perceptions of Islam
as passed down by biased political histories have become the predominant

perception of the way the West should view religious extremists and terrorists. Islamophobia now grips the West due to ignorance, propaganda, and fear.

In considering historical Islam, the Rashidun Caliphate (632–661) spread Islam under the first five rulers, or the "rightly guided Caliphs," from the Arabian Peninsula to as far east as Afghanistan and as far west as Libya. In the seventh and eighth centuries the Umayyad Caliphate ruled from Córdoba in al-Andalus on the Iberian Peninsula and spread farther still. They branched out to encompass all of North Africa, Spain, and a greater part of Central and South Asia. This was solidified by the Abbasid Caliphate (744–969). Soon after, the Crusades tore into the heart of the Islamic world and created a political split between Christian and Muslim worlds that has yet to be reconciled. In the twelfth century the Mongols came from Asia, eventually sacked and killed the Caliph in Baghdad, and caused Islam to split into three empires: the Mughal, the Safavid, and the Ottoman. In time each of these eventually fell to war, intrigue, and conquest. The Ottoman Empire was the last consolidation of the greater Muslim world, and after World War I it, too, collapsed in the face of colonialism and military technology. Surprisingly, the Ottoman's most noted losses in World War I were the defeats in Transjordan, Palestine, and Syria. These wartime losses were delivered by small asymmetric groups similar to those we face on the Afghanistan-Pakistan border today—armed tribal militants led by an experienced organizer, T. E. Lawrence (of Arabia) and the tribe of Abdul Aziz ibn al-Saud.

The key issue here is not to say that Islam was never engaged in warfare. Everyone was. It is that in its fourteen-hundred year history no one in the Islamic world ever advocated the mass murder of their own Muslim brothers or innocent non-believers to die by the thousands, tens of thousands, at a time or actively sought religious sanction to kill millions of innocent people in order to achieve perfection in God's word. No matter how it is viewed, this twist in the faith is a corruption that all who seek to know the difference between Islam and the terrorists must accept and understand.

9/11 and the False Image of Islam

NAWAL ABDUL FATAH, the forty-eight-year-old woman, stood in front of a news crew's camera and was broadcast around the world as she waved her arms and danced. She smiled a broad, almost toothless grin and held her fingers up in the "V" for victory symbol. The dozens of boys and the few men around them in East Jerusalem smiled and clapped as the boys danced in the streets. Stories of celebratory gunfire were reported at Lebanon's Ain al-Hilwah refugee camp. Video from Nablus on the West Bank of Palestine was shown as well. The images were presented raw and designed to disgust—the Arabs were celebrating mass murder. In America FOX News anchorman Brit Hume fumed as he decried that the Palestinians were dancing in celebration of the murder of thousands of American citizens. The jubilant cheers in East Jerusalem may have been of a few hundred people who tied their poor fortunes to the attack. They may have been sincere in their praise for the terror, or they may have been seeking publicity of their plight. It is possible that some were incited by Hamas militants when cameras came to shoot reactions of Palestinians. Some may have been offered cake to dance before the cameras, as Mrs. Fatah later claimed. For the American TV audience this was the scene that set the stage for hatred of the rest of the Muslim world that was not al-Qaeda. These were the scenes that rallied many Americans, blinded in rage, to nurture a prejudice against Muslims and immediately equate Islam with terrorism. Ask an American on the street where Nablus is located in relation to the caves of the Afghan-Pakistan border where the terrorists planned the attacks and you will generally face a stammering, "I don't know." Ask how the images of 9/11 and the reaction of the Arab street are connected and you will be told "they were celebrating."

The desire to seek revenge against Islam and Muslims for 9/11, not just find the perpetrators of the attacks, has been one of the open secrets of the War on Terrorism. Many have written about the sentiment, but the official denials gave cover to the hatred that spilled onto the streets of America. That very morning that I was stumbling through the smoke of the burning wreckage of the Pentagon attack site. I knew this meant a wide war against al-Qaeda, but my concerns that it would become an anti-Muslim rally point a few days later were justified. Fury and rage is a fickle servant. The hatred that the attacks inflicted on our national sense of security was going to turn into a demon that would have consequences far beyond the death of Osama bin Laden. Attuned to believing that the best and the brightest would summon caution and focus our vengeance on those who actually carried out the attacks, little did I know that this internal darkness would be made into the policies of vengeance themselves by those entrusted to check the spirit of recklessness and seek true justice for this horror.

The call for vengeance, to draw blood for the massive death and destruction inflicted on America, took on a life of its own. The sites of the attacks became touchstones upon which revenge was sworn. Within days the anger coalesced into a paranoia that encompassed violating virtually every core principle of American values. Let us quickly look at what toying with the sword of vengeance yielded over eight years.

Fantasies of Revenge:
"Success" in the War on Terrorism

SINCE SEPTEMBER 11 the Bush administration and its allies painted the Global War on Terrorism (GWOT) as a highly successful offensive operation that seriously damaged the AQ organization at every level. Though this was challenged by the political opposition and the rest of the world, the media and general public largely bought into this characterization. No less astute an outside observer than *Newsweek International* editor Fareed Zakaria claimed that the Bush counter-terror polices have been "intelligent and effective."[5]

Before we can ask the world for a new level of assistance we need to face the facts about our own misguided beliefs in what some felt was a successful period. Consider the following statements made by the Bush administration and the results that history has passed down:

The Global War on Terrorism was a success[6]: In fact, the GWOT is both an unsuccessful policy and a flawed operational concept, which has created far more terrorist recruits and generated more terrorism than existed at any time before 9/11.

Three-quarters of the known al-Qaeda leadership have been brought to justice[7]: The assertion by the former President and his administration was a propaganda talking point that could never be verified. In fact, the regeneration of AQ since 9/11 and the creation of al-Qaeda in Iraq (AQI) and other franchises throughout the Middle East and South Asia created new lieutenants and terrorist operatives who now have combat and terror skills that few of the previous generation had.

Al-Qaeda is on the run: Between October 2001 and February 2003, AQ was on the run. Their leadership expected the land invasion of Afghanistan but not the rapid fall of the Taliban. Al-Qaeda cells all around the world started feeling the pressure of law enforcement. Bin Laden remained defiant and executed his long-term plan to bring about destabilization by Takfiri militant movements throughout the Middle East and to engage in a long war against the United States. The organization was damaged and on the run until the 2003 invasion of Iraq, which bought them sympathy and support from all over the militant extremist world. With America's power split, OBL survived and thrived and reoriented AQ to support self-starting Takfiri groups around the world.

Iraq is the central front in the War on Terrorism: Iraq was not even on the AQ radar as a battlefield due to the brutality of the dictator Saddam Hussein. AQ avoided all but the uncontrolled Kurdish northern Iraq. Under the protection of the U.S. no-fly zones, Abu Mussab al-Zarqawi was able to assist the Kurdish Takfiri groups to thrive and avoid Iraqi and Kurdish intelligence agencies. After the American invasion Iraq became the central front of resistance for AQ as America's occupation motivated thousands of young men to become terrorists and head to Iraq. The Iraq war allowed AQ senior leaders the opportunity to regroup and strengthen their hand in Afghanistan and South Asia. Analyst Brent Budowsky summed up this Ahab-like obsession: "The Bush and McCain obsession with Iraq and Iran has not only done grave damage to our military force structures and deterrent, they have warped our international policy, endangered our national security and created a crisis of inattention from Pakistan to Russia that makes the world a far more dangerous place."[8]

If we fight them there we won't have to fight them at home: This is a completely flawed concept that requires AQ to buy into our philosophy that they will not plan on fighting in the United States if they are engaged in struggles with the U.S. military overseas. The opposite is true; AQ may find it easier to operate and attempt infiltration as America's attention and military strength are bogged down in wars where other militants are performing effective asymmetric warfare. Where and when AQ attacks is often left up to planning, patience, and opportunity.

Why should we not consider the GWOT a success? The entire basis of this assertion is because there have been no attacks by members of AQ on the continental United States since 9/11. Is there no reason to believe that it is a well-tuned war policy that has kept us safe for eight years as asserted by the Bush administration? No. The metric for the policy has been an absence of a direct attack on the continental United States. A more gruesome and less reliable yardstick has been the rising number of dead in Iraq and Afghanistan. This debate also completely ignores the fact that the Bush administration presided over the greatest and most devastating attack on American soil since Pearl Harbor. It happened on their watch and should have been the basis of any objective evaluation of America's overall safety.

Zakaria is correct in one core aspect of his dismissive reading of the GWOT's "Bush kept us safe" argument when he writes:

The Bush administration deserves credit for its counterterrorism policies. But it also must bear the blame for distorting the challenge. Initially unaware of the problem, Bush adopted an exaggerated view of the threat, seeing al-Qaeda as a vast global organization comparable to the Soviet Union. His conception of the war on terrorism implies that the struggle is largely military. It tends to conflate disparate Muslim groups—with differing and often opposed agendas—into one monolithic enemy.[9]

The GWOT had a singular focus in that it took all resources of government, the economy, trade, diplomacy, justice, and its core principles, and bent them into a supporting ideology that stressed almost purely military solutions for any perceived problem with regard to extremists. To ensure public political support it erroneously placed the bulk of its propaganda and media informational efforts into propagandizing the American public, not into making our friends and potential allies see the utility of their methodology. By targeting the American public before its real enemy and conflating that enemy into a threat disproportionate to all of its demonstrated capability, the Bush administration allowed extremists eight full years to dominate the zone we call the Information Warfare Battlespace (IWB).

I propose a real operational metric for success against OBL's potential terror activities: have we damaged or destroyed AQ's ability to regenerate and grow OBL's base of support throughout the Islamic world and discredited the ideological appeal of the bin Ladenist movement in the IWB? Until that question is answered in the affirmative we will be fighting a new generation of recruits to the ranks of AQ every year.

Reality: We Set the Muslim World Aflame

IF IT CAN be said that OBL and AQ knew that their attack on New York would set the region aflame, no one imagined that the American response would be to attempt to combat it with a flamethrower. The immediate response by the Bush administration to the OBL departure from Afghanistan via Tora Bora was to minimize resources to capture and kill him, not increase them. The insular Bush policies assuming American dominance in the Middle East only conflated the wild assumptions that the Taliban and the core forces in AQ were utterly defeated. The postcombat headiness, felt even though intelligence clearly indicated that bin Laden had walked off the mountain and into Pakistan, was seen by neoconservatives as a permission slip to attack, destabilize, or topple any other government that had even the slightest suspicion of AQ association, true or not.

Though many of al-Qaeda's beliefs, perceptions, and fundamental understanding of the American political structure and presidential decision-making are rudimentary, it was often the U.S. government's own actions and words that have given al-Qaeda a tangential series of side benefits, which have proven critical to their ability to expand and grow credible. The missteps of the Bush years were legion, including the following unintended consequences of neoconservative doctrine.

AL-QAEDA SUCCESSFULLY IMPLEMENTS GLOBAL TERROR ATTACKS

DURING THE PERIOD when the Bush administration was congratulating itself for defeating AQ and the Taliban, AQ terrorists carried out a series of wide-ranging demonstration attacks. Demonstration attacks are designed to show that a terrorist group's combat arm is viable and able to manifest lethal threats and should not be taken lightly. AQ groups or their extremist affiliates have carried out attacks that have killed thousands of people since September 11: they've attacked the subways of Madrid, Spain; killed almost two hundred Australian tourists and Indonesians in Bali; massacred fifty-four in the downtown London metro; carried out multiple suicide bombings in Casablanca, Morocco, and Egypt; attacked hotels in Jordan; blew up tourist sites in Tunisia; slaughtered sightseers in Yemen; and mass-murdered Indians by both suicide bomber and gunfire in Mumbai.

IRAQ BECOMES THE WORLD'S TERRORISM UNIVERSITY

ALL THE WHILE, Iraq was in full-fledged armed resistance. Both bin Laden and Saddam Hussein had independently planned for a slow, bloody war in Iraq. AQ used suicide bombers and Hussein's former Ba'athists used roadside bombs and rifles. This resulted in the slaughter of tens of thousands of Iraqis and thousands of American soldiers. By 2006 the CIA would assess that the invasion had created more terrorists than had existed before it and that they were professionalizing.

EASTERN AFGHANISTAN AND WESTERN PAKISTAN BECOME "GREATER TAKFIRISTAN"

AFTER SEVERAL YEARS of fighting in Iraq, AQ and their new extremist allies in South Asia worked tirelessly to strengthen the insurgency in Afghanistan such that by 2008 the war was at its strongest point. The FATA, a belt of provinces that extend around Afghanistan's eastern border, were in rebellion against the Bush-backed dictator Pervez Musharraf. The FATA Takfiris, assisted by OBL and his foreign fighters, inflicted punishment on the Pakistani army and allowed them to negotiate settlements that strengthened extremist control in these areas. More important, their successes and Musharraf's failure to defeat them led to significant political standing in Pakistan's population. Today, though under Pakistani army pressure, the al-Qaeda-backed Tarik-e-Taliban Pakistan controls much of the FATA, and managed to shut off much of the 75 percent of supplies NATO needs for operations in Afghanistan. Other ideological allies include the Lashkar-e-Taiba and Lashkar-e-Jangvi. When not fighting in the FATA, extremists border-dance and fight NATO forces in Afghanistan. When pressured, they retreat into the extremist sanctuary of the FATA.

A ONCE-THRIVING LEBANON IS BADLY DAMAGED

AFTER THE 2005 assassination of Prime Minister Rafik Haririr, Syrian forces left Lebanon and a period of Lebanese nationalism gave hope that the influence of the Assad regime had ended and that democracy would flourish. Soon afterward, with the blessing of the United States, Israel would launch a disastrous invasion of Lebanon. With the joint American and Israeli objective of destroying the Shiite political cum terror group Hezbollah, the Israelis decimated the commercial infrastructure of Lebanon through a wide range of aerial bombings. Both Christian and non-Hezbollah Muslim Lebanese found themselves supporting the only group that had the arms and experience to hurt the Israelis—Hezbollah. The Israelis failed to realize that a group that forced a humiliating withdrawal on Israel after eighteen years of occupation in southern Lebanon was not going to be defeated in thirty days of air raids. Israel withdrew again, but only after dropping 1 million cluster bombs in southern Lebanon during its last forty-eight hours. The war was seen as a complete failure for both Prime Minister Ehud Olmert and President Bush.

PALESTINIANS DEMOCRATICALLY ELECT
A TERRORIST ORGANIZATION

SUPPORTING AN ISRAELI policy of isolating Palestinian President Yasir Arafat, Israel, with Bush administration backing, allowed him to wither on the vine until he died in uncertain circumstances. The United States supported a UN-sponsored Palestinian legislative election in 2006. Arafat's Fatah political organization handily lost due to U.S. support of Fatah's moderate candidate, Mohammed Dahlan, and internal struggles. The Bush administration was slow to realize the error of not backing the moderate group. Assuming that democracy would put the U.S.-backed Fatah candidate in power, the Palestinians democratically elected a terrorist organization's political arm. Fighting broke out between Fatah and Hamas, and the Gaza Strip remained under Hamas's control. With 1 million people effectively cut off from all but the basic food supplies distributed by the United Nations, and under siege by direct Israeli air and ground assaults, Gaza effectively became the largest open-air prison in the world.

SYRIA BECOMES A GATEWAY
TO INSTABILITY IN IRAQ

INSTEAD OF SEEKING the cooperation of the Syrian government prior to the invasion of Iraq, America remained hostile to Syria, due to the perception that Syria is the principal client state of Hezbollah in Lebanon. This made Syria indifferent to extremist volunteers entering via Damascus. These volunteers provided the thousands of armed foreign fighters who infiltrated the border and joined al-Qaeda in Iraq. In addition, the Syrians allowed their Ba'athist Party peers from Saddam Hussein's regime to openly operate the armed resistance campaign from the Iraqi refugee–filled Damascus suburbs. This open pipeline, which could have been closed through diplomacy and cooperation, allowed suicide bombers and Iraqi extremists to flow in and out. The terrorists who plied these "resistance routes" were directly responsible for thousands of deaths in Iraq.

TURKEY FIGHTS IN KURDISH NORTHERN IRAQ

KURDISH EXTREMIST GROUPS that operated across the porous Turkish-Iraqi border find refuge in the deep mountains. Without interference from the Hussein regime, they stepped up their cross-border infiltration and mounted combat operations into Turkey. In September 2004, Turkish forces warned Kurdish forces, then commenced combat operations against them. There are continuing clashes between this NATO member on the terrain of the newly liberated Iraqi Republic.

ISRAEL MOVES TOWARD A HARD-RIGHT GOVERNMENT

FOLLOWING THE DISASTROUS Israeli invasion of Lebanon in 2006, the government of Ehud Olmert moved toward measures far more extreme than normal against Hamas. Only weeks before the compliant Bush administration would be removed from the political scene, Israel took a series of brutal and massive interventions against the Hamas regime in Gaza. In response to small-scale homemade rocket attacks the Israeli air force and army pommeled Gaza. The onslaught was surprising in its brutality and disregard for civilian casualties. Over one thousand civilians were killed in the attacks. These were brought to vivid light when a Palestinian surgeon being interviewed on Israeli television lost six relatives, including his three daughters, live on television. Surprisingly, the attacks, which Israel vowed to carry out until Hamas was destroyed, stopped twenty-four hours before the swearing in of President Barack Obama. The 2009 election saw the rise of the hard right wing led by the radical Avigdor Lieberman, who garnered 20 percent of the popular vote and formed a coalition government with former right-wing Prime Minister Benjamin Netanyahu. Lieberman became foreign minister, thus suppressing many hopes of reconciliation and forward progress on the two-state solution that would see the founding of the Palestinian nation peacefully bordering Israel.

IRAN BECOMES A MAJOR REGIONAL PLAYER

THE INVASION OF Iraq first frightened the nuclear-hungry Iran by toppling the dictatorial rule of Saddam Hussein on their western border. Believing that Iraq would gratefully become a U.S. client state and fulfill its fantasies of empire and oil, the Bush administration disregarded Iran's enormous capacity for mischief and localized influence peddling. An even greater mistaken belief was that Iraq would be so grateful that they would offer, without question, permanent military bases from which Iran would be boxed in by American might. This myopic view as promulgated by a small political elite called neoconservatives upset the regional balance of power and gave the Islamic Republic of Iran long-term strategic leverage it could never have hoped to achieve so long as Saddam was there to balance it.

HOWEVER, INDIFFERENCE TO al-Qaeda is not just the fault of the Bush administration. The public has been led by a profit-driven media and an exceptionally laissez-faire attitude to create a real difference of opinion, which crops up only when bin Laden comes out and makes a statement. The lack of personal investment by the American people and an indifference toward the wars against al-Qaeda is so markedly different from America's other global fights, such as World War II, Korea, or Vietnam, as to have almost become an issue that the press and public considers a non-issue.

America Has a Moral Case for Justice

WE SHOULD REMEMBER the depth and righteousness of the world's sympathy after the 9/11 attacks. Though this was squandered, with a little prodding perhaps the world could be persuaded again to assist us as a matter of justice. However, serious concerns will have to be addressed. The Muslim world admires the West for its technology, education systems, and even many of our freedoms. They have serious concerns about our values, but many in the Middle East desire to reach a happy medium where Western values are not forced upon their religious and cultural traditions. What they seek most, particularly since 9/11, is respect for their religion and community.

On that September day the victims were people who had done nothing wrong. They had led their lives in peace. Innocent people had gone to work or to an airport and found themselves being kidnapped, slaughtered, and burned to death. A nation so attacked on its own soil would be right to bring the perpetrators to justice. The global community should participate to ensure such an act never occurs on any nation's soil and with such horrific loss of life. To the overwhelming majority of the world, this was unquestionable and reasonable.

After bin Laden ordered and directed the mass murder of almost three thousand people from seventy-six countries it remains patently clear that America has a claim to justice.

The American counter-terror endeavor was morally defensible to the Muslim world right up until it was clear that President Bush fully intended to invade Iraq in the face of massive global opposition. For them the conspiracy theories of 9/11 being used as a thinly veiled attempt to take over the fourth-largest oil reserve in the world were coming true. Iraq was broadly seen by many as using the deaths of 9/11 in a manufactured bid to enter the heart of the Islamic world and dominate the Middle East. From the day Iraq was invaded, al-Qaeda was placed in the enviable position of having their warnings validate the suspicions and fears of many in the Middle East.

In the years since 9/11, America has killed many, many members of al-Qaeda. Before the invasion of Iraq there were an estimated two to five thousand active members of al-Qaeda and as many as ten thousand graduates of its camps who may have been sympathizers but not actively involved in terrorism. The Taliban, the radical religious government of Afghanistan, had approximately seventeen thousand men. However, there were zero members of al-Qaeda operating in Saddam Hussein's Iraq prior to that invasion. The Iraq war created an entirely new division of al-Qaeda, with volunteers coming from the Arabian Peninsula, North Africa, and Europe for suicide bombings and attacks. They had no association with the pre-invasion al-Qaeda. Thus the invasion of Iraq created a wholly new body of terrorists that formed with a few AQ diehards such as Abu Mussab al-Zarqawi. They volunteered and went to Iraq expecting to fight and die in the name of OBL. The U.S. armed forces may have killed as many as three thousand of the militants, and as many as one thousand died as suicide bombers.[10]

With a few exceptions, such as the killing of Mohammed Atef and the capture and imprisonment of Khalid Sheik Mohammed and Ramzi bin al-Shibh, the war on al-Qaeda has been failing to bring the full measure of justice to the planners and perpetrators of the September 11 attacks. But what is that metric? Is it all involved with AQ captured or killed? Is it the utter destruction of the military capacity of AQ? I contend it is breaking their ideology and exposing their corruption of Islam.

Unfortunately, the War on Terrorism's metrics for the damaging or destruction of the group have always been measured in the quantity of Muslim blood we extract, not the lessening impact or spread of their ideas. This mentality did not work in the Crusades and will serve no purpose other than to make bin Laden a bomb-throwing caricature of Saladin in the eyes of the affected populations.

Islam Has a Moral Case for Preservation of Life and Cultural Respect

AFTER ALL HAS been said and done in Iraq and Afghanistan, with hundreds of billions of dollars spent on pacifying hardened terrorist insurgencies, the United States has yet to make a convincing argument that the American victims of 9/11 have justice. There is a common cause for the Muslim world with America against al-Qaeda, but we have muddled the job so horribly as to make it almost unsalvageable.

Add on top of the ill will caused by invading Iraq, American errors in combat arms since 9/11 in Somalia, Afghanistan, and Iraq and in imprisoning Muslim suspects without due process have caused a wellspring of false moral equivalency arguments that are difficult to defend and set any rational argument into the spiral of conspiracy. Yet for all of our power, prestige, and fortune the American justifications for fighting al-Qaeda have yet to be clearly and convincingly enunciated at the street level of the Muslim community.

Many Muslim observers see the murderous actions of al-Qaeda, which are by doctrine designed to massacre large quantities of innocent people, only in light of military overreactions of the United States that are often as equally lethal and terrifying as anything a suicide bomber could render. As a nation, America cannot and should not allow our mission to eliminate al-Qaeda and to secure ourselves from harm lose the common goal of securing the safety of all who could come to harm in our pursuit of justice. The choices we have to make in the fight with Osama bin Laden's brand of heretical Islam may seem a situation where, as Thomas Jefferson wrote, "We have the wolf by the ears; we can neither hold him nor can we safely let him go." The situation need not necessarily be so dire. We do have the wolf by the ears, but what must we do to gain local allies that can grab him by each of his legs and tail? We need the Islamic world as allies from those who may become the wolf's next dinner to help bring about its destruction. We must convince the Islamic world that AQ is an existential threat to their religion.

Islam, like all great religions, has been filled with debate, controversy, and movements. The debates have often been tranquil, hushed, sonorous, as they have sometimes been revolutionary, fiery, and the source of furious discussion. From the first days after the death of the Prophet there have been sects from both inside and out that have been determined to reinterpret the Qur'an and Mohammed's words in an ever-increasingly puritanical manner. To the casual student of Islam, one can barely detect the vortex of swirling religious controversy, theological debate, and personal fractiousness that make up the lives of those who discuss the meaning of the Qur'an. As noted before, most scholars, politicians, writers, and adventurers, particularly from Christianity, have managed to create an image of Islam that is wholly one-sided. These images have been borne through the literature of the post-Crusades Europe of the Middle Ages, the nineteenth-century European Orientalism movement, and modern popular media. Apart from the exhaustive world of academia, the Western populist perception of Islam has almost exclusively equated to the false image of war, dissent, intrigue, and expansion through power. Although many observers gave accurate and sympathetic accounts of this monotheistic, multicultural society, such as the Swiss explorer Johann

Burckhardt and English adventurer Sir Richard Francis Burton, the negative images of Islam as rival and adversary endure.

Although Islam is traditional, it is also a highly diverse religion due to the nature of its multicultural essence. It does have competing ideologies that have existed since the first days after the death of Mohammed. The first of these were the great Sunnah-Shiite split that occurred in the seventh century. The effects of this great cleaving of Islam remain today.

The first Caliph was challenged by the first cousin and son-in-law of the Prophet, who believed that because he was related by marriage and was a cousin he should have been chosen leader of the Muslims. A civil war split Islam into two denominations: Sunnah and Shiite. Shiite Islam settled in what is modern-day Iran, southern Iraq, southern Lebanon, and spots in the Gulf states of Bahrain, Pakistan, and Afghanistan. Today they constitute 15 percent of all Muslims. However, despite the fact that Sunnah Muslims are the overwhelming majority (85 percent), the two worship similarly and perform the same basic Islamic rites. Still other "splinter" branches of Islam exist within both Shia and Sunnah, such as the Deobandis, Sufis, Barelvis, and Ibadis. Within Sunnah Islam itself the most prominent reformation movement is Wahabism, spread largely due to the global missionary work of Saudi Arabia.

Generally, there have always been two schools of Islamic scholarship: traditional and revolutionary. Mainstream Islamic practices can be said to be traditional and largely cohesive in their conservatism. Fourteen centuries of tradition have yet to be successfully challenged on a large scale. The center of Sunnah Islamic tradition rests at the al-Azhar Mosque and University in Cairo, Egypt, a seminary and finishing school for Islamic scholars. Its blessings and guidance are an absolute must to teach and remain respected in the mainstream of Islamic orthodoxy. The ulema is *the* body of Islamic jurists who have progressed to positions of note and authority by a rigorous series of advancements in which they learn the traditional basis of Islamic thought and jurisprudence.

One Islamic law scholar in the ulema described his education this way: "I have an unbroken chain of knowledge from the Prophet to his Companions to myself." In essence, the résumé of the Islamic scholar is proof positive of his understanding and maintenance of the traditional line of Islamic thought as it has existed since the time of the Prophet. Scholarship in the ulema requires that one study and advance through years of rigorous debate, writing, and creating a body of scholarly work until one earns the standing and respect to be heard. Established in 972, al-Azhar literally embodies the slow, conservative, and centrist basis of all Islamic thought. Some claim to have this respect but are actually outsiders; others, like OBL and his ideological followers, have no standing among the ulema at all.

Within the Islamic conservatives there are deeper levels of Islamic ultra-conservatism. Some people erroneously refer to the ultraconservative Muslims as Islamists, Islamic fundamentalists, militants, or religious radicals. Each of these terms could be correct if evaluating the Islamic conservatives and ultraconservatives through the rigidity they seek in worship but incorrect if referring to the adoption of armed political resistance. Islamic ultraconservatives take a much harder view of cultural and spiritual matters within their religion but see it as strictly Orthodox to work within the faith and the religious political system to correct the failings of their friends, family, and government. It should be noted that like Christian and Jewish conservatives/ultraconservatives they may espouse narrow opinions to the point of sexism, racism, intolerance, and xenophobia. But, by definition, just being Muslim and ultraconservative does not make a Muslim a terrorist any more than being a conservative Christian evangelical or an ultraorthodox Jew does. Within the spectrum of Islam are wildly varying shades of adherence to the rules. AQ, on the other hand, operates outside of these rules.

However, the commonalities between all Muslims are what the West notes most and best. We see people worshiping their God in a manner that many from outside the religion view as fundamentally different. The singing of the muezzin, calling Muslims to prayer; the obligation of five prayers a day together with other Muslims or alone on a side of the road, this is what the West thinks of when they picture Islam. Unfortunately, they now also see another image.

Yet there is a third group within Islam I call the cultist fringe. They are the focus of my thesis. Identifying the cultist fringe ideologues is difficult because they generally operate in relative secrecy.

Around the world, there are many armed militant nationalist and political groups that perform acts of armed resistance and even terrorism for political or nationalist goals. For example, the Iraqi Sunnah Insurgents, the Revolutionary Armed Forces of Colombia, the Real Irish Republican Army—they all resort to terror. Other groups have even carried out suicide tactics, including Hezbollah, Hamas, the al-Aqsa Martyrs Brigade, and the Tamil Tigers. However, al-Qaeda may be unique in the pantheon of historical terrorist groups.

An Islamic Cult

THE IDEOLOGY OF AQ is an extreme ultraconservative interpretation of the Qur'an that goes beyond religion and into the realm of cultism. AQ seeks to achieve complete domination of Islam or will die trying. They establish armed sanctuaries, call them earthly Islamic emirates, and live in a messianic dreamworld where mass murder and the warrior ethos is a trait of love for God. This is the fantasy world of the cultist fringe.

The AQ cultist fringe is wholly unlike mainstream Muslims. They see Muslims as unpious and often believe they are no longer members of Islam. The AQ cultist fringe may share some of the religious fervor of the ultraconservative Muslims, but they see them as insufficiently motivated for their cause. Only the blooded members of the cultist fringe are trustworthy and acceptable to live and rule in their fantastic world. They represent a fraction of a fraction of the mainstream population.

The cultist fringe often hides behind religious rhetoric that is ignored because their ideas are too extreme for the conservatives. They are often insular organizations or groups who represent virtually no parts of a religion. But they seek influence and power to impose their interpretation of godliness on others. The cultist fringe rarely seeks acceptance but are often quick to exercise and pass judgment. Their outsider status often gives them a green light for radical action, sometimes including armed militancy or terrorism. In the West these cult groups tend to revolve around the personality of one man, who usually seeks to convert followers through a puritanical reading of their sacred texts but manages to apply only his interpretation upon his followers.

In this reading of AQ it is not helpful to apply a religious label to them. The cultist fringe creates their own standard of piety and will interpret religious texts to suit their political or personal ambition. Cultism is rare within Islam, but there is a compelling argument that the cultist fringe is resurgent and that the al-Qaeda organization is beyond the pale of even the most conservative readings of the Qur'an. Many in the Muslim world have already called them heretics and outsiders, murderers and apostates.

Ideologies and charismatic leaders who have claimed God's guidance and harked to his orders to the detriment of others are as old as mankind. AQ and their allies fall into the pantheon of revisionists to a mainstream religion. They are led by a charismatic leader who extols apocalyptic salvation only through death.

On the one hand, Osama bin Laden's peers include Jim Jones, who had over a thousand of his followers drink cyanide in their religious retreat in Guyana; David Koresh, the man who claimed he was Jesus Christ and battled the American FBI with hundreds of automatic weapons; and Soko Asahara, the Buddhist cult leader who created a sarin nerve gas factory and wanted to destroy the government of Japan for his own religious purposes. On the other hand, bin Laden is also akin to the late Velupillai Prabhakaran, the terrorist leader of the Tamil Tigers, pioneers of the suicide bomb. Prabhakaran ran a cult of personality and a twenty-six-year nationalist terror campaign that extended to making all of his militants carry cyanide capsules around their necks.

However, AQ is trying to evolve from a terrorist cult into a mainstream movement. They have slowly inched away away from their twenty-year mission of being a terrorist command center to becoming an ideological corporate management and coaching consultancy for many other Sunnah Muslim terror and militia groups that have taken up arms. AQ now advises a wide range of battlefield and near-battlefield actors in the Middle East, Europe, Africa, and South Asia, including warlords, drug gangs, politicians, and educators. These localized ideological followers, who are closer to the mainstream than the body of terrorists, hold sway in their public areas of influence. Many who work under or near them are well aware of the radical philosophies they espouse, but the beauty of al-Qaeda's doctrine is that it is based on a debate that has raged throughout Islam for at least the past two centuries. Can Islam be more perfect and pure? It is often preached in such a way as to be compatible with the ultraconservative Wahabist ideology of Saudi Arabia. Many on the Muslim street, from imam to student to merchant, understand this is merely a puritanical reading of the most traditional facets of Islam. This seemingly unshakable faith is, in fact, admired on many levels. However, the ideology takes a clever, almost unseen twist on the issue of suicide and mass murder. It is precisely there, at the murder of innocents and the permissibility of suicide, that the AQ extreme becomes a cult.

The core belief of the AQ terrorists is that they must bleed the enemy dry in order to stop oppression. To do this they must completely disregard Islam's basic tenets. Once the enemy is vanquished, they, as victors, will decide which of Islam's values will be obeyed.

The Greatest Threat Is to Islam Itself

THE WORLD'S MUSLIMS are now pawns in a game started by a man who claims religious scholarship and piety and to be a devoted slave and servant to the one God. He claims to pray five times a day, or more, and live purely by the word of God as passed down to the Prophet Mohammed and as enshrined in the holy Qur'an. He claims to lead a life where he has freely given up his fortune in doing Allah's works. If it were true, it would be admirable. Yet as the blood of Muslims dries on the hands of his men they know that they are willfully violating many parts of Islamic jurisprudence, in the name of not God but their prince, Osama bin Laden. They must know that they are guilty of being rebellious to the word of God; thus they are considered Zalimun—evildoers.

The ulema consensus is that "enjoining good and forbidding evil is one of the most important obligations of the Muslim society."[11] In this instance the Afghan Taliban, the Pakistan variant Tarik-e-Taliban, and al-Qaeda have formally decided that enjoining evil and forbidding good except as they allow is an important obligation in their Muslim society. It raises the question: are they a part of Muslim society or something different?

The Qur'an says that there are two ways to adhere to Islamic ideology: stay true to Sunnah and reject Bid'ah. "The word Sunnah is also applied to Sunnah acts of worship and beliefs that are proven in the Sunnah. The opposite of Sunnah is bid'ah (innovation/heresy)."[12]

Perhaps the AQ variant of Islam, where they can murder at will, defile a married women in public, mutilate a body of a Muslim without proper burial, hang children in front of their homes without judicial review, and execute lethal judgment (which the Qur'an states must be left only to God), is not Islam at all but Bid'ah.

President Barack Obama, speaking before the Turkish parliament in 2009, summed up the multinational character of the United States and its new face toward the Muslim world this way:

I also want to be clear that America's relationship with the Muslim community, the Muslim world, cannot, and will not, just be based upon opposition to terrorism. We seek broader engagement based on mutual interest and mutual respect. We will listen carefully, we will bridge misunderstandings, and we will seek common ground. We will be respectful, even when we do not agree. We will convey our deep appreciation for the Islamic faith, which has done so much over the centuries to shape the world—including in my own country. The United States has been enriched by Muslim Americans. Many other Americans have Muslims in their families or have lived in a Muslim-majority country—I know, because I am one of them.

This was the first shot in the new battle for the support of the mainstream Muslim world. It was a good one, but an organized strategy to break the link between Islam and AQ needs much more support. Al-Qaeda recognizes the threat that such a newly adopted mind-set could have in the battle for the hearts and souls of the Muslim community. No less than AQ's second-in-command, Dr. Ayman al-Zawahiri, gave us the key to their defeat. Remove the fractional support of the Muslim world and AQ will end: "In the absence of this popular support, the Islamic mujahed movement would be crushed in the shadows."[13]

Part II

Coup de pointe:
The Ideology of Mass Murder

3.

Companions of the Fire:
The Corrupted Framework
of al-Qaeda's Ideology

But whoever of you turns away from his religion and dies in disbelief,
his works will come to nothing in this world, and in the world to come.
Such are the companions of the Fire, where they will stay forever.
—QUR'AN 2:217

MY OWN EXPERIENCE with modern suicide terrorism began a full eighteen years before September 11. It was in Lebanon in 1983 that I witnessed Hezbollah's terrorist group, the Islamic Jihad Organization (IJO), destroying first the American embassy in West Beirut, killing sixty-four people, including the entire CIA contingent. A few months later, while we were still studying the motivation of the first attack, they then flattened the multistory marine barracks at Beirut Airport. The attacks used just one man, each driving a large SVBIED, what we now call suicide truck bombs. The suicide bombers were trained and sponsored by the Iranian Revolutionary Guard (IRG), an official arm of the government of Iran. The IRG provided technical assistance to the IJO in order to drive Israel and the West from political and military interference in Lebanon. The two attacks on the American presence were soon followed by a third against the new American embassy. In just two years the IJO killed over three hundred Americans.

America was not alone in the onslaught. The French and Israeli armies would soon suffer similar attacks and add more than one hundred more dead to the total of suicide truck bomb victims. The IJO was not the first terrorist organization to use such tactics; they had been used regularly by the Sri Lankan Tamil insurgency's "Black Tiger" suicide units. They delivered these attacks with cars, trucks, boats, and individual bombers. Their tactics were soon being mimicked in the terror world even as they had copied them from the Japanese army kamikaze pilots of World War II. Without aircraft at the time but using their bodies or vehicles as bomb platforms, these terrorists tapped the vein of a new form of fear—a simple method where one man and one bomb would fuse together into a human-guided weapon system and devastate their enemies with ruthless effectiveness.

Ten years after my traumatic introduction to militant suicide extremism I would see the emergence of a different group of terrorists. Wholly unlike their Shiite brethren in the Lebanese IJO, the Sunnah Muslims of AQ were motivated not by nationalism or fighting occupation or deposing tyrants—though they feigned that this was their reason for being. These men were fighting, they claimed, to reestablish a Muslim Caliphate, from Morocco to the Philippines. To do this they were calling for a grand defense of Islam to avenge offenses suffered by Christians and Jews that they claimed harkened back to the Crusades. The terrorists claim not to fight for themselves but directly for the sake of God and draw themselves as holy knights engaged in an honorable war. This is a war of choice that they themselves have started. These "knights" see themselves as nomadic Islamic scholars, living a harsh, austere life away from "unpure" Muslim and non-Muslim civilizations. Embracing a gypsylike lifestyle where only their brothers and God reign, they go and fight wherever they perceive injustice or Muslim lands under attack. Like the Ronin of feudal Japan, they have been forsaken and seek to find redemption through a more pure love of God and action by arms. Philosophically, this has always been an appealing ideology in the Muslim world, the stuff of heroes and from *A Thousand and One Arabian Nights*. It came about in Saudi Arabia during the Ikhwan uprising of the nineteenth century, then in the Egyptian underground with the Muslim Brotherhood; finally it found a global voice after the Soviet invasion of Afghanistan. They fought there and when it was complete they spread globally to first Somalia, then Bosnia-Herzegovina, Indonesia, Chechnya, Uzbekistan, the Philippines, Kyrgyzstan, Tajikistan, Pakistan, and on and on. Like a band of religious mercenaries, they swore oaths to live as "jihadists"—religious war combatants. They networked and formed a constellation of guerrilla groups, insurgent cells, and terrorists. They used technology of the Internet, the fax machine, and the cell phone to organize into a unified network called al-Qaeda, under the leadership of the Saudi national hero Osama bin Laden.

It was during the tumultuous early 1990s when AQ-supported "jihadists" flitted from war to war that OBL tasked his lieutenants to develop a global jihad strategy. This would be the combat and ideological doctrine on which AQ would base their training curriculum for the next decade.

A secondary goal of his battle staff was to maintain continuity in coordinating or providing technical assistance for a wide-ranging series of global attacks with acolytes who would be inspired by al-Qaeda's daring raids, or *ghazwahs*, on their enemies. Nothing would be discounted; all weapons and tools would be brought to bear on the Americans. Anyone who stood in al-Qaeda's way, particularly if they were Muslim, would be fair game. In a perfect al-Qaeda world, new recruits would learn to conduct their own anti-American operations, from the most simple hand grenade attack to massive suicide strikes within America itself, without direct al-Qaeda assistance. This was called the self-starting jihad.

In February 1993 a small band of Egyptian terrorists, inspired by Egyptian cleric Omar Abdel-Rahman and led by an al-Qaeda bomb maker named Ramzi Yousef, delivered a fifteen-hundred-pound bomb into the World Trade Center in New York City and detonated it. Six people died but the Towers did not collapse as planned. America was not amused. In the three years that followed, a near-textbook counter-terrorist operation made the arrests and convictions of all but one of the members. The master bomber Ramzi Yousef was later captured in Pakistan.

It was only after this attack that American and British intelligence agencies finally awakened to the fact that the U.S.-backed Afghan war had started a pan-Arab extremist movement that was going global. It was found to be specifically targeting the West and Saudi Arabia.

OBL's objectives were clear to him—with his brave martyrs positioned around the world he would strike, strike, and restrike at America long enough to make it clear that occupying any Muslim land, particularly having any presence in Saudi Arabia, the Land of the Two Holy Shrines, was not acceptable. If he won that concession (and he did in 2004), no matter; he would restrike the World Trade Center just to reemphasize the point.

In bin Laden's estimation, when America had enough bloodshed they would sever their ties to the Saudis. When that occurred, his decades-long radicalization campaign of Saudi terrorists would rise up and bubble to the boiling point. A true Islamic revolution would occur. His jihadists would take back Mecca and Medina as the Prophet Mohammed had done fourteen hundred years before. Once that happened, bin Laden or his followers of another generation could purify Islam and return it to the practices not seen since the last days of the Prophet. Bin Laden only needed to strategically communicate his message to the world and bring Islam along with him.

In 1988 the AQ leadership established a working philosophy for the group based on pan-Islamic jihad against the West and its supporting Muslim nations. By 1992 they had developed long-range goals and a strategic plan of action through which to achieve them. The defeat of America and Zionism cannot be achieved until Islamic unity and jihad is accepted throughout the constituency AQ seeks to influence the most—the 1.5 billion Muslims on earth. With the exception of a small portion of Pakistan, the acceptability of AQ's acts has made virtually no major inroads in the Muslim world. However, the fastest method to gain new recruits is to pierce through the heart of traditional Islamic devotion and piety and perform bold, daring acts.

Raiding the Crusader Camp

WHEN HE MADE his 1997 "Declaration of Jihad" against the United States, bin Laden was well aware of what was in store for America. Bin Laden planned a multidecade operation, a "long war" for an "Islamic renaissance" that would see America itself brought low and the Islamic Caliphate rise again. The early attacks on America, including his critical assistance to the 1993 World Trade Center bombing, were merely the youthful brilliance of his lieutenants stretching their legs. True, he had failed to destroy twelve U.S. airliners over the Pacific Ocean that same year, called Project Bojinka, or Chaos. True, he had aborted crashing a hijacked airliner into the CIA headquarters. Also true, he had failed in an assassination plot to kill the Pope, blow up President Clinton and Secretary of State Madeleine Albright, and destroy the Los Angeles airport, but no matter; during the 1990s bin Laden had a battle staff working on other plots to damage America and its allies full-time.

OBL had foreknowledge of all this, but more immediately a series of large-scale suicide bomb attacks were in planning to destroy two U.S. embassies in East Africa. These would be the last lethal signal that he would send to America. The 1998 Kenyan and Tanzanian dual suicide bombings were in the final stages of logistics and surveillance. He only had to light the fuse.

Men were being vetted for the year 2000 millennium attacks and an operation involving the hijacking and crashing of aircraft into New York's twin skyscrapers. There was precedence for this plot. In 1995 al-Qaeda's Algerian brothers had succeeded in hijacking an Air France airliner to crash into Paris but were stopped by French commandos in Marseilles in a storm of bullets.

As the time and circumstances of OBL's ideological war have changed, al-Qaeda's strategic goals have changed as well. But America's weakness is a belief that bin Laden banks on. Based on reports that he had received from Somalia in 1992, bin Laden developed the belief that the American army and people were individually and collectively weak. Speaking in 1998, he stated that "We believe that America is much weaker than Russia, and we have learned from our brothers who fought in the jihad in Somalia of the incredible weakness and cowardice of the American soldier."[1]

OBL had secondhand information gleaned mainly from allies in the Somali militias and intelligence reports from his aides in Mogadishu that were fatally tainted. In fact, no fight in Somalia where a militia was pitted in a stand-up battle against U.S. soldiers was won by insurgents. Even the bloody Battle of Bokara Market, which was idealized in the book and movie *Black Hawk Down* (a favorite movie of the Iraqi insurgents), was a devastating example to an enemy skilled in irregular combat of how tough U.S. soldiers could be in a face-to-face infantry battle. Whether by rifle or RPG, the Americans had prevailed in Somalia with only seventeen deaths to as many as one thousand militiamen massacred. Still, it was the media that provided this impression to OBL. The disgust that the Americans had displayed at the dragging of the dead soldiers' bodies had formed in him a dismissive opinion of American resolve. He calculated that in the face of massive suicide attacks from his legion of militants armed with the Qur'an and religious zeal, America could easily be defeated in an insurgency similar to that of Russia in Afghanistan. His strategy was to push America into an Afghanistan war. Afghanistan is known as the graveyard of empires. OBL banked on Afghani animosity to non-believers so he could lure in American soldiers and watch them die by the hands of his foot soldiers.

Al-Qaeda's Ideological Formation

OSAMA BIN LADEN was born on March 10, 1957, in the al-Malazz neighborhood of Riyadh, Saudi Arabia. He was just one of fifty-two children (he had twenty-four brothers) of Sheikh Mohammed bin Oud bin Laden. Mohammed bin Laden was not a local Saudi but a native from neighboring Hadramut

Province of Yemen.[2] Mohammed had left Yemen in the early 1920s and settled in the Hejaz region of Saudi Arabia in 1932. There he made his fortune as a businessman. He founded the Bin Laden Construction Corporation. Bin Laden Construction grew during the oil boom of the 1970s into a power-house in the western provinces. As a favor for a loan to the Kingdom, Mo-hammed was given exclusive rights to renovate all religious buildings in the Kingdom. Most important, he was granted the honor to renovate and mod-ernize the Grand Mosque in Mecca. In 1976 the company went through a reorganization and was renamed Bin Laden Brothers for Contracting and Industry. Mohammed was an engineer and architect who had eleven wives. With this brood he created one of the richest families in the Kingdom. Mo-hammed died when his son Osama was ten years old. Osama would come to inherit a share of the bin Laden family wealth that was estimated at approxi-mately $20 million upon the death of his father.[3] At nineteen Osama entered King Abdul Aziz University in Jeddah, where he majored in management and economics.

Like most terrorist leaders, Osama bin Laden developed his working ide-ology at the hands of mentors and professors who had a great influence on him. During his university years bin Laden became deeply religious. It was while studying there he became a student of Mohammed Qutb, the brother of Sayyid Qutb. Sayyid Qutb was a member and religious ideologue of the Egyptian Muslim Brotherhood. Executed by the Egyptian government, Qutb is hailed as the father of the philosophy that called for a complete rejec-tion of the West and its values. Qutb was also the author of radical books that form the philosophical and operational heart of al-Qaeda militancy, includ-ing *In the Shade of the Koran* and *Milestones*. These books were mandatory reading for all in their insurgent camps.

Bin Laden was profoundly impacted by the writings of Qutb and his indoctrination into the militant ideology. Sayyid's brother tutored OBL in a radically revolutionary interpretation of Islam that claimed jihad was an of-fensive tool to be executed in the face of the land of the "ignorant," as the non-Islamic world was called. They also believed the West had been interfer-ing in the Islamic world since the Christian Crusades. To them this made the modern "offensive jihad" actually "defensive," as the militants were address-ing a long list of past grievances that had never been resolved. Sayyid also preached that all Christians and Jews were the death enemies of Muslims and were destined for damnation, contrary to what is written in the Qur'an.

Another of OBL's mentors at the university was the scholar-warrior

Abdullah Yusuf Azzam. A Palestinian with a Ph.D., he had come to teach after a stint fighting the Israelis from Jordan. Azzam believed in an internationalist jihad where arms were the salvation of Islam. OBL seized these and other more radical concepts and worked them into his code of belief.

Islamic Schisms, Movements, and Cults

ISLAM HAS HAD schisms, movements, and even fringe cults before. Most perversions of Islam were usually snuffed out by traditionalists well before they had a chance to flourish. Others became true minority movements, existing for centuries in isolated geographic regions. For example, the Yazidis are a Kurdish religious sect with a mix of practices from several ancient religions, including Zorastrianism and Islam. Believing they are descended from supporters of the second Umayyad Caliph, Yazid ibn Mu'awiyah, in the seventh century, they are often erroneously said to worship the devil, due to their belief that the devil had repented his sins before God and had been forgiven. In South Asia, the followers of the nineteenth-century leader Mirza Gulam Ahmed formed the Ahmadiyyahs, a largely Pakistani sect that claims its leader Ahmed is also a Prophet. A group that could be said to be more denominational than a sect is the Sufis. Sufis are orthodox interpreters of the Qur'an who diverge because of their use of mystical Islamic practices, in the form of dance and music to worship God.

There have been past Islamic sects that resembled the modern al-Qaeda. Some of the components of these ideologies appear to have been co-opted by bin Laden in an attempt to make past fringe thoughts, rejected for centuries by most Muslims, a historically based alternative to mainstream Islam.

The Khawarij–the First Takfiri Extremists

A PAST GROUP that reflects some of the characteristics of the ideology of modern-day AQ terrorists was the fringe al-Khawarij of the seventh-century Hijaz (modern-day western Saudi Arabia). This Muslim group split into a dissident sect during the reign of the third leader after the death of the Prophet Muhammed, Caliph Uthman ibn Affan. These Muslims initially backed the succession of the Prophet's son-in-law Ali Ibn abi Thalib, but they soon rebelled and formed a series of complex rules for their tribesmen that doctrinalized an ultrapuritanical interpretation of Islam.

After the Battle of Hunain, in 630, the Prophet divided the spoils to the participants. A larger share was given to the non-Muslim participants as an enticement to come to Islam. One Hurqu ibn Zubair complained about the division of the takings and was rebuked by the Prophet. Mohammed said:

> There will come a time when a group of people will leave our ranks. They will recite the Quran with fervour and passion but its spirit will not go beyond their throats. They will leave our ranks in the manner of an arrow when it shoots from its bow.[4]

The Prophet Mohammed died in 632. His closest companions met to choose a successor. One of the Prophet's closest companions, Umar ibn al-Khattab, nominated another close friend of Mohammed's, Abu Bakr. Along political lines, Abu Bakr was overwhelmingly and democratically chosen a righteous Caliph (rashidun). He ruled until 634. Unfortunately, at the time of Mohammed's death other companions and friends of the Prophet supported his first cousin and son-in-law, Ali Ibn abi Thalib, to be a bloodline successor to the Prophet. The hard feelings of all parties after the succession of Abu Bakr would eventually split Islam in two, but only after the Khawarij were through. For now Abu Bakr reigned. He was soon followed by two more elected Caliphs, Umar and Uthman ibn Affan.

The Khawarij in the First Islamic Fitnas (Civil Wars)

BY THE TIME of the election of the third Caliph, Uthman, the Islamic world extended from western Persia to the western Algerian coast. But all was not peaceful. In 656 an armed rebellion against Uthman was incited by the Egyptians. They converged on the city of Medina and called on dissident forces who came from as far east as Kufa and Basra in Iraq. These rebels laid siege to Uthman's palace, and after several days of fighting they finally succeeded in assassinating him.

After Uthman's murder and suppression of the rebellion, Ali, the Prophet's first cousin, was finally elected Caliph. He established his Caliphate in the Iraqi town of Kufa, outside of Karbala. Though he was finally elected Caliph, many refused to support him. One was Mu'awiyah, the governor of Syria. Mu'awiyah wanted the murderers of Uthman brought to justice. He believed that Ali was unwilling to do that and should be deposed. Mu'awiyah formed an army in his province and marched toward Iraq, intending to overthrow Ali. Ali responded and called on Muslims to defend the Caliphate. The two forces met near the Syrian village of Siffin on the Euphrates. After three days of indecisive battle that killed several of the Companions of the Prophet, a clever ruse by Mu'awiyah's men brought Ali's forces to near mutiny. They placed pages of the Qur'an on their spear tips and dared them to attack. This gesture forced Ali to meet Mu'awiyah in negotiation. The two leaders were met by a *Shura*, a guidance council that ruled that Ali was to return to his duties as Caliph and Mu'awiyah would return to his governorship. The *fitna* was ended, or so it appeared. While the negotiations played out, twelve thousand men in Ali's army rejected any talk of negotiation. In a sign of rebellion, they laid down their weapons and abandoned their positions. It is here that the militant extremist dissident soldiers, later called the Khawarij (which means "those who went out" or "outsiders") effectively tore the first hole in the unified Caliphate and started the Sunnah-Shiite split in Islam.

After departing from the main forces at Siffin, the Khawarij leadership based their decision on the literal reading of the Qur'an—it stated clearly that there could be no ruler but God. This meant the Khawarij demanded the immediate excommunication of Ali, Mu'awiyah, and anyone who had taken part in the negotiations at Siffin.

It was an anarchist approach to Islam. They effectively rejected both Ali's and Mu'awiyah's claims to earthly leadership. As the Khawarij left the battlefield, Ali sent forces to intercept them before news of their wild words got into the Iraqi cities. His emissaries managed to convince eight thousand to return to his forces. The other four thousand, including Hurqu ibn Zubair, the early dissenter to the Prophet's generosity, were defeated in 658 at the Battle of Nahrawan in Central Iraq. It left only a handful of survivors.[5] It was a singular slaughter. Nine survivors of the battle escaped. They later radicalized and organized to assassinate Ali. In 661 they were successful, but for Islam it was too much. The Khawarij treachery on the battlefield and the assassination of Ali effectively split the Islamic world in two.

After the murder of Caliph Ali his supporters believed that he and his following imams should have held political and spiritual control over Islam, not the chosen Caliphs. As followers of the "Faction of Ali" (Shi'atul Ali) they are popularly referred to as Shiite, or the faction.

The philosophy of Shiite Islam is not just an argument over the Prophet's succession but a discussion of who can become a Caliph, what he represents, and what functions he can perform. The Shiites' largest denomination is called the Twelvers, for they believe the first twelve imams, all bloodline descendants of the ahl-al-Bayt, or house of the Prophet Mohammed (all of whom are infallible and sinless), are the true leaders of Islam. Interestingly, a more significant difference between the two denominations is that the Shiite believe that the last of the twelve imams, Mohammed Mahdi, who "disappeared" in 937, is expected to return at Judgment Day as savior of mankind.

The views of the Shiites are wildly divergent from the mainstream, traditionalist Muslims, who call themselves the Sunnah. They believed that any good Muslim was capable of becoming Caliph. Already three Caliphs had served before Ali, so the precedent was set, but to the Shiites the restructuring of Islam was just beginning and they rejected the authority of the three Caliphs. After the death of Ali, his nemesis, Mu'awiyah, became Caliph and the first of the Damascus-based Umayyads to rule the now-split Islam.

The Khawarij managed to remain viable and grow into an insurgent tribe who saw themselves as the only true Muslims in Islam. They eventually broke down into fifteen distinct sects generally named after their founders and with varying levels of militancy. The most powerful of their mini-states was in the al-Yamamah region of Saudi Arabia and communities in Oman, Zanzibar, Berber Tunisia, Libya, Algeria, and Morocco.

Some Khawarij would impose strict penalties on sins and leave other sins without punishment. It depended entirely on the sect. The most influential after the original Muhakkiah were the Azariqa, named after Nafi' ibn al-Azraq, a surviving dissenter of the *fitna*. Followers of al-Azraq were also among the most extreme, adopting positions that are now seen among AQ including:

Mandatory Hijrah: Khawarij true believers asserted that they should emulate the Prophet and move away from non-believers in Hijrah (emigration).

Mandatory isolation: According to literal readings of the Qur'an, the known world is in a state of ignorance from the word of God. Only communities where Muslims immigrate and establish Sharia law are legitimate. Therefore, isolation is the only guarantee from ignorance.

Right of Takfir: The Khawarij reserved the right to declare anyone, Muslim or not, a *kufir*, or a non-believer, and kill them.

Universal excommunication: In some sects they ruled that all people but the Khawarij in their sect were deemed *kufir*.

No innocents to be spared: Some Khawarij, particularly the Azariqa, believed that children and women were an equal threat. Though the Qur'an specifically disallows this, the Azariqa wanted no blood feuds to come back on them, so they did not spare children.

Rigorous interrogation: Interestingly, like today's al-Qaeda terrorists the Khawarij were internationalist Muslims. However, anyone seeking to join the group was subjected to a severe and rigorous interrogation to determine that he was not a spy.

Covert operation and dissimulation: One sect of Khawarij, the Sufriyya sect in Basra, gave up armed rebellion and stayed underground in southern Iraq in order to survive the anti-Khawarij raids of the Caliphate. To survive they practiced Taqiyya, the Qur'anic-inspired tactic of espousing one faith and hiding one's true beliefs in order to infiltrate or survive a hostile country.

The second Islamic *fitna* started in 680, at the death of Mu'awiyah. During this time Islam was in chaos and the Khawarij spread to Iraq and the Arabian Peninsula. By 730 they were eliminated in large part by the Umayyad Caliphate.

The Qaramita and the Desecration of Mecca

DESPITE THE SUNNAH-SHIITE split, there formed divisions within Shiite Islam itself. The Ismali sect believe that the line of succession split after the sixth Shiite imam, Jafar al-Sadiq, and passed onto Ismā'īl ibn Ja'far and that he was the end of the line of succession. They also believed that Imam Muhammad bin Ismail was the living Mahdi, or savior who would stay on earth and prepare it for Judgment Day.

One of these early converts was Hamdan al-Qaramat of Kufa. His followers were commonly called the Qaramita (anglicized to "Caramathians" or "Qaramitians"). The radicalism of the group started in 874 when Hamdan and his brother-in-law, Abdan bin al-Rabit, desired to militarily prepare southern Iraq for the return of the Mahdi. The Qaramita created other armed communities in eastern Arabia. After a senior imam claimed to have succeeded the person assumed to be the Mahdi, Imam Muhammad bin Ismail, Hamadan publicly renounced the practice of Ismailianism. He is said to have separated from his own rejectionist group after his brother-in-law, Abdan, was killed during the fighting over the succession of Imam al-Mahdi. Hamdan al-Qaramat is said to have abandoned his fellow travelers and sided with the Fatimid Caliphate. Yet the sect retained the name Qaramita even after the original followers were defeated in 906. They would create a formidable Bedouin power in eastern Arabia.

The Qaramita inhabited the island of Bahrain and the entire eastern region of the Arabian Peninsula. They had a chain of connected oases and communities, skilled at desert navigation and control of trade routes, from Basra to Muscat.

During the heyday of Qaramita ascendancy from 906 to 929, hajj attacks had been a lucrative form of raiding by Bedouin tribes in the Arabian Peninsula and Syria. Hajj pilgrims did hire protection armies, but the large groups of raiders would slash through them, wreak terror, and pillage the caravans. The Qaramita took up this trade and the Abbasid Caliphate could do little about it. Some observers believe that the Qaramita filled a role for the Bedouin raiders of Bahrain who were excluded from chance of working for the Abbasid government and in its military service.[7] No matter, they took to banditry and insurgency as a faster route to riches. The Qaramita raided also to spread their variant of Ismailianism and to secure a Gulf port for a maritime protection racket for the hajiis in order to safeguard them from the eastern Arabian raiders, namely themselves.[8]

As the hajj was a major economic event and many hajiis from Persia and South and Central Asia had to transit across the Qaramita's domain, it was an opportunity made for raiding. Ironically it was the Qaramita that broke the rule of the Ibadi sect, the descendants of the surviving Khawarij clans, in Oman.[9] They also cut the line of communication from Kufa in south-central Iraq to Palmyra in western Syria, thus isolating all trade between Baghdad and Damascus.

In 922 the hajj was again raided for the second year running and the victims were mounting into the thousands. An attack on Basra in 923 killed the governor, Sabuk al-Mufhli, who thought the Khawarij attackers were just Bedouin raiders. There they burned mosques and killed hundreds.[10] This insurgency could not continue, and the Abbasid Caliphate entered into negotiations and managed to pay the group to secure unmolested passage for the hajj. Unfortunately, the new Caliph, al-Muqtadir, cut the subsidies.

Some historians believe the Qaramita, under the leader Abu Tahir, were forced to make a point about the loss of their economic subsidies and their rejection of Sunnah Islamic practices. The Qaramita proclaimed that the hajj had devolved into a form of idolatry by Muslim hajiis worshiping at the

Kaaba and the black stone inside.[11] Either way, they declared war on Islam. In 930 a Qaramita raiding force entered Mecca and utterly desecrated the holiest spot in Islam for seventeen days. During that time they seized the Kaaba, the center of Islam, and stole the black meteorite. It is said they killed many and dumped dead bodies in the holy well of Zamzam. The raiders took the stone to their base at Hajar and entered into negotiations for its ransom. Infuriated, the Fatimid Caliph wanted justice. Abu Tahir received a letter from the top Fatimid imam that stated:

> It is a contemptible matter that you have committed a grave sin under my name. Where did you commit? You have committed in the House of God and its neighbours. This is a sacred place, where the murder was unlawful even in the age of ignorance; and the defamation of the people living in Mecca is considered inhuman. You have violated that tradition, and even rooted out the Black Stone, and brought it to your land; and now you expect that I may express my gratitude? God curse you, and be again accursed and execrable. May peace be upon him (Prophet Muhammad), whose sayings and deeds are the source of the integrity of the Muslims, who may be ready to answer hereafter what they have committed today.[12]

Although the Fatimid argument was supposedly persuasive and Abu Tahir promised to repair the damage, the stone was not returned for twenty years, until 950. The new Fatimid Caliphate, based in Tunisia, had no better luck with the Qaramita, who had become even more powerful. They fought a series of clashes for control of the Syrian and Arabian trade routes. The Fatimids eventually restricted control of them and managed to finally marginalize the Qaramita into central Iraq. Over time they withdrew to Bahrain, where they effectively ended their reign in 1077.[13]

Juhayman bin Seif al-'Uteybi— *Grand Mosque Siege, 1979*

AQ ARE NOT the first terror group to perpetrate mass violence in the modern Kingdom of Saudi Arabia. In 1979 a Salafist extremist group of two hundred armed men, led by a former member of the Saudi Arabian National Guard, Juhayman bin Seif al-'Uteybi, seized the Grand Mosque in Mecca.

Al-'Uteybi sought to fulfill the prophecy of the return of the Mahdi, the holy redeemer who would return to earth at the end of days and assist Jesus in slaying the anti-Christ. These Sunnah militants became convinced that one of their fold, Mohammed bin Abdullah al-Qahtani, was the Mahdi, based on dreams Islam recognizing al-Qahtani as the Mahdi. They sought to proclaim his return in the fourteen-hundredth year after the birth of Islam. On the first day of the new Islamic year, two hundred al-'Uteybi's militants seized the Grand Mosque and trapped hundreds of worshipers inside. They fought a pitched battle that lasted two weeks, until the militants were finally gassed out with a toxic riot agent supplied by the French. The al-'Uteybi militants killed over 60 Saudi soldiers while losing 75 of their own and 170 captured, including al-'Uteybi.

The man assumed to be the immortal Mahdi, al-Qahtani, was killed in combat. Sixty-three terrorists were later executed by beheading. It is believed that several of the surviving members joined the al-Qaeda movement. One of its leading modern ideologues, Abu Mohammed al-Maqdisi, author of the militant tome *Clear Proofs That the Saudi State Is Infidel*, mentored and shared a cell with the man who would become the leader of al-Qaeda in Iraq, Abu Mussab al-Zarqawi.[14]

Core Religious Tenants of Fringe Islamists

SALAFISM

"SALAFISM" IS THE much-maligned term used for adherents to the fundamentalist Muslim practices that were developed by the first three generations of Muslims. "Salaf" is Arabic for "forebears." The original Salaf were the immediate friends and associates of the Prophet. The Saudi ulema defines "Salaf" as "those who came before you of your forefathers and relatives who are your elders and betters."[15] The Muslims of that era are collectively called the Righteous Companions of the Prophet Mohammed (*al-salaf al-salih*). Understanding this group is critical to understanding the behavior of militants who base their militancy on their religious devotion and the principles of Salafism today. Salafism is an ultraconservative variant of Islam that encourages one to emulate, in modern life, the acts and behaviors (to literally follow the words) of the Prophet and his Companions. Although the Companions were always revered, as we have seen in the previous section, this interpretation formed mainly under the eighteenth-century scholar Mohammed ibn 'Abd al-Wahab al-Tamimi.

However, some scholars view Salafists as distinct from Muwahiddun (e.g., Wahabists) in that it is a far more fundamental creed in Islam and is much less tolerant of opinions and religious diversity.[16] Modern-day followers of these practices are often referred to as Salafiya. The Saudi ulema calls it "a term of praise for everyone who take the Salaf as an example and a method to follow, and the Salaf were the best of this ummah, according to the hadith of the Messenger."

The Saudis also contradict claims that Salafism is just a fad and not an Islamic school of thought. They believe the entire basis of Salafi religious jurisprudence is rooted in two core Islamic principles of the Companions of the Prophet: "good example and correct methodology."[17]

Salafism has been unfairly associated with terrorism due to its adoption as a core principle in al-Qaeda's ideology. Appeals for Muslims to adhere to the Salaf are repeatedly used by OBL and his subordinates to convince Muslims of the righteousness of their activities. However, the methodology of emulating the Salaf themselves has never advocated violence and political revolution. This is where confusion about what AQ stands for ideologically gets mixed up with traditional Saudi Salafism and, as we will see, what many call Wahabism.

NEO-SALAFISM

AQ'S IDEOLOGY AND their extremist use of Salaf is a terrific corruption of Islam. Writing for the U.S. Army War College, Christopher Henzel identified this simple difference as the main reason the Salafist world has currently split ideologically.[18] Incited by the rise of the terrorist fringe adopting ultraextreme positions and verbiage, then labeling it Salafism, the practitioners are engaged in a global religious showdown between the two schools of thought; the pro-Establishment or "moderate" Salafist camp in contrast with the "fighting revolutionary" or ultraextremist Salafist camp. The moderate Salafist camp is led by the government of Saudi Arabia, and this brand of Salafism is practiced by the overwhelming majority of Muslims on the Arabian Peninsula. The fighting revolutionary Salafist camp is led by Osama bin Laden and his ideologue-in-chief, Dr. Ayman al-Zawahiri.

This is not a completely new split, as it has a basis in history. The antecedents of the revolutionary camp have been in flux with mainstream Islam since the nineteenth century. Christopher Henzel writes:

The revolutionary Salafists are outsiders. Their movement, from its origins a century ago until today, has been at odds with the Sunni establishment . . . the experience of their movement drives them to view their opponents within Sunni Islam including the governments of Egypt, Saudi Arabia, Jordan, et al.—"the near enemy"—as more important than non-Muslims in the West—"the far enemy."[19]

Traditions die hard in every society. The Muslim world is no different from those of Christianity and Judaism with regard to the internal struggles for interpretations of core beliefs. That said, what is occurring within the Muslim world today is not so much a discussion about the traditional interpretation of the words of God as narrated by the Prophet Mohammed as an attempt by the terrorist fringe to reinvent the meaning for more sinister purposes.

One consideration is the intensity and irreconcilability of AQ. Many Muslims who reject their brand of worship call it neo-Salafism (Salafiyyah Jadeedah). The fighting neo-Salafist revolutionaries struggle with the illusion that they are striving to be equal in piety and deeds to the original Companions of the Prophet through war. The revolutionaries believe they can bring honor to themselves by discussing among themselves and reminding all who hear their voice of the characteristics of their forefathers and then corruptly use these same characteristics of peace, loyalty, and bravery as the basis for excommunication and murder.

It is noteworthy that throughout the AQ literature the militants use the word "Tawaagheet" to define their enemies. It is an early Islamic word that means "idolaters (the polytheists that worshiped in Mecca at the time of the Prophet)." To the militants, all non-believers and any entities that support the political goals against AQ, such as the Saudi government and Arab states, are given this designation. They also associate quotes from the historical confrontations in the Qur'an against enemies of the Prophet in the Hijaz with modern-day application to justify their animosity and aggression against the West. A popular example is found in Qur'an 9:73: "O Prophet! Strive hard against the disbelievers and the hypocrites, and be stern towards them. Their resting place is Hell, and worst indeed is that destination." With this verse alone, they justify their entire repertoire of terror.

Takfiri Ideology

A POWERFUL IDEOLOGICAL tool for a religious terrorist is a belief in the necessity to violate fourteen centuries of sacred law. Takfir is a core ideological belief of the al-Qaeda organization and its followers. It is the belief that a

Muslim can declare any other Muslim, no matter how devout he or she may be, a *kufir* or "non-believer." Islamic law, when taken literally, states that a Muslim who leaves or rejects Islam should be sentenced to death. This convoluted argument originated in the writings of Taqi ad-Din Ahmed Ibn Taymaiyya and 'Abd al-Wahab, who wrote on Takfir:

> . . . we do not make takfeer of anyone whose religion is correct, whose righteousness, knowledge, piety, and asceticism is well-known, whose life is praiseworthy, and who made his sincere effort for the ummah by devoting himself to teaching the beneficial sciences and writing about them, even if he was mistaken in this matter or in other matters.[20]

Takfiris cite many of the classical scholars after the period of Salaf, particularly after the Mongol invasion, as saying the Islamic world reverted to a state of pre-Islamic enlightenment the "ignorance." Technically all Muslims who do not support jihad against invaders are considered apostates who have given up Islam. Therefore, the followers of Takfir ideology can kill at will or justify the deaths of anyone they designate. The modern usage of Takfir is a clear throwback to the seventh-century Khawarij's brutal decision to excommunicate and kill any dissenters to its rebellion. Takfir became a tool that justified for tribal expansion under 'Abd al-Wahab and the al-Saud tribe in the eighteenth and nineteenth centuries.

AQ members also believe that they have the ability to declare Muslims who cooperate with any entity opposing their strategy or ideology Kufir as well. By adopting Takfir, murder is transcended to a divine rite and removes all possible appeals to humanity. The executioner is simply applying God's pre-determined judgment, which absolves him of any guilt for murder. Pulling a trigger to kill a human being is harder than one would think, and violating the Qur'an requires a special set of tools for a Muslim to get beyond the sinfulness of the act that could result in the death of one or more believers. Takfir is that tool.

Al-Wala' Wa al-Bara'
 (Devotion and Disavowal)

IN SALAFISM, AL-WALA' Wa al-Bara' is a depiction of "Love and Hate for Allah's Sake." It is a process where the intimate devotion to God (al-Wala') is shown through complete and utter disavowel (al-Bara') of all things and associations with non-believers. The Wala' is complete, unquestioning love and loyalty due to God. Advocates demand the complete withdrawal from anyone who is not a true believer in Islam. It asks that concepts, practices, and ideas of non-believers must be abandoned in order to attain purity. Believers must refute and avoid friendships with Christians and Jews.

Many radical proponents of al-Wala' Wa al-Bara' (AWAB) justify this mind-set using Qur'anic verses, particularly verse 3:28 ("Let not the believers take disbelievers for their friends in preference to believers. Whoever does this has no connection with Allah unless you are guarding yourselves against them as a precaution. Allah bids you to beware [only] of Himself. And to Allah is the journeying") and verse 5:51 ("O you who believe! Do not take the Jews and the Christians for friends. They are friends of one another. And whoever of you takes them for friends is [one] of them. Surely Allah does not guide wrongdoing people"). OBL and his followers take these verses quite literally. Simply put, many Salfist jurists who advocate al-Wala' Wa al-Bara' emphasize that any contact or friendship with non-believers has consequences. ("He will be an infidel akin to them.")[21]

In an early interview after 9/11 the concept of al-Wala' Wa al-Bara' was spelled out by bin-Laden. He issued a direct threat to all who continued to know or interact with non-believers.

> So I tell the Muslims to be very wary and careful about befriending Jews and Christians. Whoever helps them do so with one word, let him be devout to God, and to renew his faith so he can repent about what he did . . . even one word, whoever upholds them with one word . . . Falls into apostasy, a terrible apostasy, and there is no might nor power except with God.[22]

As we have read before, in Islam the Qur'an gravely cautions against the introduction of heresy; somehow al-Wala' Wa al-Bara' has been given a loophole against this warning. In practice, Muslims are being given a litmus test in the form of having their behaviors with regards to non-believers watched and checked. Taken to the extreme, it is a loyalty test for the level of devotion to the AQ and affiliated organizations as well.

Joas Wagemakers, a Dutch scholar who has studied the life of Abu Mohammed al-Maqdisi, the compatriot of Abu Mussab al-Zarqawi, leader of

AQI, discusses how jihad is then worked into the formula of al-Wala' Wa al-Bara' to make it essentially al-Wala' Wa al-Bara' plus jihad:

> The theory of al-wala' wa'l-bara' as a means to brand rulers and their legislation as forms of polytheism is further developed in al-Maqdisi's other works. Relying on the example of Ibrahim used in Qur'an 60:4, in which believers are encouraged to show their enmity and hatred of polytheism, he stresses that all Muslims must disavow politicians and their laws. Al-Maqdisi considers the highest form of this disavowal to be jihad.[23]

Yet mainstream Salafists do acknowledge that the AWAB rejects outside influence but not in the same way that the neo-Salafist Takfiri militants believe. The fireburning fundamentalist orator, Sheikh Abdulaziz al Rayyis of Saudi Arabia, speaking on the matter, said about being in contact with non-Muslims:

> . . . On the contrary [a Muslim] should abhor them and their way of life. His abhorrence of them being in turn an act of obedience to Allah and His Messenger.[24]

However, there are limits AQ ignores. It is critically important to note that where mainstream Salafists differ with al-Qaeda on this confession is they are adamant that al-Wala' Wa al-Bara' is not a license to kill. Sheikh al Rayyis emphasizes that the violence espoused by al-Qaeda is illegitimate. In the same speech where he notes the necessity for a Muslim to avoid non-Islamic ways, he immediately contradicts bin Laden on resolving the matter with murder:

> It is not in the meaning of "abhorring the Jews and Christians" in any way that we oppress them or Endeavour to kill them. Definitely not! This is not permissible in the true Islamic teachings. On the contrary it is forbidden in the utmost! and is something that should be prevented. Being as the Sharia' extremely honors contrasts and agreement and orders us to commit ourselves with the utmost commitment thereto.

Defining Historical Events for Al-Qaeda

THE CRUSADES (1050–1350)

OSAMA BIN LADEN believes that now is the time for a reckoning with the West. He believes that Islam is in a perpetual jihad against the original sinners, the Crusaders of the Middle Ages and Jews of the Qur'anic age. Interestingly, his reading of the history of the Crusades is almost as corrupt as his understanding of Islam. OBL believes that Christianity, aided by the Jews, has been on a ten-century plan by the Crusader nations and their colonies to insidiously work their way around to finish the vanquishing of the Muslim world. He does not see the Crusades as having effectively ended after the recapture of Jerusalem by Salahudin al-Ayyubi in 1187 A.D. OBL skips nine centuries in between and refocuses the issue on when American forces entered Saudi Arabia in 1990 after Saddam Hussein's invasion of Kuwait. To him, this was the Crusaders infiltrating the heart of Islam to finish the job Richard the Lionhearted and Louis IX did not.

A quick review is in order. It is widely agreed that the Crusades began when Pope Urban II called upon French and German nobility to allegedly assist Christians of the Byzantine Empire who were about to succumb to the rise of Islam. In fact, many historians note that economic and trade concessions were a greater motivating factor than religion. The First Crusade took place between 1096 and 1099 and the major combatants included Geoffrey of Bouillon, Raymond of Toulouse, Robert of Normandy, and Baldwin of Boulogne. In 1099 Jerusalem fell to the Crusaders and they established Christian mini-states from northern Syria to southern Palestine. The Second Crusade was called in 1147 and lasted until 1149, with French and German armies under Conrad III and Louis VII. In 1148 the Crusaders laid siege to Damascus but failed to win it due to lack of water. By 1187 the Muslim ruler of Egypt recaptured Jerusalem and settled the withdrawal of the Crusaders. The last significant Crusade (out of nine) was the third, between 1189 and 1192, where a combined Franco/Anglo/German army under Richard I (the Lionhearted), Frederick Barbarossa, and Philip Augustus of France made an effort to retake Jerusalem by winning victories down the coast, including the brutal massacre of civilians in Acre. After the army came within visual range a treaty was made with Salahudin, as the force was essentially spent and broken. The terms allowed and respected Christian pilgrimages to Jerusalem.

All in all, the nine Crusades were mercenary, ill-advised, and poorly executed campaigns that led to painful losses. They could best be described as overzealous feudal lords leading unskilled and ignorant peasants to take lands that did not belong to them for the benefit of avaricious traders. All of these ventures were supposedly done for religious honors. Granted, some of the leaders did embark on the mission with a quest for pious duty—this was the Age of Faith—but many invested in the righteousness of the task only when promised grants of lands and limitless looting. Other participants wanted a life of adventure and warfare and the honor to serve as knights in what would become a culture-smashing quest.

Professor Emeritus of Near Eastern Studies at Princeton Bernard P. Lewis believes that the Crusades were the opposite of what OBL asserts. That they were a dying stab at holding back the natural political tide that was the cresting of Islam. He notes:

> "Crusade" still touches a raw nerve in the Middle East, where the Crusades are seen and presented as early medieval precursors of European imperialism—aggressive, expansionist and predatory. I have no wish to defend or excuse the often atrocious behavior of the Crusaders, both in their countries of origin and in the countries they invaded, but the imperialist parallel is highly misleading. The Crusades could more accurately be described as a limited, belated and, in the last analysis, ineffectual response to the jihad—a failed attempt to recover by a Christian holy war what had been lost to a Muslim holy war."[25]

The Crusades were never truly a European victory of any note except, on occasion, in arms. The Muslim world at the time was indisputably more advanced than Europe. Islam had contributed greatly to the world body of knowledge, especially in the sciences, including astronomy, cartography, navigation, and meteorology; algebra; geometry; trade management; fortification building; and arts and literature as well as medicine and health.

The question is, how did the Crusades come to be considered a Christian victory that would burn its way into the psychology of modern Muslim terrorists? Certainly much of bin Laden's ideological rhetoric related to the Crusades is far-fetched. These small, brutal expeditions may have accidentally brought with them the stuff to spark European industry and guide it from out of the Dark Ages and eventually to global preeminence. These gains arguably directly contributed to the Renaissance. Perhaps the answer lies in the fact that through the centuries of incursions and trade the Europeans acquired learning and technology that helped them leapfrog to future greatness during the latter second millennium leading up to the Enlightenment (which was a period of Islamic decline that led to 'Abd al-Wahab's Islamic revivalism). For modern-day terrorists with a poor grasp of history this is justification enough to do as much damage as possible to the descendants of the Crusades in order to restore the respect the terrorists feel was lost one thousand years ago.

THE MONGOL INVASION OF ISLAM

ANOTHER HISTORICAL EVENT that influenced militant ideology was the invasion of the classical Islamic world by the Mongols. These nomadic herders of the Mongolian steppe were led by Genghis Khan. They were highly skilled horsemen and warriors who defeated fragmented Chinese dynasties in the thirteenth century and then turned west to start conquests that soon enveloped all the lands from the eastern Mediterranean to the South China Sea. Though they eventually became Muslim, many classical theologians, and their modern followers, invalidate the Mongols' conversion. They believe the Muslim world reverted back to a state of pre-Islamic ignorance.

The Mongols conquered much of the Islamic world in two major expeditionary thrusts. In the first, between 1206 and 1227, the Mongols under Khan rampaged across Central Asia, leveling the Islamic empire of the Kwarzim Shah, Muhammed II, in Persia, and then marauded across the Caucasus via Daghestan. In 1220 the Islamic cities of Samarkand and Bukhara fell, followed by Persia. The war-fighting tactics of the Mongols, based on speed and powerful, accurate horseback archery, cut through the infantry of their adversaries. They were not always successful. The first Islamic victory against the tide of Mongol invasion was in 1221 at Parwan in what is now central Afghanistan. The son of the Muslim ruler of the Kwarzim, Jalal ad-Din, mustered an army of remnants, engaged the Mongols, and inflicted a rare defeat. Genghis Khan himself was so astonished that he led a an army down to personally defeat Jalal in the Battle of Indus and force him to flee to India.

Under Gen. Ogodei Khan the second thrust into Islam reduced a resurgent Kwarzim Shah, then cut through the Trans-Caucasus region of present-day Daghestan and Georgia. A successful winter invasion of Volga Bulguria lands in Russia, the Eastern Principalities, Poland, Hungary, and the Balkans followed.

The final major conquest occurred under Hulegu Khan, the grandson of Genghis. Under orders from his brother Mongke, the ruler of the Mongol

Khanates, Hulegu set out from Balkh and fought his way into the Abbasid Caliphate. In 1258 he took Baghdad, the center of the Abbasid empire and the greatest city of the Islamic world. Hulegu imprisoned and then killed the Caliph, al-Musta'sim, and his sons, thus punctuating an abrupt end to the five-hundred-year Abbasid rule.

Hulegu Khan then invaded Syria. The Syrian cities fell in rapid succession as he worked his way from across the north and turned southward to invade, via Aleppo, Homs and captured the second major Islamic power center, Damascus. There is evidence that some Shiite Muslims and Christians welcomed the Mongol invasion as an alternative to the yoke of the Sunnah Caliphate.

In 1260 Hulegu's forces were stopped from entering Egypt when they were defeated at Ain Jalut north of Jerusalem by the Egyptian Mamluks. They were shock troops of the Abuyyid Caliphate, where the heart of Islam moved after the fall of Damascus. The Mamluks were trained and specifically equipped to defeat the Mongol army due to their extensive knowledge of Mongol battle strategy. In response to this strategy they had developed counter-Mongol field tactics including the use of explosives, handheld cannons, and body-worn pyrotechnics that frightened the Mongol horses.[26]

Indeed, by the time they were stopped at Ain Jalut the Mongol invasion had destroyed much of six centuries of Islamic economy, learning, and trade infrastructure and brought it into direct internal conflict with Buddhism. Although the Khanates eventually became Muslim, the damage from pillaging mosques and universities from China to Palestine was done. The miracle itself is that Islam was not destroyed completely under the Mongols.

However, many Muslim theologians rejected Islamic rule under the Mongols, or the Tartars, as they were often called. The hate has been cited to this day to reveal among militants that Islam has been impure since the fall of Baghdad. For example, Egyptian militant Muhammad 'Abdus Salam Faraj included this story from Ibn Taymaiyya, the classical scholar who endured the sacking of Damascus, in his book *Jihad: The Absent Obligation*:

"No one would join their government unless he is one of the most evil of people. Either a hypocrite who does not believe in Islaam inwardly but professes Islaam outwardly, or is one of the people of bid'ah [innovation] such as the Rafidhah [Shiite Muslims] . . . Whoever enters into their [non-Islamic] and Kufr laws will be regarded as their friend and

whoever opposes them, he will be regarded as their enemy, even if he
is from amongst the best of Muslims."[27]

Ibn Taymaiyya, being a witness to the fall of the Caliphate in Baghdad and
his own city being overrun by non-believers, was an opponent of all who
sided with the Mongols, adding that Muslims who accepted the subsequent
Mongol conversions to Islam were essentially collaborators:

> . . . Also they are fighting for the reign of Jengiz Khan (their King's
> name). Therefore, whoever obeys them they befriend even if he is a
> "kaafir," and whoever rebels against them they regard him as their
> enemy even if he is one of the best Muslims. They are not fighting for
> Islaam and they do not impose Jiziah and abasement (on the kuffaar).
> The aim of most Muslims amongst their leaders and ministers is that
> the Muslim becomes like those whom they glorify from the polythe-
> ists, such as the Jews and Christians.[28]

THE END OF THE ISLAMIC CALIPHATE IN 1924

IN THE WORLD of the al-Qaeda militants the end of the Islamic Caliphate
under the Ottoman Empire was the final straw for the interference of the
West in Muslim affairs. Not even the creation of Israel in 1948 ranks higher
than what they view as the treachery of Kemal Atatürk.

The last Islamic Caliphate was based in Istanbul. It lasted from 1517 after
defeating the Mamluks of Egypt until the advent of the modern Turkish
state. After the defeat of the Ottomans in World War I, very little of the Islamic world was left under their control and what remained was signed
away in the Treaty of Sèvres. The partitioning of the empire by the Allied
states led to the rise of a young war hero, Mustafa Kemal Atatürk, who established the Turkish National Movement in the Turkish War of Independence. This war would force the European victors to break the Treaty of
Sèvres and negotiate a treaty with the nationalists in Lausanne, Switzer-
land, in 1923.

Atatürk wanted to create a modern secular republic. To effect this, the
last vestiges of the Ottoman Empire needed to go. He formally eliminated
the Ottoman Caliphate on March 3, 1924. It is this date that often springs up
in Islamic extremist literature and discourse. In a manual on the combat doctrines and tactics of al-Qaeda found in England, the significance of the end of
the Caliphate was outlined:

After the fall of our orthodox caliphates on March 3, 1924, and after expelling the colonialists, our Islamic nation was afflicted with apostate rulers who took over in the Moslem nation. These rulers turned out to be more infidel and criminal than the colonialists themselves. Moslems have endured all kinds of harm, oppression, and torture at their hands.[29]

The modern militant sees this rejection of the Caliphate as the pinnacle of betrayal of Islam.

Historical Antecedents

FOURTEEN CENTURIES OF radical Islamic scholars, jurists, activists, and terrorists make up the foundations of the AQ revolutionary philosophy. Understanding those who came before and laid the ideological underpinnings of bin Ladenism can help identify how and why AQ has chosen to corrupt large portions of traditional Islamic scholarship.

Taqi ad-Din Ahmed Ibn Taymaiyya (1263–1328) was an influential and prolific Islamic scholar of Kurdish origin, who was of the Hanbali school. His philosophy was grounded in the precept that jihad was a duty of every Muslim to reject the invasion of the Mongols, who were then crushing the Abbasid Caliphate. Ibn Taymaiyya disbelieved their conversion and issued a fatwa declaring the Mongols infidels despite their apparent embracing of Islam. He was also critical of man-made law in place of Sharia law. He saw the Mongol enforcement of their laws, not Sharia, as an example of their illegitimacy and thus made their occupation a reason for an Islam-wide jihad. He died in prison for extremist views. According to the West Point Combating Terrorism Center, Ibn Taymaiyya "is the single most influential medieval authority"[30] for modern-day militants and was the most respected of the Salafist scholars. Militants revere his writings about defending Islam against the disaster that was the Mongol invasion.

Ibn al-Qayyim al-Jawziyya (1292–1350) was the closest disciple and student of Taymaiyya. Born Muhammad Ibn Abi Bakr ibn Sa'd in Damascus, he was the son of the *qayyim* of the al-Jawziyya school. Ibn al-Qayyim became a scholar in theology, Sharia law, and science. He was the editor of Ibn Taymaiyya's written works and an ardent supporter. Both were arrested and imprisoned in the al-Qala prison in Damascus. Ibn al-Qayyim became a scholar in Islamic jurisprudence and eventually became the imam of the al-Jawziyya school. Al-Jawziyya is respected by scholars because "his interpretations are unique in accuracy."[31] He was a fundamental developer of Salafi Sunnism. He was imprisoned along with Ibn Taymaiyya for extremism in his views.

Ibn Hajar al-Asqalani (1372–1448) was born in Egypt of a Palestinian family from Askalan (modern-day Ashkalon in Gaza). He is said to have memorized the Qur'an at age five. Al-Asqalani rose to prominence as a jurist and scholar, writer of the famous classical tract *Fath al-Bari*, a series of commentaries and debates on the Sahih al-Bukhari. The great Islamic scholar al-Albani wrote of him that "Ibn Hajar was the strongest of those 'Ulammaa who had memorised hadith." He is seen as a symbol for striving to continue seeking more Islamic knowledge.

Mohammed ibn 'Abd al-Wahab al-Tamimi (1703–1792) was born in Najd, Saudi Arabia, and became the ideological inspiration for a wing of worship that emphasized ultraconservative, almost rabidly puritanical practice of Islam. During his life in the eighteenth century he observed what he believed were continuing signs of the paganist and polytheist activities in some Muslim communities on the Arabian Peninsula that had been thought banished at the time of the Prophet, some one thousand years earlier. Some tribes continued to pray to objects such as trees and rocks, as well as to individuals. He believed and stressed the monotheistic basis of Islam, the unity of the one God (Tawhid), and that anyone living under rulers, jurists, or imams who allowed such polytheist activities had the right to disobey them. 'Abd al-Wahab also advocated rejecting the practice of human intercession with God, swearing to anyone but God, the worshiping of saints and other honored people, and celebrating non-divine anniversaries such as the Prophet Mohammed's birthday. He pointed out that good Muslims in such communities had the right to emigrate (Hijra) and separate from these societies, such as the Prophet Mohammed had done when faced with polytheism in Mecca.

A strict constructionist of the Qur'an, 'Abd al-Wahab believed that the Qur'an was God's dictation to the Prophet and the words meant exactly what was written. In addition, the Qur'an held that issues not specifically authorized in the Qur'an and the early practices of Islam were heretical innovations. 'Abd al-Wahab's thoughts on the matter of what is pure Islam concluded that only the first centuries of Islam were pure. He particularly stressed the need to emulate the first Muslims, the Companions of the

Prophet Mohammed. 'Abd al-Wahab wrote: "Moreover, from what we are upon is that bid'ah (heretical innovation), which is everything that was introduced into the religion after the three generations, is in all of its forms blameworthy, as opposed to those who say that there are good and bad bid'ahs, or who divide them into five categories; unless we can harmonise by saying that the good bid'ahs are those that as-Salaf as-Saalih were upon, and that they include that which is obligatory, recommended, and permissible."

'Abd al-Wahab's philosophy was a marked change from the traditionalist juridical thought, scholarship, and law. He essentially dismissed the works of a century of Islam and supported new concepts such as al-Wala' Wa al-Bara'. He wanted to push Islam hard to the right of the traditional hard right. His position on complete and total enmity to all non-believers and those who associate with them is captured thus: "A Muslim is not right in his religion, even if he rejects everything other than Allah, unless he feels enmity towards the disbelievers and makes this known to them . . ."[32] He gained favor among the East-Central Saudi tribes under their sheikh Muhammed ibn Saud. Over the next two centuries the al-Saud tribe would grow, first through a series of mini-jihads sanctioned by 'Abd al-Wahab in the eighteenth century. In the early twentieth century the Saudis expanded into the dominant tribe with strategic alliances with the British. The Saudis' aid in World War I to the Allies led them to regional dominance. The discovery of oil and its strategic necessity in World War II and the late twentieth century turned the Saudis, with American assistance, into the economic powerhouse they are today. However, despite the non-traditionalist appearance of some of the modern al-Saud family, the state has sponsored and evangelized 'Abd al-Wahab's practices, in state-run schools and seminaries.

MODERN IDEOLOGUES (NINETEENTH CENTURY)

Jamal Ad-Din al-Afghani (1838–1897) received his education in Kabul and Tehran and India. Close friend and student of Mohammed 'Abduh (see next entry), al-Afghani traveled throughout Persia, the Ottoman Empire, and Russia and established himself as an intellectual power in Paris. He is considered to be a father of the modern pan-Islamic unity (al-Ittihad al-Islami) movement. Living under the Ottomans in Istanbul, al-Afghani exhorted Muslims to rise up, unite, and defeat British rule in Egypt, Anglo-Egyptian Sudan, Hadramut (Yemen), Oman, the Arabian Gulf emirates, and India. Ibrahim Kalin of the Canadian Center for Islam and

Science writes that al-Afghani espoused that "modern Western science and technology are essentially separable from the ethos and manners of European nations and can and should be acquired by the Islamic world without necessarily accepting the theological and philosophical consequences emerging from their application in the Western context . . . science should be understood in the light of this general program of Islamic 'reform' or renewal (*islah* or *tajdid*)."[33]

Mohammed 'Abduh (1849–1905) was a pioneer of modern ultraconservative Islamist philosophy. Born into an impoverished family from lower Egypt, he studied at the al-Azhar University as a jurist and scholar. Strongly influenced by al-Afghani, 'Abduh was exiled to Lebanon after participating in revolt against British rule in Muslim nations. 'Abduh is believed to have popularly adopted the term "Salafiyah."

Mohammed Rashid Ridha (1865–1935) was a student, scholar, and successor to Mohammed 'Abduh. An ardent pan-Arab nationalist, Ridha was "concerned about Arab backwardness and weakness of Muslim societies with regard to western colonialism." He blamed Sufi degeneracy, stagnation of the ulema, and failure to achieve progress in science and technology.[34] Ridha became popular with his call to believe that all flaws in Islamic society and unity could be corrected by a return to the past traditions of Islam.

MODERN IDEOLOGUES (TWENTIETH CENTURY)

Hassan al-Banna (1906–1949) was the founder of the Egyptian Society of the Muslim Brothers (al-Ikhwan al-Muslimun), a religious nationalist movement established in Cairo in 1928. Al-Banna's ideology was that of unifying the Muslim states into a utopian Islamic Caliphate ruled by the Qur'an and Sharia law. He wrote that Islam was "at a cross roads of . . . The Way of the West and the Way of Islam." The Muslim world had to soon choose and al-Banna advocated the Egyptian nation be the first to return to and become strong to spark the revival of "International Islam."[35] The movement rose to become a powerfully influential political party in Egypt and was disbanded in 1948 and 1954. It maintained a secret militant wing to effect religious change to the founding ideology through political assassination and terror. After the 1948 assassination of the Egyptian foreign minister, al-Banna was killed by Egyptian security service agents. In 1981 Egyptian President Anwar Sadat was assassinated by members of a brotherhood splinter group, the Jihad Group.

Abu al-A'la Mawdudi (1903–1979) was a Pakistani intellectual and founder of the Jamaat-e-Islami, the oldest Pakistani religious-based political party.[36] Mawdudi was a prolific writer and religious lecturer who helped spark a Salafist revivalist movement throughout the Islamic world in the 1960s. A follower of 'Abd al-Wahab, Mawdudi was also a student of the school of thought that the Islamic world had fallen back into Jahiliyyah (the state of pre-Islamic ignorance) and had betrayed their ignorance by not understanding and respecting the concept of monotheism (Tawhid). However, Mawdudi did not believe in declaring Muslims apostates; hence he was not an advocate of Takfiri. But he did believe in using Islamic populism to move his party into position to eventually take control of the government and establish a theocratic democracy.[37]

Sayyid Qutb (1906–1966) was born in Egypt and became a member of al-Banna's Egyptian Society of the Muslim Brothers, also known as Muslim Brotherhood. Qutb was an author, critic, and philosopher of modern Islamic radicalism. His writings and beliefs are said to be the foundation stones of modern neo-Salafist rejectionist terrorism, which is sometimes referred to as Qutbism. Qutb became active in the Egyptian Muslim Brotherhood movement during the 1950s as editor of their weekly newsletter, *Muslim Brotherhood*. During this time he had the opportunity to travel to America and the West. Not impressed with what he saw, he wrote with amusement and disgust that America was the "peak of Advancement and the Depth of Primitiveness." He opined that it was America's mixing of cultures, races, and religions that brought about its sexual permissiveness, disinterest in religion, and poor quality of Hollywood movies, and he even criticized the crudeness of American football. He rejected American churchgoing values and thought the only way to salvage the West was to destroy it.[38]

In Qutb's writings, most notably the landmark book *Milestones*, he spelled it out clearly that he believed, like 'Abd al-Wahab and his students, that the Muslim world had reverted to Jahiliyyah because Islamic law (Sharia) had been replaced by Western law or ignored, and he showed disdain for civil government and religious structures as being man-made artifices that were abhorrent to God, and extorted Moslems to fight Jahiliyyah through the "Call to Islam" (Dawa') and destruction of government and religious structures through armed struggle via Holy War (jihad). One of Qutb's most popular core principles was that all modern Muslim societies were illegitimate and, in fact, apostate due to the fact that there was not absolute compliance with Sharia law. To effect this revolution he called on the creation of a "Vanguard" organization to take charge and fight Jahiliyyah and apostasy. It needs to be noted that these concepts were thoroughly rejected by mainstream Islamic scholars. No less great an authority than the al-Azhar in Cairo, the top juridical authority in Islam, stated that *Milestones* was heretical and the work of a "Kharajite."[39]

Qutb included all non-Islamic states within this definition of Jahiliyyah and Muslim nations were apostate dictatorships run by complicit stooges. Since the regimes of Islamic countries did not live by Sharia law Qutb assessed that they were apostate governments and could be considered *kufir* (unbelievers) and excommunicated (Takfir)—preferably through death. Qutb did not advocate killing all Muslims, just those who lived as apostates and outside the ideological state of grace (non-believers). Some prominent organizations believe this is because he had a faulty understanding of the Declaration of the Faith (Kalima) and the meaning of Hakimiyyah, or Allah's sole right to legislation. Many view Qutb's assertions as a grossly heretical innovation.[40]

Qutb also agreed with 'Abd al-Wahab's philosophy of emigrating from the unjust and ignorant lands to a land where Islam was performed correctly. Qutb believed that if such a land did not exist, it must be created, or at least true Muslims must separate themselves from non-believers and the impure.

Sayyid Qutb was truly revolutionary in thought and it's easy to see how modern Takfiris have seized his philosophy as a role model for armed insurrection and defiant change. Qutb, like nineteenth-century theologian al-Afghani, saw technology as non-antithetical to Islam, particularly in spreading the message of the coming revolution. The greatest problem Qutb saw with traditionalist Islam was its determination that Islam was restricted to "Defense Jihad." He called this defeatist.

Like many revolutionary firebrands, Sayyid Qutb was sentenced to death, and he died by hanging in 1966 after being accused of conspiring to overthrow the government of the popular Arab nationalist President Gamal Abdel Nasser. Qutb's writings were popularized by his brother Mohammed Qutb, a teacher at King Abdul Aziz University. Both Osama bin Laden and Dr. Ayman al-Zawahiri were students of Mohammed Qutb. They were both deeply affected enough by Sayyid's writings to make them part of the foundation of al-Qaeda ideology.[41]

Shukri Mustafa (1942–1978), a member of the Egyptian Muslim Brotherhood, became a radicalized follower of the Qutbist ideology while imprisoned. He formed his own organization called the Muslim Society (Jama'at
al-Muslimun), which became popularized in media as "the Excommunication and Emigration group" (al-Takfir w'al-Hijra) because of their extremist view that Takfir was appropriate for the Muslim world and good
Muslims should emigrate away to a pure Muslim country or isolation.

Mustafa's group was to execute a strategy of going into isolation to
avoid contamination from the Jahiliyyah, gain strength and resources,
and then launch a jihad to assist in forming the Caliphate.

The Takfir w'al-Hijra took the extremist views of Qutb one step further, claiming that not only was the Muslim world in a state of Jahiliyyah,
but Egypt as a nation was an apostate state due to its failure to establish
Islamic law also. He declared they were no longer Muslims. Thus he called
to excommunicate any Muslim for any offense identified by his armed
vanguards. Note that this ideology was extremely similar to that of other
cultlike religious sects as they demanded extreme standards for piety and
loyalty. Mustafa called for cutting ties to the family, and the liberal use of
Takfir in ways that had not been seen since the radical Khawarij in the seventh century. It was quickly embraced by modern-day Takfiri militants,
including al-Qaeda adherents. The group was found out after a failed
armed raid and Mustafa was executed in 1979 for rebellion against Egyptian President Anwar Sadat for making peace with Israel.

Abdullah Yusuf Azzam (1941–1989) was a Palestinian, born in the West Bank
in the village of Asba'ah al-Hartiyeh near Jenin. Educated in Damascus,
he earned his degree in Islamic law. He became radicalized and moved to
Jordan to join the Palestinian resistance but found he had little in common with the Palestinian nationalists of the PLO. He left after Black September, the ruthless smashing of Palestinian terrorist camps by Jordan's
King Hussein in 1970. Azzam traveled to Cairo to study at al-Azhar University and earned a doctorate in the principles of Islamic jurisprudence.
A close follower of Sayyid Qutb, Azzam popularized the idea of the
continuous internationalist Islamic jihad as a means to restore the New
Islamic Caliphate.[42] Azzam asserted that "Jihad must not be abandoned
until Allah Alone is worshipped. Jihad continues until Allah's word is
raised high. Jihad until all the oppressed people are freed. Jihaad to protect our dignity and restore our occupied lands. Jihad is the way of ever-
lasting glory."[43]

Azzam later became a professor of Islamic studies at King Abdul Aziz University in Jeddah, Saudi Arabia, with the brother of Sayyid Qutb, Mohammed Qutb. He was OBL's professor and became his mentor in Islamic studies. After the Soviet invasion of Afghanistan, Azzam left the university to fight and OBL soon followed him. With the war raging across the Afghan-Pakistani border Azzam organized an international network of Arab volunteers to fight the Soviets, called the Mujahideen Services Bureau (MSB, Maktab al Khadimat al-Mujahideen) which would inspire, recruit, and train Muslim men who would come from around the world to Pakistan and fight in the Afghan jihad.

Azzam's lectures, filled with stories of personal heroism, devotion to God, and romance of martyrdom, were overwhelming for many. Volunteers were publicly recruiting at MSB offices in America, Europe, and the Middle East. Bin Laden was an early supporter of Azzam, and once they met in Peshawar, Pakistan, the two quickly joined forces. Though they were preaching a radical form of Salafism, they were financially supported by public donations and direct money from Saudi intelligence. Azzam and bin Laden made the call to "Join the Caravan" of war, sacrifice, and martyrdom. Together they extolled the virtues of establishing the New Islamic Caliphate. They praised those who died trying and honored those who desired to die. Azzam and bin Laden's efforts were legion in the Kingdom of Saudi Arabia and the Arabian Gulf states. They became celebrated figures in the media.

Omar Abdul Rahman (1938–present) was a radical Egyptian cleric and best known for his role as the ideological godfather of the first World Trade Center bombing. He lost his eyesight to diabetes in childhood and became an Islamic scholar. Rahman studied the Salafist writings of Ibn Taymaiyya and the neo-Salafist Sayyid Qutb in Braille.[44] A former member of the Egyptian Muslim Brotherhood, Rahman was a compatriot of Abdullah Azzam. Rahman was arrested and tortured by Egyptian authorities after the assassination of Anwar Sadat but was later released. He worked as a traveling recruiter, lecturer, and ideological policy maker with Azzam and bin Laden during the anti-Soviet Afghan insurgency. As a leader in Azzam's Mujahideen Services Bureau, Rahman went to the United States following Azzam's assassination to lead the MSB offices that were established there in the 1980s. Rahman became the spiritual leader of the Egyptian terrorist group the Islamic Group (al-Jama'a al-Islamiyya) soon afterward.

A firm believer that Qutb was correct in his assessment of the role the West played in the destruction of the Muslim world, Rahman called for the development of a strategy to strike the far enemies such as Russia and America. He wanted to neutralize them before attacking the near enemies such as Egypt and Saudi Arabia. With America reduced and out of the way it would simplify the creation of the New Islamic Caliphate.

Abdul Rahman may have played a significant role in the establishment of OBL's campaign to destroy the American economy by striking economic targets in New York. In a speech he gave in Europe, Abdul Rahman demanded that Muslims "cut the transportation of their countries, tear it apart, destroy their economy, burn their companies, eliminate their interests, sink their ships, shoot down their planes, kill them on the sea, air, or land."[45]

In the early 1990s Rahman managed to move to the United States despite being on the U.S. State Department terrorist watch list and established a Takfiri-based Islamic study group, which planned and executed the first World Trade Center attack in 1993. Rahman was quickly captured and convicted. He is now serving a life sentence on terrorism and murder charges.

According to the West Point Combating-Terrorism Center his release from imprisonment in Colorado is a top demand by Takfiri terrorist groups. In 1997 the Egyptian Islamic Group killed fifty-eight European tourists and left leaflets demanding the release of Rahman.[46]

Muhammad 'Abdus Salam Faraj (unknown–1982) was the Egyptian founder of the Islamic extremist terrorist group the Jihad Group (Jama'at al-Jihad). Inspired by the Salafist movement of Abu al-A'la Mawdudi, Faraj formed a terrorist group that would serve as the action arm of Sayyid Qutb's Islamic revolution. Faraj was a firm supporter of the philosophy of Sayyid Qutb and believed jihad was the highest of the pillars of Islam. Faraj's work *Al-farida al-gha'iba* (Jihad: The absent obligation) is a forceful call to action for militants. He rejected Shukri Mustafa's al-Takfir w'al-Hijra philosophy of wanting to isolate themselves from the Jahiliyyah.[47]

Faraj advocated infiltration into the political systems of government and, once in place, to engage in direct armed combat. He formed the Jihad Group in 1980 and gained followers from other terror cells who wanted action. The Jihad Group carried out a number of terror attacks, which led to brutal suppression of all Muslim organizations. Their highest achievement occurred when a cell of their military followers, led by

Lt. Khaled Islambouli, attacked and assassinated Pres. Anwar Sadat in 1981 during a military parade. Faraj was arrested and executed in 1982.

THE MODERN FOLLOWERS of eighteenth-century imam Mohammed ibn 'Abd al-Wahab's Salafist revival are often derisively and mistakenly called Wahabis. Muslims themselves reject this term as an example of how non-Muslims often label a religion or practice of worshiping in one man's name (for example, the eighteenth- and nineteenth-century depictions of Islam as a religion called Mohammedanism). These Muslims prefer to be called just Muslims, some accept "Salafists," and still others prefer "Muwahiddun" (believers in the One God—or Tawhid). Despite Western media perceptions, Salafism in Islam is not a religion or cult but a means of showing denominational respect for 'Abd al-Wahab's puritanical method of practicing Islam.

The ideological teachings of 'Abd al-Wahab were and continue to be widely popularized by the government of Saudi Arabia in Muslim communities across the globe. Starting in the late 1960s and early 1970s the Saudi government started a massive evangelical mission. 'Abd al-Wahab was the religious and spiritual leader of the al-Saud tribe. His beliefs and writings, particularly the *Kitab al-Tawhid* (The book of monotheism) were influential throughout Islam. The al-Saud family, who managed to rule the Arabian Peninsula using 'Abd al-Wahab's religious teachings as pretext for justifying armed invasions of neighboring lands because they were considered pagan or polythesist, was greatly in debt to the 'Abd al-Wahab doctrine. This relationship gained the al-Saud family political and religious control over the peninsula as well as the title of Stewards of the Two Holy Shrines (in Mecca and Medina).

The government of Saudi Arabia today builds thousands of mosques and Islamic schools (madrassas) worldwide and performs missionary and charity work dedicated to spreading Salafist ideology. Though this is the dominant method of practice in Saudi Arabia, modern Salafist Muwahiddun are hardliners in their worship of God. Their social-political machine supports state-run religious activities Westerners find disturbing, such as the funding and enforcement of morals by an authoritarian governmental religious police force, indiscriminate corporal punishment for the slightest personal infractions, public humiliation, and severe restrictions on women's rights.

Let's be clear: no matter how the Saudi Salafists run their religious nation, which is the heart of Islam, they are an order of magnitude more liberal and tolerant than the Takfiri variant. Neo-Salafist philosophy is far deeper and more sinister than the Qutbism that many ascribe to the heart of the ideological problem. The ideology of AQ marries modern political goals with a military triumph over bin Laden's coreligionists in order to re-create a holy nation-state on earth. Again, this can only best be described as bin Ladenism.

Transforming bin Ladenism into the Victorious Denomination

OBL CREATED WHAT could best be described as Bin Ladenist Victory Ideology (BLVI). The group itself has a name for it, the Victorious Denomination (al-Ta'ifa al-Mansoura).[48] I will call it bin Ladenism. The late leader of AQAP Saleh al-Oufi describes the fundamental Bin Ladenist Victory Ideology thus:

> Rejoice! The strangers are a few, and in the end the "Victorious Denomination" [Al-Ta'ifa al-Mansoura] will be the few left. Islam will be strange [*sic*] as it started, and a denomination from Muhammad's Ummah will keep fighting for the truth. They will not be affected by those who deceived or disagreed with them. I remind you that victory comes with patience. It is an hour of patience. Those who fear God will have either one of two beautiful fates: Victory or Martyrdom. Both fates are noble.[49]

In summary the bin Ladenist insurgency would be based on the classical warning about rejecting the false Islam of the Mongols and the ignorance of the Crusaders and the necessity to go back to pre-twelfth-century Islam.

The call for an international choice between Islam and the West and fighting colonialism was uttered by 'Abduh, Ridha, and al-Banna. The revolutionary Kalashnikov-Takfir-Hijra philosophy of Mawdudi, Qutb, Azzam, and al-Zawahiri guided the war fighters like Faraj, al-Zarqawi, Khalid Sheik Mohammed, Abu Anas al-Libi, Sayf al-Adl, and Mohammed Atta, who would kill until they achieved their goal. This was to be a revolutionary armed struggle, and time was irrelevant, be the New Islamic Caliphate established in twenty years or fifty years.

As one can see, this is not just rhetorical Bid'ah; it is a flamethrower to the last millennium of Islamic history.

Neo-Salaf Takfiris believe in an Islam that will confront communism and Western civilizations and best them in a global showdown. Communism has already collapsed; Russia proved simple for them to defeat in Afghanistan. America's failure is next on their agenda—in their eyes the

United States is already losing in Iraq and Afghanistan. Once vanquished, Israel will follow. To do this they will fight in two arenas, the streets of the Muslim world and, most important, the minds of the Muslim youth.

From the center of the "New Islamic Caliphate," now coalescing in the Hindu Kush, they believe their militancy will defeat and cleanse the Emirates of Afghanistan and Pakistan of the Americans, after which they will rapidly spread their message of Salaf, Takfir, Jihad, al-Wala' Wa al-Bara' through the Muslim world and prepare for the final showdown with their most hated enemy—the Saudi royal family.

4.
The Political Objectives
of bin Ladenism

There are but two powers in the world, the sword and the mind.
In the long run the sword is always beaten by the mind.
—NAPOLÉON BONAPARTE

IT IS A common misperception that AQ has no real goal beyond terror. In truth, OBL has very specific short-term and long-term political objectives for the group. Most observers have been focused on the organization's violence and their burning anti-Western rhetoric. There have been hundreds of books and analyses on the political impact of the group, but few focus on the terminal geopolitical objectives as stated by its own membership. How does AQ seek to achieve their political objective of destroying the current power structures of the Islamic world? Is it possible to govern while imposing Takfir and managing it through a literal reading of Sharia law? It would be foolish and dangerous to dismiss these words as mere fanatical utopianism. Their dream is powerful and the political and military strategy to make this a reality is being played out, no matter how foolhardy. The AQ goal is not just a Takfiri jihad for the sake of jihad; it involves creating a godly Islamic nation on earth, a New Islamic Caliphate. The lengths to which the Takfiris will go to achieve this cult-led superstate would make most Muslims blanch if they knew precisely what OBL intends.

A Clash of Civilizations?

MANY IN THE Muslim world point to an interesting event in the ideological struggle that they believe contributed to AQ's war on the West. They believe that the Western world is executing a plan to dominate Islam based on the theories of Samuel P. Huntington, author of *The Clash of Civilizations and the Remaking of World Order.* Huntington espoused that at the end of the Cold War new lines of conflict would emerge based less on ideology and more upon the differences in cultural and religious identities. Huntington referred to clashes of what he called fault-line conflicts. He remarked that these conflicts "are particularly prevalent between Muslims and non-Muslims."[1]

In the Muslim world his ideas have devolved into an all-encompassing conspiracy theory: The West is out to destroy Islam in a clash of civilizations. OBL exploited this conspiracy theory well. In an interview with Al Jazeera television he lauded its accuracy:

> I say that there is no doubt about this. This [clash of civilizations] is a very clear matter, proven in the Qur'an and the traditions of the Prophet, and any true believer who claims to be faithful shouldn't doubt these truths, no matter what anybody says about them. What goes for us is whatever is found in the book of God and the hadith of the Prophet. But the Jews and America have come up with a fairy tale that they transmit to the Muslims and they've unfortunately been followed by the local rules [of the Muslims] and a lot of people who are close to them, by using "world peace" as an excuse. That is a fairy tale that has no substance whatsoever![2]

Huntington's Clash of Civilizations concept was a well-meaning attempt to prognosticate future conflict. It was not intended to be the blueprint for Western domination. However, this conspiracy theory is one with legs, and OBL often just repeated what many on the Muslim street believe.

In AQ's canon, it validates what Sayyid Qutb wrote about the incompatibility of the West and Islam in the book *In the Shade of the Quran*:

> The truth about the battle in which the Jews and Christians have engaged the Muslim Ummah in every corner of the earth, and in every age, is that it centers upon our belief or creed. Although they may quarrel amongst themselves, they are forever united in the struggle against Islam and the Muslims . . . They have used every kind of wickedness, perfidy and treachery in this struggle ever since they have experienced, firsthand, the zeal of the Muslims for their religion, having previously confronted them in the fullness of their creed.[3]

In the 1991 ramp-up to the first Gulf war many notable Islamic clerics, including Safar al-Hawali, dean of Islamic studies at the Umm al-Qura University in Mecca, announced that the American interventions in the Middle East, particularly their presence in Iraq, were part of this clash. He said: "It is not the world against Iraq, it is the West against Islam."[4] This is precisely how the Takfiris see the world: Islam is under attack in a clash of civilizations against the West and communism. After the failure of communism, they believe Islam and the West will fight it out on a global scale. Their duty is to be the tip of the spear that eliminates Western dominance.

The War To Control Islam

THE BEHAVIOR AND policies of the West since the Crusades is a modern invention by the Takfiris—a poor attempt at justification to harness the Muslim world to join their side of the debate. All of OBL's talk of a unified Western conspiracy against Islam is merely a convenient distraction—interesting, but a head fake from the far more important and real conflict under way.

The heart of the real ideological conflict is not a war between believers and non-believers. It is about control of Islam itself. The stakes are no less critical to the discussion. It is about determining who will control the hearts, souls, and minds of Muslims. There is no Western conspiracy to destroy and dominate Islam, there is an active plan—under way for more than twenty years—for the neo-Salafist terrorists of AQ and their allied groups seek to destabilize and eliminate traditional Islam. This slow-speed coup d'état has been stated publicly and repeatedly by virtually every neo-Salafist militant since the founding of al-Qaeda. There is a real and open global anti-Islam insurgency under way by AQ and they fully intend to win on battlefields of both the arms and of the mind. The ideological war has been declared and the target is nothing less than the destruction of traditional Islam.

The historical basis for AQ's ideology is rooted in some of the major schisms within Islam, including beliefs at the Khawarij, Qaramita, and al-Otaybi sects. This struggle is no different from other cults', except that this particular sect wants both political and spiritual control of one-quarter of the world's population.

The greatest obstacle to OBL's chances of success is America and the West. Therefore, all of the wild rhetoric about both the West's and Israel's involvement in the ideological battle is merely a straw man, a convenient whipping boy to motivate the politically frustrated Muslims bin Laden needs as a recruiting base. The political obfuscation is intended to remove any legitimacy for Western support to mainstream Islam while its traditions are attacked and corrupted by al-Qaeda's bin Ladenist ideology.

OBL requires the Muslim world to see through the limited prism of political dissent but intends them to join AQ to achieve the hidden goal of his group—to topple traditional Islam and replace it with his own fringe model. This simplistic view may not gain favor in the intellectual pantheon desperate for a deeper and more satisfying reasoning as to why mass murder has been done in the West. For AQ's leaders there is no less important goal than mobilizing the Ummah to populate the Takfiri insurgent base. If that means millions of Americans or British or Saudis must die—so be it. OBL has demonstrated he will do anything to bring Muslims to his side, even killing thousands of other Muslims.

The "clash of civilizations," according to OBL, has been a millennially long and bloody one. The recent adoption of this theme by some in the Western intelligentsia has allowed AQ the opportunity to use it in their ideology—in AQ's propaganda effort it represents a perfect example to the Muslim world of how the West wishes to view all of its actions against Islam. It also allows OBL the opportunity to say "I told you so" any time there is a rift between the Islamic world and the West in media, foreign policy, or popular culture.

For example, OBL expounded on the two sides of the "clash" after he was attacked by American cruise missiles in 1998. His earliest public missives and interviews (1994–1997) had centered on Saudi Arabia, America, and Israel as the conspirators in the plot to destroy Islam. However, after the Clinton administration attacks on Iraq in Operation Desert Fox and on his base in Afghanistan in Operation Infinite Reach, bin Laden adjusted his opinion to tap into a broader outrage in the Muslim world. In 1998 he stated:

> I say that there are two sides in the struggle: one side is the global Crusader alliance with the Zionist Jews, led by America, Britain and Israel, and the other side is the Islamic world. It is not acceptable in such a struggle as this that he [the Crusader] should attack and enter my land and holy sanctuaries, and plunder Muslims' oil, and then when he encounters any resistance from Muslims, label them terrorists.[5]

The question for this statement is, when exactly did the "Crusader alliance" attack Saudi Arabia and occupy it? It's a deft spin in semantics, but OBL frames the invitation by the Saudi government as part of the plot to invade, as key to the clash of civilizations. In fact, OBL himself offered to mobilize an Islamic army to retake Kuwait through the exact same jihad he now cites as the basis for a Crusader conspiracy. To buy into his assertions, Muslims must wholly reject the fact that Christians and Jews were tribal countrymen and shared the same communities for over fourteen centuries and that the Qur'an has, even at its most fiery, always dictated tolerance and patience toward them.

To work outside of those restrictions OBL desperately needed the physical presence of the Americans to enable him to use the confused rhetoric about Crusaders again entering Muslim lands to destroy Islam and impose Christianity.

The Political and Religious Transformation of Islam

THE AQ STRATEGY to ultimately transforming Islam can be considered both neoreformational and revolutionary in scope. It is neoreformational because they are making a new push to further the cause of the original Salafist philosophers. In addition, their strategy within nations they operate in is revolutionary as they intend to change governments and behaviors of people that they deem not sufficiently Islamic by terrorist actions from within. They also have the revolutionary goal to transform the whole Islamic world to follow their Salafist variation.

As part of this effort, al-Qaeda strategy divides their enemies into two categories, far enemies and near enemies. The terms were originally for those who opposed Islam during its period of birth in the seventh century. However, as used by AQ it describes their operational attack strategy for those nations that pose a greater threat to the organization or their strategic vision as a whole.

After the 1988 inaugural convention in Peshawar, bin Laden commissioned a political subcommittee to doctrinalize and promulgate the strategic goals of the organization. From that time AQ's political strategy has been in a state of constant development and refinement. The localized political goals against the "near enemies," or governments that were deemed insufficiently Muslim, necessitated the speed and intensity of an underground guerilla war that would be waged throughout the Muslim world. The "far enemies," those nations that facilitated or directed the "oppression" of the Muslim world, would be struck with the intent to shock them out of supporting the near enemies.

Al-Zawahiri, like Faraj, was an early advocate of attacking the near enemy, which at that time was Egypt.[6] The largest and oldest Salafist movements were in Egypt, and many saw the Sadat regime as more apostate than any before. Al-Zawahiri stated that the road to Jerusalem passes through Cairo, an allusion to recovering Islam's third holiest shrine, not to winning Palestinian statehood. He laid out the argument for attacking the near enemies, saying: "The battle will not be won and Jerusalem will not be conquered unless Cairo is conquered and the battle in Egypt and Algeria is won."[7]

Despite his forceful nature, Al-Zawahiri was overruled by OBL. During the early 1990s AQ would shift from the Near-and-Far strategy and adopt the Far-Near Strategy. It would create consternation among Egyptian groups who had been working for decades to launch revolution and waiting for outside support.

STILL, AQ'S GOALS needed to be prioritized. In his statement about the foundations of the AQ movement Dr. Ayman al-Zawahiri called for several fundamental principles that AQ would strive to achieve.

PRINCIPLE ONE—ESTABLISH A
NEW ISLAMIC CALIPHATE

"ESTABLISH AN ISLAMIC nation" is one of the top objectives of the original AQ charter signed in 1988. The penultimate objective of the organization is to re-create and return to a single nation, a new Caliphate, based on the Takfiri interpretation of Islam.[8] That this Islamic nation already exists spiritually in the widely diverse Ummah is notwithstanding. The AQ mission is to reunify the Muslim world back into a single Caliphate without national borders. The role of this new nation will be to continue the struggle until the world accepts Islam. Many Western analysts misinterpret this heavenly mission as proof positive that the AQ organization seeks global subjugation. It is merely an exceptional foil. What they seek is control of Islam.

The militants view this as a century-long mission that will reach its culmination in the next decade or two. The organization seeks to convert members within the global Islamic community and motivate them to help remove the political and social obstacles to bring about a perfect Islamic state. This is done through sacrifice of their lives for the AQ objectives through the adoption of Bin Ladenist Victory Ideology.

After the 1996 triumph of the Taliban in Afghanistan, OBL came to believe that Afghanistan was a perfect example of a purely Islamic nation. He believed that it and Pakistan were going to be the heart of the New Islamic Caliphate. This is the principal reason he maintained a sanctuary there and chose to fight from there. He believes that Afghanistan will provide the base for the expansion outward and across the Muslim world:

> This is our goal, to liberate the land of Islam from unbelief and to apply the law of God almighty in it until we meet Him and He is pleased with us.[9]

However, OBL has an expansive view on what is his responsibility in the defense of Islam. He views any presence or attack in any Muslim country as attacking the New Islamic Caliphate's sovereign soil. Furthermore, any non-believer who attacks any Muslim is by definition embarking on a "New Crusade." Every other religion in the world is "Pagan," "Polytheists," or "Jews." In bin Ladenism he harnesses these Qur'anic terms to draw lines where there can be no in-between, no compromises, and no room for anything but his interpretation of Islam. However, there is always room for death to anyone who demurs.

OBL's comments are often dismissed as rhetoric, but statements such as those evoking the Crusades, fighting for defense of the Muslim lands, and defending the helpless pious Muslim are powerful stuff on the Muslim street. They tap into the deep feelings, folktales, and myths found throughout the Muslim world and the belief that something was taken from Islam when the Crusades penetrated into the Levant.

PRINCIPLE TWO—MOBILIZE THE ISLAMIC WORLD TO MAN AL-QAEDA'S JIHAD

SPEAKING TO THE Qatari-based Al Jazeera TV news network after the American cruise missile attack on his terrorist training center in 1998, OBL reiterated another of his principal objectives that he had espoused in his private interviews and then in his formal declaration of war:

> Our duty, which we have undertaken, is to motivate the ummah to jihad for the sake of God against America and Israel and their allies. And we are still doing this, motivating people; the popular mobilization that happened in these last months is moving in the right direction to remove Americans from Muslim countries.[10]

OBL sees the Muslim world as simply sleeping in the face of the tragedy that was the loss of the Caliphate in 1924. He believes Muslims cower in fear of the autocratic regimes that were engineered by the Europeans to divide the Middle East. He repeatedly and often calls upon the Muslim world to join his jihad for these reasons.

From the earliest days of the anti-Soviet insurgency the Salafist volunteers' call to "join the jihad" was built on the Qutbist philosophy of motivating the rest of the Muslim world to continue the mission started in Afghanistan and to spread out to restore the Caliphate. In 1988 OBL formalized the organization to do just that when he stated, "You know, we are linked to all of the Islamic world, whether that be Yemen, Pakistan, or wherever. We are part of one unified Ummah, and by the grace of God the numbers of those who have conviction have set out to wage jihad are increasing every day." The perception by the Takfiri insurgents is that they have the Muslim world on their side.

PRINCIPLE THREE—REMAIN IRRECONCILABLE

THE NEO-SALAFIST TAKFIRIS believe that the Muslim traditionalists have an elitist and privileged view of Islam. They believe their power structure will be responsible for the fate of what is happening today, that they adhere to "safe" interpretations of Islam and ignore criticism. Nothing could be further from the truth. The ulema is engaged in a constant and near-never-ending debate about what is and is not acceptable Islam. The error may be in believing the newest usurpers will eventually come around and moderate their radical views over time.

There is no question that the Takfiri militants prefer to operate on the outside of the Islamic mainstream. Their perception is that they can excite within the Muslim community the rebellious nature of the people. With the right mixture of grievance, complaint, piety, and aggression they can invoke the furies of defending their faith by showing they always express a love of God first and foremost—then they can kill at will. Religious militants of all stripes believe that they can change the opinions of the community from the outside in. By violent acts they often seek incremental concessions that may be granted in the face of popular outcry against these same acts. Although from time to time this has occurred, there is scant evidence that the current challenge to the Muslim world as presented by bin Laden is understood in its true form. They seek dynamic, revolutionary change.

Nor is concession the goal of the neo-Salafist revolution—complete and total victory over their ideological and combatant opponents may be a more realistic assessment. Engulfed in their militant fervor, the Takfiris seek to violently overthrow traditionalist Islam and establish the ultrapuritanical interpretation in its stead. Their goal is decapitation, to overturn the current model at the head while still allowing the traditional power structure to maintain continuity of debate in their slow, ponderous fashion. This way the revolution will overtake them by events. AQ states there is no room for compromise—they view the world as divided into two camps: dictators and unbelievers. Al-Qaeda recognizes that there are innocents among them, but they must be converted to Islam. The AQ position is uncompromising, as their charter states: "We will not meet them halfway and there will be no room for dialogue with them or flattery towards them."

AQ's Strategic Communications Strategy— Hijack the Opinions of the Muslim World

AQ CLAIMS TO speak for many in the Muslim world who hold non-extremist opinions. Most positions that AQ espouses are mainstream Islamic values that have been surreptitiously hijacked to make it appear that the Muslim world supports AQ's positions. Scholar M. J. Akbar notes that al-Qaeda is the beneficiary of Muslim dissatisfaction in the political and personal realm. The terrorists have managed to attach themselves to the popular opinions that connect to their political ideology. The anger in Islam is politically oriented not so much against individual Westerners but against national policies and activities that Muslims see their coreligionists suffering from. To a very small few, supporting or participating in some offensive action could represent an option for the disaffected and angry. The *"jihadi* knight" image that AQ tries to project lends a romantic glow to their angry actions. On occasion their acts of terrorism do force some nations to take corrective action to address legitimate social complaints from the public. However, violent action has almost always led to a brutal backlash from their governments, which of course fuels the anger.

Alec Gallup, of the Gallup Poll, noted:

I think many people in the U.S. were surprised to find out just how negative the Islamic nations were toward us. The conventional knowledge was that it was just [the] radical fringe that was anti-United States, but didn't go very deep into the population. Our numbers indicated that wasn't the case.[11]

Negative public opinion polls about America in the Mideast are almost always political. There is broad respect for Western technology, education, and sciences. Where there is great divergence between the Muslim world and the West, AQ has attempted to point to anti-Muslim sentiment as a wedge. It was not difficult, as the Tafkiris have been successful in message control down at the street level. Most ideological statements of AQ target specifically the issues where there is conflict between Islam and the rest of the world. Their exploitation of natural tensions in the political sphere between Islam and the West has given them the ability to project their opinion as speaking for the entire Muslim world, particularly after they have conducted a tragic slaughter.

There are many issues on which the Muslim community differs politically from the United States and the West. At the top of the ticket are the negative perceptions of disrespect. As Gallup said:

> First, it is evident that these respondents simply don't think that the United States and the nations of the West have respect for Arabs or for Islamic Culture or religion.[12]

It should be noted that Muslims, even in sizable numbers who agree with goals that are similar to (if not the same) as those espoused by AQ, are not agreeing with AQ themselves. For example, Palestine, corruption, Western values, and American behavior in war are all issues the average Muslim finds grief with. The expression of that grief by OBL does not mean the average Muslims are in league with AQ. AQ strategic communications harnesses a mélange of populist views within the Islamic world and intersperses them throughout their fringe ideology. Gallup also notes:

> The people in the Islamic nations also believe that Western nations do not respect Arabs or Islamic values, do not support Arab causes, and do not exhibit fairness towards Arabs, Muslims, or in particular, the situation in Palestine.[13]

On that point, OBL struck the chord early in his campaign. In a 1997 interview with Peter Arnett of CNN, bin Laden explained his group's terror goals as being a mix of populism and Islamism:

> The reaction came as a result of the U.S. aggressive policy towards the entire Muslim world and not just towards the Arabian peninsula. So if

the cause that has called for this act comes to an end, this act, in turn, will come to an end. So, the driving-away jihad against the U.S. does not stop with its withdrawal from the Arabian peninsula, but rather it must desist from aggressive intervention against Muslims in the whole world.[14]

I. FIGHT INJUSTICE AGAINST MUSLIMS, PARTICULARLY IN PALESTINE

THE PERCEIVED INJUSTICES against the Islamic world are a platform from which AQ members can strike out at their enemies. The 9/11 attacks were described as punishment for a litany of alleged offenses, from the Crusades to the economic boycott against Iraq in the 1990s. The ideological basis for this goes back to the classical period when Ibn Taymaiyya, speaking of the Mongol invasion, stated:

> The obligation of the believer is to choose both his friends and his enemies for the Sake of Allah. Whenever there are believers, he must ally himself with them, even if they have wronged him, since no personal offence can absolve one of the obligations of alliance in faith. Allah has said, And if two groups of believers fight then seek a settlement between them.[15]

This is the heart of their gypsy knight concept, by which combatants travel from country to country to fight for Islam, Palestine being the holy grail of combat theaters. AQ understand that Palestine has a high level of popular support in Muslim opinion. It is not only the confrontation state against Israel, but it is the site of the third holiest shrine in Islam, the Dome of the Rock in Jerusalem and also the place of Ain Jalut, where the Mongols were halted.

In fact, polls have shown that the closer the Muslim country is to the situation in Palestine, the higher the level of political awareness. For example, a sample of Jordanians, residents of a country that borders Palestine and Israel, shows that over 90 percent watch for news about the situation. The situation is most closely followed (at a higher level of watching TV news on Palestine than watching entertainment programming) in Arab nations, many of which form the recruiting base of AQ, including Kuwait, Saudi Arabia, Morocco, and Lebanon. OBL knows this, and his statements almost always praise the people of Palestine no matter how little he contributes to the resolution of the problem. When OBL says, "Palestine will be restored to us, with God's permission, when we wake up from our slumber and adhere to our faith and sacrifice our souls and belongings for it,"[16] it gains him a base of support, which yielded him 56 percent approval in Palestinian territories in 2009.

Gallup even found a relationship between those Muslims who pay attention to the situation in Palestine and those who harbor a negative view of the West. By 2009 majorities found U.S. involvement as intrusive and malignantly supportive of expanding Israel and its territories and opposing a solution to Palestine. In his first statement after 9/11, OBL essentially attempted to justify 9/11 by claiming the hijackers attacked New York and Washington in the name of Palestine:

And they have done this because of our words—and we have previously incited and aroused them to action—in self-defense, defense of our brothers and sons in Palestine, and in order to free our holy sanctuaries. And if inciting for these reasons is terrorism, and if killing those that kill our sons is terrorism, then let history witness that we are terrorists.[17]

2. RIDDING THE MIDDLE EAST
OF AMERICAN FORCES, PARTICULARLY IRAQ

AFTER PRESIDENT GEORGE Walker Bush decided to invade Iraq, AQ was given an easy propaganda advantage. With al-Qaeda capitalizing on Arab anti-American sentiment and tacit approval of their armed attacks, Iraq quickly became an unmitigated disaster for American interests and propelled AQ into becoming an arbiter of what a superpower could or could not do in the Middle East. Any goodwill after 9/11 quickly evaporated and approval of armed resistance attacks had high public approval. AQ sought to seize on what would be an easy mission for them once Iraq was invaded. Over in Islamic countries, it was not hard to achieve 71 percent agreement with AQ's generic goal of ridding the Middle East of U.S. forces in Islamic countries averaging 71 percent was not hard to achieve. However, after the massacres in 2003–2007 by al-Qaeda in Iraq (AQI) the effect was lessened, with mounting Muslim disgust at beheadings and suicide bombings that killed many more Muslims than soldiers.

Six years afterward opinion polls in the Arab world noted that in 2009 "significant numbers approve of attacks on U.S. troops based in Muslim countries, presumably as a means to apply pressure for their removal."[18] In 2009 Egypt and Morocco, both U.S. allies, sentiments in favor of attacking Americans in Iraq ran as high as 83 percent and 68 percent respectively. In supposedly hostile Pakistan it was a surprisingly low 26 percent, which was equaled in Indonesia. Vast pluralities opined that withdrawal from Iraq would decrease the chance of an attack on the U.S. mainland.

A rhetorical goal for AQ is getting the United States to stop favoring Israel. The organization consistently propagandizes and seeks to co-opt this strong opinion in the Muslim world. However, they have little reach in Palestine and it is a region where they have never actively participated in terrorist operations. No matter; through their rhetoric OBL holds a 70 percent approval rating in the Palestinian territories.

OBL is effusive with his praise of small localized conflicts involving Muslims, and this gains him a measure of popular and material support. From Somalia to Kashmir to Bosnia, OBL always made sure his support was with the Muslim street. The only goal that was not broadly approved by the Muslim poll respondents was the United States stopping support of Saudi Arabia, Jordan, and Egypt. Only 47 percent approved of that goal.[19]

Much mistrust exists despite the fact that the United States and its NATO allies have come to the aid of numerous Muslim nations, including Kuwait and Saudi Arabia, and, most important, stopped with armed force the Serbian genocide of Muslims being carried out in Bosnia-Herzegovina. On that note the ground was also conceded to al-Qaeda. OBL is prolific in his reinterpretations of history related to the Balkan Muslim states:

> Then there is the genocidal war in Bosnia that took place in front of the whole world's eyes and ears. For several years, even in the heart of Europe, our brothers were murdered, our women raped, and our children slaughtered in the safe havens of the United Nations, and with its knowledge and cooperation. Those who refer our tragedies today to the United Nations, and want us to resolve through it, are hypocrites who are trying to deceive God and His Prophet and those who believe.[20]

OBL ALSO FORGETS about the Kosovo war in 1997, when NATO applied all of its might to free the minority Muslims from the Serbian nation. Top this off with completely dismissing the very war he and his compatriots feign to have fought for the good of the people of Afghanistan against the Soviet invasion and one can clearly understand that his ideology requires as much selective disappearing of key historical events as challenging the best propaganda of the former Soviet mouthpieces.

The selective reading of history and bin Laden's ability to use his propaganda system to seize opinions that existed before his rise to infamy may not work in the Islamic world despite his understanding of his brethren. The level of political knowledge on a day-to-day basis in the Muslim world is impressive and too deep to whitewash except in the poorest classes. Again, the popular opinions that AQ has attempted to hijack existed well before the beginning of the organization. This theory is put to the test in most polls since 9/11 when pollsters asked if people shared AQ's goals and methodologies. Most respondents noted that they shared some of AQ's goals and opinions about the U.S. government but did not approve of their tactics of killing civilians. Support for AQ and their tactics dropped since 2007 from a low 16 percent to an even lower 13 percent, generally speaking.

3. PROTECT ISLAMIC UNITY AND VALUES

SAYYID QUTB WROTE in his first book, *The America I Have Seen: In the Scale of Human Values*, that America was culturally and morally bankrupt.[21] This common theme was again noted in the earliest poll on the Middle East and mirrors Qutb's commentary on the West. Gallup stated that the people across the Islamic world "have deep-seated disrespect for what they see as the undisciplined and immoral lifestyles of people in Western nations."[22] OBL notes this when he commonly refers to Americans and Westerners as "a vile people who have never understood the meaning of values."[23]

OBL piles on and manages to connect the perceived negative values with threats of action to stop them:

> But when after 80 years, the sword comes down on America, the hypocrites rise up to lament these killers who have scored the blood, honor, and holy places of Muslims. The very least you can say about these people is that they are immoral, dissolute, apostates, who helped the butcher slaughter his victim and helped the oppressor against the innocent child. May God Almighty protect me against them, and may He give them what they deserve.[24]

AQ has effectively managed to co-opt the role as protector of Islamic values from Western decadence. Each appeal from OBL to defend Islamic values is couched in terms of the state of the world at the time of the Prophet Mohammed's first Muslim campaign. AQ doctrine consistently calls on the

Ummah to unite against the "state of ignorance" (the state of the world before Islam and in the lands of all non-believers) that Salafists believe has permeated their society. At the same time, al-Qaeda chastises the Muslim world for allowing the disaster of Western thought and "Israeli colonization" to occur without a fight. An original AQ training manual stated:

> We cannot resist this state of ignorance unless we unite our ranks, and adhere to our religion. Without that, the establishment of religion would be a dream or illusion that is impossible to achieve or even imagine its achievement. Sheik Ibn Taimia—may Allah have mercy on him—said, "The interests of all Adam's children would not be realized in the present life, nor in the next, except through assembly, cooperation, and mutual assistance. Cooperation is for achieving their interests and mutual assistance is for overcoming their adversities. That is why it has been said, 'Man is civilized by nature.' Therefore, if they unite there will be favorable matters that they do, and corrupting matters to avoid. They will be obedient to the commandment of those goals and avoidant of those immoralities. It is necessary that all Adam's children obey.[25]

This is where OBL's ideological hijack excels in co-opting the opinion of the Muslim world to the point where it appears al-Qaeda speaks for all of Islam. When people in the Muslim world are asked about what level of support they have for keeping Western values out of Islamic countries, the poll shows 72 percent of respondents thought this was a worthy goal.

Overwhelming majorities of Muslims believe the United States wants to weaken and divide Islam. Almost eight out of ten 2009 World Opinion Poll respondents claimed that this was the military objective of the U.S. government in the Middle East. This was followed by the same percentage who said that the United States wants to spread Christianity.[26] This is almost never missed when OBL speaks. Virtually each statement he makes relates to how America wants to divide or destroy Islam, usually for the benefit of Israel. In addition, al-Qaeda formulates each statement to make their illegitimate offensive jihad speak for Islam, as in this statement:

> The infidels know that when Muslims realize what is truly expected of them in their religion, about fighting the infidels, it will mean the end

of their amoral rule. Consequently they fight against Fundamentalism in every sphere and struggle to dislodge Jihad from its proper role in Islam.[27]

The "Defense of Values" concept was enshrined in the AQ charter. The charter discusses the necessity to "Get Rid of Evil," defined in Takfiri doctrine as all enemies to the organization, its mission, and its interpretation of Islam. All who do not accept AQ are, by definition, "evil."

4. RECOGNIZE AND SPREAD ISLAM AND ESTABLISH SHARIA LAW

ANOTHER CORE VALUE in the AQ founding charter was to use ideological warfare and strategic communications to "establish the truth," the "truth" being the belief in the purity and infallibility of God and His word as passed down to man through the Prophet Mohammed. This is the fundamental basis of Islam. This is embodied in the Witness, or Shahada, which reads: "I witness that there is no god but God and Mohammed is His messenger." AQ's interpretation is that there is no other basis of truth but this core value. It is a solid and simple testament that lays the bedrock for the volunteer to tie him- or herself to the core faith. Alternatively, this truth, known to all good Muslims, is immediately corrupted by one who swears an oath, or Bayan, to al-Qaeda.

The call for Islamic jurisprudence to resolve legal issues is another issue that is hijacked readily by Takfiri militants. Opinion polls asking if the goal of implementing "strict Sharia law in every Islamic country" was worthy yielded an average 66 percent, with 76 percent approval by Pakistan, a nation undergoing a severe insurgency, and 76 percent approval by Morocco, a nation with a French-based infrastructure, high levels of Western investment, and a fledgling AQ problem.[28] These polls may have encouraged militants to believe they have broad-based popular support.

5. ESTABLISH NEW PRIORITIES FOR NEO-SALAFIST ISLAM

AS WE HAVE seen, Salafists are divided into two camps. In the moderate camp, God's words are absolute, but His laws moderate the severity and the hadiths lend assistance to interpreting them. In the revolutionary neo-Salafist camp, God's words are absolute—unless they can be twisted or parsed into an entirely new meaning to justify a violent fracturing away from the traditional Salaf into a "purer" variant. This includes justifying human acts of brutality against any and all Muslims and non-Muslims. For the revolutionary Salafists, if it's even slightly mentioned in the Qur'an, particularly if the opinion can be split, it's legal. This method of interpreting the Qur'an is evident in how they choose to justify terrorism and behaviors toward Christians and Jews. For example, a favored quote from the Qur'an for Takfiris is one where the Prophet Mohammed describes the retribution one should inflict while conducting missionary works:

> God's Saying: "And if you punish (your enemy, O' you believers in the Oneness of God), then punish them with the like of that with which you were afflicted . . .

Using their parsing technique, OBL, who justified the 9/11 attacks with this line from the Qur'an, leaves off the remainder of the verse and with it all reference to patience, tolerance, and leaving actions in God's hands. The above quote from the Qur'an, which Muslims believe is the exact word of God, has been cut short, and the remainder states:

> But if you endure patiently, verily, it is better for As-Sâbirûn (the Patient one).[29]

To achieve their political goals al-Qaeda must infect the consensus beliefs of the Muslim world with the fringe characteristics of the Takfiri insurgency. Repeat a lie long enough or a partial verse of the Qur'an and it becomes the truth.

AQ goes far beyond the confines of Islam. They are more along the lines of a privately funded superpower led by a man with charisma and devotion. The goals: liberation of the Islamic Homeland and return of Islam to its former pure state. In AQ ideology, this struggle would encourage the true believers using all means necessary to bring about the fall of the political systems that they believe oppress the Muslim population and prevent their seeing and understanding the call to the Salafist philosophy. This jihad would be not just among Muslims in the Muslim world but global. AQ calls for establishing political leaders who have, as Ayman al-Zawahiri stated, "Qur'an-based authority to govern." That leadership will be made up of Takfiri commanders.

Compulsory Duty to Armed Jihad
In the NIC all Muslims will have a duty to fight in jihad. Although AQ reverses the Qur'anic meaning of the "lesser jihad" (the jihad of self-defense)

and makes it of more importance than the "greater jihad" (the internal struggle to know oneself and Allah better), AQ view themselves as dedicated
to removing regionalism and tribalism from the members brought to the
struggle. They desire the manpower for combat on a global scale. AQ views
the armed jihad as better than the greater jihad as they "struggle to agitate
them [the Muslim street] so that they will be in the rank of al-Jihad because
they are fuel for the battle."

Takfiri-Designated Qadis Will Administer Islamic Law

The organization supports all rules and beliefs according to the Qur'an and
their interpretation of it. The government of the Taliban was called by bin
Laden the purest example of Islam on earth and an Islamic Emirate. This
means laws and rules, punishments, and oppression seen under the Taliban
will be made and enforced in the NIC. In 2007 the Swat Valley was overrun
by Pakistani Taliban militants to achieve this very goal.

Resistance to Non-Islamic Leaders (Near Enemies)

Al-Zawahiri called this the "Liberation of the Human Being" to resist and
cast off leaders who violated Islamic law—"we shall not accept the rule of
anyone but God and His Prophet." Invoking this fundamental principle is
their way of influencing the potential of the jihadist to infiltrate and topple
the "corrupt" systems of governments they live under.

Spreading the Word: The Network-Centric Global Media System

THE INTERNET HAS become a critical tool in AQ's ability to conduct strategic
communications to the Muslim world and to spread the propaganda and spiritual materials to their constituency. Despite the large-scale media and news
operations in the West and the advent of Middle Eastern–originated chan-
nels such as Al Jazeera, Al Arabiya, and MBC, the key to understanding why
there has been such a rapid spread of populism within the Salafi world is that
they already had a solid grounding in their message based on books, pam-
phlets, lectures, and letters. These materials were spread by hand first,
handed out at conferences, and made into cassette tapes and widely distributed throughout the Muslim world through supporting Islamic bookstores
or charities.

By the mid-1990s the rapid spread of materials could be done between intellectuals and theologians, particularly through college students who had access to the early Internet. The Internet's free-flowing and rapid communications, with virtually no policing or monitoring at that time, made its strategic ideology and intelligence a perfect distribution system for jihadists. AQ also saw it as the perfect covert communications system. It was cheap and relatively secure and documents translated into Arabic could be sent with little fear of interception. Computer media also were prime movers for the transmittal of papers, posters, and other forms of propaganda. The growing size and geographic distribution of the organization lent themselves naturally to the Internet. The relative youth of the organization's members meant that even some of the poorest and least-educated members were tech-savvy in the handling of electronic media.

The Internet allows the message of insurgency to travel without its owner handling incriminating data on his person. In a mass-storage device such as a laptop, data-carrying wristwatch, electronic planner, or flash memory stick, such data was undetectable unless opened.

AQ always understood the importance of strategic communications to the street level. Theirs would be a grassroots revivalist Islam, and the media outlets in the confrontation states that supported America were not to be trusted. They also understood that printing houses in Pakistan and England were being raided and their material was being prohibited. The Internet gave them the natural idea that a network of like-minded individuals could become a constellation spreading the word about the goals of the Takfiri militants and keep them informed of the activities of their enemies. It also lent itself to the al-Wala' Wa al-Bara' creed of disassociating from the nonbelievers and their methods.

Yet it was Sayyid Qutb, an early proponent and admirer of Western technology and its usefulness to the movement, who allowed them to overlook its being one of the very important methods of violating the disassociation (al-Bara') from the Western world's materialism that the Takfiris reject. It was a religious tool and a weapons system all in one—like a page from the Qur'an on the bayonet of a Kalashnikov. It gave the members the power of inspiration and harnessing, debating, and spreading ideas. It gave the prospective terrorist the information he needed to carry out attacks and then popularize them with association to a global network of like-minded men. It was a channel for people who had nothing to have something and a way to be somebody. It was a fantasy, a quest, a charge, and a triumph, all starting with personal anonymity and then being so inspired that one would strive to be known among one's peers. The system was perfect, as it allowed the Takfiris to spread a lethal mental virus without really standing out from the clutter of pornography and ranting that swirled all around them on the Internet. It was a Western machine that would be the cause of the West's own demise.

OBL took the individual members who were working on distributing materials and information on the Net for over ten years and created As-Sahaab (The Clouds) Media. This network had four roles: propaganda for the street, intelligence for the raiders, education for the desirous, and preaching to the unbelievers or apostates. It was quiet and effective.

On a personal note, my first brush with the Takfiri network came in 1995 while I was attending an Arabic-language program in Garmisch, Germany. The World Wide Web was so new only the library had a computer configured for it. Apart from the few media outlets and the rapidly expanding pornographic industry, I stumbled onto a treasure trove of jihadi literature at a Web site called Azzambrigades.com. Long since defunct, it was the heart of the new network distribution systems for al-Qaeda, which had just arrived back in Afghanistan. It was a powerful collection of materials, lectures, and videos, the most important of which was the only one of its kind at the time. Chechnyan guerillas had shot amateur video of a Russian soldier being held down to the ground and his throat being cut like a goat at Ramadan. It was graphic and horrific. It was also the most popular download on the Web at that time. Virtually every person I know in the military saw that video at one time or another.

The propaganda arm would collect materials, videos, and news releases of all like-minded Takfiri organizations and bring them under one umbrella for distribution. If one hub of the network was arrested or put out of commission, the next would have the same material on multiple servers. The news would always make it to the Web sites or press contacts. The very nature of the Net ensured that whatever was up would not be taken down in time for a copy not to have been made.

Finally, the covert communications and intelligence collection structure would also be network-centric. After the fall of Afghanistan to American forces in late 2001, AQ had to shift to a more secure covert system of communications. Distribution of inspirational media including images, videos, and audio recordings would naturally allow intelligence, reports, and messages to piggyback on the same information technology structure.

As-Sahaab, however, is not directly responsible for the myriad of support

Web sites and forums. As-Sahaab does support the Shebaka al-Ansar, or "Partisans Network," of AQ global sympathizers and wannabes. These sites appear to have been part of a secondary militant and personally inspired system, similar to computer gamer fan sites, which has sprung up since 9/11. These supporters would find, read, distribute, and produce materials related to the Takfiri cause or provide the thousands of other points of distribution. They were to create and participate in a "virtual jihad" where they would prepare themselves religiously and operationally for joining the physical jihad in the new Caliphate or take part in actions in their own countries. An entire repertoire of information is available for anyone wanting to learn or participate in their cause.

Many of these sites are forums where members post questions and share information. Several well-known sites are those of al-Ansar, *Al-Tawhid*, al-Firdaws, al-Hisba, and al-Buraq. In them they share media including Glory of Martyrdom videos, in which as-Sahaab uses raw combat video to create dramatic music videos with speeches and imagery of stunning attacks. They also attempt to capture the romance of being a Takfiri raider by posting combination music and speech video biographies of al-Qaeda suicide bombers from across the globe. Each of these well-edited videos is supplemented with personal messages and inspirational poetry, tributes, and well-wishes before finally ending with live video of the suicide attack.

Members to Be Honored/In Memoriam videos are tributes to militants who were killed in the wars of Afghanistan, Pakistan, Yemen, and Iraq and other parts of the world. They are honored with short biographies and videos or photos of their corpses before burial. These videos often emphasize the romantic and even the mystical qualities of their deaths. People would claim to touch the cold corpses and say they were still warm or contort the cheeks and claim that the men died smiling. These videos and articles are designed to show how deeply honored men who have fallen in battle are within the organization. This organizational respect is powerful and many join the terror wars for just this reason—to be a man among men, as the old Saxon phrase put it, is a deep appeal to disaffected Muslims of all ages.

"Path of Jihad" battlefield communiqués are popular, as are video newsreels of live combat and interviews on the satiation in the Pan-Islamic war against the West. These "official" communiqués from the battlefield often claim (wildly exaggerated) deaths and attacks on enemy forces and are issued daily with the intent to make the terrorist movement appear to have the aspects of a military campaign that has continuing momentum.

The virtual jihad is the ether space on the Web where people who have an interest in joining the cause can watch and receive "How to Join the Jihad" instructions and gain hints and personal guidance on how to come directly to the battlefields of Afghanistan, Iraq, Saudi Arabia, et cetera. In many of the deeper Web sites, after vetting one can receive instructions on where to go and how contact can be made for activists who truly want to seek connection. AQAP created a virtual militant training camp and magazine called *al-Battar Camp (Mu'askar al-Battar)*. There they played instructional videos and answered questions from students. They also post extremely graphic video and photo warnings about the fate of infiltrators to deter the insincere or the curious.

A study carried out by the Norwegian Defence Research Establishment notes that the Internet is less of a virtual training camp than many believe and more of a militant library. Though information on how to prepare can be found, it takes an enormous amount of data, much of which is included in a jihadi encyclopedia such as the *Encyclopedia of Preparation*, which was updated until 2004 (researcher Anne Stenersen notes that this encyclopedia had "300 Arabic-language documents and manuals of various length, adding up to some 10,000 pages"[30]). Other Web sites include multivolume sets of information, thousands of videos and photos, and enormous quantities of religious material. Although militants are aware that the Net is being monitored by intelligence agencies and amateur "counter-terror" vigilantes, who often will hack and take down a Web site, they still use the Net for personal enlightenment and communications.

Despite efforts to curb their usages, e-learning remains popular in militant circles. The Internet is a significant learning structure for members who are interested in the jihadi lifestyle but cannot connect to a group. Those members can connect to videos created for the purpose of instructing them in the combat arms aspects of al-Qaeda. AQ-inspired e-learning includes lessons on using weapons: photos, manuals, and even practice marksmanship programs can be found on these Web sites. In 2006 the famous American sniper Col. John Plaster found his own shooting videos from the "Ultimate Sniper" series bootlegged and widely distributed on an extremist Web site in order to teach the fundamentals of sniper marksmanship. Bomb-making was not ignored. Many virtual, highly graphic e-lessons on finding and assembling bomb components, mixing ingredients, and properly deploying the bombs for terror are often hidden and shared among trusted people on the server. The militants also produce media on how to hack and conduct Internet piracy. These computer-based efforts key off of the successful Hamas campaign against Israel in the 1990s. The networks reveal tips and tricks for those who cannot join the jihadists to disrupt or harass Web sites and networks that oppose them.

More important than all of the bombs, videos, and lectures has been the very fact that al-Qaeda are capable of continuing to inject their message directly to their supporters and bypass the media filters of the West. There are several monthly online magazines in Arabic and English that support the effort, including *Sada al-Jihad* (Echo of jihad); *Qadaya Jihadiyya* (Jihadi issues); *Majallat al-Fath* (Magazine of the conquest), a magazine formerly distributed by al-Qaeda in Iraq; *Dhurwat al-Sanam* (The pinnacle); *Mu'askar al-Battar* (al-Battar camp); and a Syrian magazine called *Risalat al-Mujahideen* (Letters of the mujahideen).

After 9/11: The Corporate Strategy Consultants of Fourth-Generation War

THE POST-9/11 GLOBAL push to destroy AQ has led to their third major transformation, which could be called a back-to-the-future campaign. As part of the 9/11 attack plan, the al-Qaeda Senior Leadership (AQSL) immediately reverted back to their Afghanistan war posture of holing up in their Pakistan FATA sanctuary, the NIC. Once the American push moved them out of Afghanistan, OBL was back on familiar turf with almost the exact same scenario as the Soviet invasion playing out. Gone were the days when AQ members stood in public parade at the terrorist training camps and cheered OBL's arrival. The AQSL understood that the United States would unleash its Global War on Terrorism strategy and reveled in the idea of fighting on these terms. The major core of trained volunteers that fought in Afghanistan, Somalia, Chechnya, and Bosnia would be called upon to act as lieutenants and trainers of new and old recruits. The AQSL would take a commanding, high-profile role to focus the American operations upon themselves. Although they push a religious-based ideology, AQ is not living in a military doctrine–less bubble. In 1989 four Marine Corps officers wrote an article explaining that the history of warfare had developed into four distinct generations. The first three were conventional war, but the fourth generation was of the type fought by U.S. forces in Somalia, Vietnam, Iraq, and Afghanistan. An AQ strategist writing under the name of Abu 'Ubeid Al-Qurashi recognized this style as a brilliant description for the war that would be waged for the New Islamic Caliphate. Al-Qurashi commented:

In 1989, some American military experts predicted a fundamental change in the future form of warfare. . . . They predicted that the wars of the twenty-first century would be dominated by a kind of warfare they called "the fourth generation of wars." Others called it "asymmetric warfare . . ."

Al-Qurashi understood and made clear to his followers that this is the battlefield that AQ has been and would continue to be operating on:

The Islamic nation has chalked up the most victories in a short time, in a way it has not known since the rise of the Ottoman Empire. These victories were achieved during the past twenty years, against the best armed, best trained, and most experienced armies in the world (the U.S.S.R. in Afghanistan, the U.S. in Somalia, Russia in Chechnya, and the Zionist entity in southern Lebanon) and in various arenas (mountains, deserts, hills, cities). In Afghanistan, the Mujahideen triumphed over the world's second most qualitative power at that time . . . Similarly, a single Somali tribe humiliated America and compelled it to remove its forces from Somalia. A short time later, the Chechen Mujahideen humiliated and defeated the Russian bear. After that, the Lebanese resistance [Hezbollah] expelled the Zionist army from southern Lebanon.[31]

While providing leadership, AQ would also supply command and control to the broader world of sympathizers through propaganda statements, commentary, videotaped remarks, and written analysis of their role against America. Though George W. Bush called the post-9/11 campaign the Global War on Terror, OBL had already declared and struck out in what could be called the Global War on Kufirs well before he released his intentions in a 1997 press release. Hence, by 9/11 OBL had a substantial twelve-year head start on the Americans in his campaign.

STRIKE AND DAMAGE THE AMERICAN ECONOMY

INSTEAD OF JUSTICE being levied by a righteous and focused effort, al-Qaeda is running free and growing stronger. Of course, this was always AQ's plan. Osama bin Laden knows he cannot defeat America by military force. He needed to wave the red flag before the bull and lead it to his saber in order to pierce its most vulnerable part: the economic heart of America.

One of bin Laden's goals, like Ronald Reagan's for the former Soviet Union, is to let America exhaust itself economically chasing one phantom after another.

Bin Laden's awareness of America's unquenchable thirst for cheap oil would prove a critical weapon in his plan.

Dr. Gail Luft, director of the Institute for the Analysis of Global Security, testified before the Senate that

> ten years ago, Osama bin Laden set a target price for oil at $144 a barrel. At the time, crude oil prices stood at $12 a barrel and his figure, aimed to compensate the Muslims for what he called "the biggest theft in the history of the world," sounded delusional. Four years ago, just prior to the U.S. elections, when oil prices stood at $38, bin Laden explained his economic warfare strategy: "We bled Russia for ten years until it went bankrupt and was forced to withdraw in defeat. We are continuing the same policy to make America bleed profusely to the point of bankruptcy."[32]

OBL realized that America's invasion of Iraq for oil had given al-Qaeda the fulcrum to push America to the brink of military and economic failure. The global oil market is easily swayed by political volatility and high oil prices. Bin Laden and his organization would provide some of that volatility. Luft continued:

> Today, with oil prices above bin Laden's stated goal, his economic warfare strategy seems like a resounding success. At a time al-Qaeda is on the run, $144 oil is a major morale booster and the best birthday present for its 20th anniversary next month.[33]

This suited al-Qaeda perfectly. In Osama bin Laden's game of strategic backgammon, the Tawla board was laid out, the pieces were in place, the first roll of the dice allowed for impressive moves, and bin Laden's opponent believes he is playing checkers. How could bin Laden not win this game?

OBL was quick to link the American lust for oil with the failed Bush policies:

> And it all shows that the real loser is you . . . It is the American people and their economy . . . the darkness of black gold blurred his vision and

insight, and he gave priority to private interests over the public inter-
ests of America ... So the war went ahead, the death toll rose, the
American economy bled, and Bush became embroiled in the swamps of
Iraq that threaten his future.[34]

INITIATE A GLOBAL, DECENTRALIZED
SELF-MOTIVATING "INTIFADA" CAMPAIGN

ONE MISSION OF OBL and his command team became perfectly clear in the
year after 9/11. In a shift away from central planning and decision making
about individual terrorist operations, the organization would decentralize in
the face of the global onslaught. OBL and his senior staff would fund and
equip groups where possible, but they were going to fight by inspiring the
insurgency to start lashing out where they could. The AQSL would remain
the key ideological leader in the global movement to return to a single Islamic Caliphate through the use of insurgency and terror.

The AQSL also knew that they would be assisted in another way by a new
group of militant jihadists. These would be the young men who were especially motivated to strike in the very countries in which they were born and
raised. They would be radicalized through their own education, often online, many through dismay at the policies of their own countries. AQSL knew
and encouraged many to "self-start" terrorist operations in the Western
countries from which they came. They wanted individual Muslims to now
rise up and create their own individual Intifadas against the West. The offensive jihad was now a defensive one and individuals had to fight as a religious obligation.

OBL saw the value in the self-starters. Minimal resources were needed for
these operations, with the exception of an occasional blessing, perhaps a distant relative who could channel the righteousness of what they were doing.
These missions were the future, but AQSL would keep the communication
lines open and their managers operating in order to keep the global franchise
alive to establish as many parts of the new "Islamic Caliphate" in as many
geographic regions of the Muslim world as possible. Al-Zawahiri put out the
order in a February 2007 message where he stated:

> You are not facing individuals or organizations, but are facing the Ji-
> hadi Intifada of the angry, alert Muslim Ummah. Therefore, you are
> just wasting your time and effort by claiming to seek to eliminate this
> person or that or such-and-such group or organization.[35]

These inroads to the psyche of the average Muslim who shared some of OBL's feelings were revealed when the evangelical mission of AQSL was brilliantly achieved after the invasion of Iraq. Men from all over the Middle East and Europe, who could not go to Afghanistan via Pakistan, poured into Syria and joined the Iraqi insurgency. The smaller cells that cropped up there self-started their own Takfiri terror groups eventually and/or aligned themselves with AQ's centralized leadership team under Abu Mussab al-Zarqawi. In one poorly formed decision by George Bush, AQSL instantly had a working model of its Global War on Kufirs working and killing Americans.

The Consultants of Global Jihad

AQSL NOW PROVIDES the centralized base of incorporated terror knowledge of over twenty years of direct hostility to the West and over thirty years of insurgency against large military forces. This is a formidable edge, but the recruitment and arming of militants require that the mission be popularized. They need to bring on board more than a few thousand suicide bombers as they did in Iraq. AQ needs to seize a broader swath of the minds of the men and women on the Islamic street. To that effect AQ has been less than effective but has made eight years of inroads.

Al-Qaeda is not just a terrorist group but a theocratic political collective. They inspire, fund, and maintain organizations that cooperate as harmoniously as possible to achieve the goal of creating the New Islamic Caliphate. From 2001 to the present AQ has been under daily pressure and losing men and manpower at an astonishing rate. However, they recover with equally astonishing flexibility. As many as a thousand have been arrested, killed, or weaned from al-Qaeda's upper-and middle-level echelons. Thousands more foot soldiers have been killed, principally in Iraq, Afghanistan, and Saudi Arabia.

AQ has transformed itself from a global terrorist operations entity into a global terrorism management consultancy for neo-Salafist irreconcilables. Since the invasion of Afghanistan and the capture of many AQ camps and facilities the organizational structure changed itself from a physical chain of camps, schools, workshops, and "guesthouse" residences into a virtual network of identical minds. All working for the same mission. All ready for the same goal: death.

Al-Qaeda's brand of terror is far more lethal than a gaggle of the stereo-typical armed Muslim extremists because AQ maintains a seductive global ideology with concrete political objectives. Without an active counter-ideological defense they may break out into an alternative option to traditional Islam that will always end with their members resorting to violence and corrupting the words of the Qur'an. Interestingly, bin Laden's direct call for the complete transformation of Islam has become a part of a dual goal of the training and redeployment of Takfiri followers throughout the Muslim world to challenge the near enemies and strike the far enemy of America.

Soon after his bastion was destroyed at the Tora Bora mountain, Osama bin Laden escaped safely into his Pakistan sanctuary in December 2001. George Bush decided the "next big push" would be in Iraq. It's been said that the decision to invade Iraq after September 11 was the strategic equivalent to America invading Mexico after the Japanese attack on Pearl Harbor in 1941. In the mind of the simple rich Texan, al-Qaeda became irrelevant. With B-52 bombs exploding behind him, Osama bin Laden walked off a mountain and into legend as possibly the greatest warrior in Islam's history. He had survived the worst America could throw at him and now it was time to start the long campaign. With George Bush's help bin Laden would eventually spread jihad in ten different regions of the world and create a new, covert rejectionist identity, al-Qaedaism, and an alternative to the Kingdom of Saudi Arabia. He would establish a new nation and from there launch a new phase in his global insurgency for Takfiri control of Islam.

5.
The Cult of Death

AQ's POLITICAL IDEOLOGY is truly run on the high-octane fuel of their seeming devotion to their ideological antecedents. This flame, in turn, fires the engines that seek to destroy the Muslim world's political power structures and establish a new Islamic nation atop the bones of the current one. Once this is complete, this new Muslim world, led by warriors who transformed one of the three major religions, will then go out and conquer the world.

These goals may be considered lofty and nearly impossible to achieve by all counting, but it is not the Western world's belief of what is possible and what is not that matters. By AQ's reckoning, they are well on their way to victory.

In 1997 bin Laden made an open declaration of war against the United States in which he promised vengeance for their political policies in the Middle East. On August 2, 1998, over 250 people were killed when AQ suicide bombers drove truck bombs into the American embassies in Nairobi, Kenya, and Dar es Salaam, Tanzania. The United States struck back by attacking bin Laden in a cruise missile attack on their Zawar Kili terrorist training base in Afghanistan. This strike, called Operation Infinite Reach, missed killing bin Laden by minutes. Soon afterward detailed planning for suicide attacks in America as well as Jordan were planned for the millennium celebrations at New Year's Day in 2000. This was the way it was going to be. OBL had chosen the new oath for his men, and their means of combat would be the gun and the bomb. It would be terror for the love of God.

Al-Qaeda's Jus ad bello: Jihad for a New Islam and Ending Old Islam

A CRITICAL ERROR that the neo-Salafist Takfiri extremists make is their misinterpretation of the meaning of jihad. In bin Ladenism, jihad is the center of all aspects of life, worship, and love of God. However, the Qur'an and traditional Islam have a different interpretation that the militants reject out of hand. Islam has five main commitments that all Muslims must practice: bearing witness to God (through the recitation of the Shahada: "I witness that there is no god but God and Mohammed is His Messenger"); Salat (praying five times daily); Zakat (giving alms to the poor); Sawm (fasting during the month of Ramadan); and hajj (pilgrimage to Mecca, at least once in a lifetime). Egyptian militant Faraj called jihad "the Sixth Pillar of Islam."

Jihad is a state of conflict (which is just and righteous), and that has strict limits and controls in Islam. Those limits and controls are not just arbitrary; they are dictated quite clearly in the Qur'an. In verse 190 of the hadith al-Baqara: "Fight in the cause of Allah those who fight you, but do not transgress limits; for Allah loveth not transgressors."[1]

Jihad is legal and authorized warfare between states or where one fights in self-defense, to aid other Muslims. The Islam Project notes that:

Jihad as an institution of armed struggle against non-Muslims can be undertaken only by a government under the limitations on legitimate conduct of war. Its use is conditional, not persistent or open-ended, nor is it directed against people because of religious differences.[2]

Bernard P. Lewis notes "the laws of jihad categorically preclude wanton and indiscriminate slaughter." The warriors in the holy war are urged not to harm non-combatants, women and children, "unless they attack you first." Even such questions as missile and chemical warfare are addressed, the first in relation to mangonels and catapults, the other to using poison-tipped arrows and poisoning enemy water supplies.[3]

Lewis continues:

Here the jurists differ—some permit, some restrict, some forbid these forms of warfare. A point on which they insist is the need for a clear declaration of war before beginning hostilities, and for proper warning before resuming hostilities after a truce.

OBL's letter of declaration of war in 1997 was an attempt to provide a clear line that would protect him from charges of waging illegal warfare. However, since he has no Islamic government, scholarship, or judicial standing as a government or Islamic scholarship or juridical standing he was in violation of the Qur'an the instant he chose terrorism and called for jihad. OBL is, in fact, a trained civil engineer.

> What the classical jurists of Islam never remotely considered is the kind of unprovoked, unannounced mass slaughter of uninvolved civil populations that we saw in New York two weeks ago. For this there is no precedent and no authority in Islam. Indeed it is difficult to find precedents even in the rich annals of human wickedness.[4]

The Qur'an Doesn't Apply to the Neo-Salafist Jihad

THE MENTOR TO OBL at King Abdul Aziz University and his combat commander in Afghanistan was Abdullah Azzam. Writing in the 1980s for the resistance magazine of the Harakat al-Mujahideen, Azzam described his interpretation of jihad for the modern Salafist:

> Offensive Jihad is when the Muslims launch an offensive attack. If this attack is on the Kufir who have previously received the message of Islam, then to call them towards Islam before commencement of the attack is considered preferable. However, if the message of Islam has not reached them, then the Kufir will be invited towards Islam. If they reject this true faith, then they will have to pay Jizyah [tax for Christians and Jews]. If they refuse to submit to the payment of Jizyah then the Muslims are to fight against them. With this type of Jihad the Kufir who plot against the Muslims are repelled and their hearts are filled with fear, so that they do not succeed in their plans.

Azzam's widely shared philosophy covered all bases for the militants. It allowed them to carry out offensive jihads on behalf of the Islamic world and even covered the base that the offensive jihad would count as a defensive jihad for the rest of the Ummah:

> The offensive Jihad is Fardh Kifayah [collective duty for Muslims], the purpose of which is to ensure the Kufir remain terrorized and away from mischief, thereby, allowing the message of Islam to be conveyed without any obstructions. If one group of Muslims fulfill

this obligation then it will be sufficient on behalf of all Muslims, but if there are no Muslims fulfilling this obligation then everyone is considered sinful.

In Azzam's terms, the terrorizing of the non-believers was sufficient reason to carry out violations or innovative acts on behalf of the rest of the Muslim world.

Azzam notes that in Fatwa Shami all that is required of Muslims is to "dispatch the army routinely once or twice a year towards the Kufr countries. In his interpretation he creates a rhetorical trap. According to the Vanguard philosophy, if the leadership do not conduct jihad, then they are considered sinners and essentially subject to the wrath of the militants. It's a perfect catch-22.

Azzam also outlined that

> the majority of Jihad undertaken at the time of our Prophet Muhammad (S.A.W.) was within the category of offensive Jihad . . . The Quran has called upon the Muslims to undertake the offensive Jihad and when this obligation is satisfactorily fulfilled there would be no apparent need for the defensive Jihad. When Muslims neglect this important obligation then they are subjected to the defensive Jihad and this has become, with regret, widely common in our time.[5]

OBL himself sees Qutb's Vanguard movement and Azzam's beliefs in the internationalist brigade variant of jihad as the basis for the entire modern Takfiri movement. OBL stated clearly in 1996 the necessity of fighting in all areas of operations, not just combat arms:

> What bears no doubt in this fierce Judaeo-Christian [sic] campaign against the Muslim world, the likes of which has never been seen before, is that the Muslims must prepare all the possible might to repel the enemy on the military, economic, missionary, and all other areas. It is crucial for us to be patient and to cooperate in righteousness and piety and to raise awareness to the fact that the highest priority, after faith, is to repel the incursive enemy which corrupts the religion and the world, and nothing deserves a higher priority after faith, as the scholars have declared, for this cause, it is crucial to overlook many of the issues of bickering in order to unite our ranks so that we can repel the greater Kufir [non-believer].[6]

According to Azzam, defensive jihad is only when "the Kufir enemy attacks the Muslims forcing them into a defensive position." In the evolving ideology of AQ, the Islamic world is enveloped in both offensive and defensive jihad at the same time. Therefore, they can remain at war until they reach the goal of the New Islamic Caliphate.

In the Bin Ladenist Victory Ideology any Muslims can perform jihad so long as their activities support the warrior out in the field. However, it must have action associated with it. There is no talking the jihad talk without walking the jihad walk among the militants. There are ways that one can support the Takfiri mission from the rear. This rear-echelon support of total global war comes in many forms. Azzam outlined them in specifics:

> The Jihad does not only consist of one person firing a gun. It consists of a large and complex structure that includes: the one who organizes the weapons and ammunition, the one who cooks the food, the one who cleans the toilets, the one who looks after the sick and injured, the one who sits in the radio communications room, the one who maintains the motor vehicles, the one overseas who raises the money, the one who brings or transfers the money, the one sitting in a Western country who locates and purchases highly sophisticated equipment such as High Frequency Radios, etc., etc. Education, especially that gained in the West, can be a tremendous help to the Mujahideen.[7]

Of course, the militants needed manpower, and Azzam was the best single recruiter of the 1980s. Even in the United States he drew in hundreds of volunteers:

> Obviously the best way of helping Jihad and the Mujahideen is by actually going to the lands of Jihad and physically fighting. This is the only action that lifts a person from the punishments mentioned in the following Ahadeeth: "Whoever dies and did not fight in battle, nor did he have the sincere wish to fight in battle, dies on a branch of hypocrisy."[8]

What is truly Bid'ah or innovative is the Takfiri concept of the jihad as a form of worship to God. The pillars of Islam are clear in saying that prayer is the only practice of worship. The al-Wala' Wa al-Bara' comes close, as it is a lifestyle of religion, but to consider warfare and by extension suicide bombing as a form of prayer and a sacrifice to a higher power is really beyond reason. Again, Azzam is a central character in the furtherance of this concept. He stated:

> Jihad is a mentally and physically strenuous act of worship, for which a person can only prepare by strengthening his Iman [faith]. Allah (SWT) will not give the victory to a people that are continuing committing sins, such as missing prayers, not praying in the mosque, failing to learn how to recite the Quran properly, following the obligatory acts of the Sunnah (e.g. keeping a beard and raising the lower garment above the ankles), having bad character, etc.[9]

Predictably, bin Laden's use of jihad as a tool for determining one's qualifications for practicing Islam is one to which he often resorts. He interprets the Qur'an and hadiths to mean his jihad, versus the correct reading to mean the parameters in the Qur'an: "Whoever meets Allah without any mark of jihad on him, meets Allah with a defect."[10]

Here in an interview bin Laden asserts that even challenging the legitimacy of his jihad removes one from the religion, whereby he immediately becomes a pagan and subject to earthly and heavenly punishment:

> I command you to do five things that God has commanded me to do: to gather, to listen, to obey, to emigrate, and to perform jihad for His sake. For whoever splits the group even a little has removed the noose of Islam from his neck, unless he repents, and whosoever calls for paganism is but one for the corpses of hell, even if he fasts and claims that he is a Muslim.[11]

Al-Qaeda Jus in bello— ## Asymmetric, Lethal, Merciless

ATTACK ANY ENEMIES WITHOUT WARNING

THE LEADER OF the Egyptian terrorist group the Islamic Group, Muhammad 'Abdus Salaam Faraj, agreed with the Takfiri cultivation of the concept to attack anyone at any time for any reason. "It is permissible to make a raid on the disbelievers whom the call of Islam has reached without prior warning,"[12] according to Faraj.

KILL INNOCENTS WITHOUT REGARD TO ISLAM OR REGRET

EARLY ON IN his written statements and interviews OBL claimed that innocent elderly women and children, who were not conducting the occupation of Saudi Arabia would be spared his men's operations: "We differentiate between men and women, and between children and old people. Men are fighters; whether they carry arms or merely help our struggle by paying taxes, they are fighters."

By 2001 OBL had ruled that this policy of restraint was out the window. He specifically ordered attacks that would kill anyone, including Muslims, in all places. He justified this in a statement where he said: "Yes, so we kill their innocents—this is valid both religiously and logically."[13] The Takfiri militants often attempt to justify their murders by claiming that it was the intent of God to have the victims die when God said:

> You killed them not, but Allâh killed them. And you [Mohammed] threw not when you did throw, but Allâh threw, that He might test the believers by a fair trial from Him. Verily, Allâh is All-Hearer, All-Knower.[14]

KILL MUSLIMS FIRST AND OFTEN

AL-QAEDA AND their ideological allies have added this new twist to war, but they have removed something from the millennium and a half of traditional Islamic practice. They do not seem to care to offer warning or consider the piety of their victims, weigh mercy, or even factor that their actions may be unlawful. Their philosophy is absolute, but in making this choice they apparently do not accept that what was written in the Qur'an is inviolable.

Islam has held a steady and compassionate policy on acts of barbarism and banditry, particularly in war. Fourteen centuries of traditional Islamic jurisprudence saw the murder of innocents as being not only unjust but also expressly prohibited. In addition, any localized calls were limited in scope as to historical time line and cultural norms in tribal Islam. The scale of bloodlust that we see within the modern terrorist community is in direct contradiction to traditional Islam. No one is asking for the keeping of the women and children of their vanquished as slaves, like the Khawarij or the Qaramita. In bin

Ladenism killing the innocents is the objective in and of itself. This is a heretical innovation where the extremist parties teeter into a form of cultism in which they proclaim that mass-murdering women and children is a form of worship or act acceptable to God.

Without any question, the victims of the AQ terrorist ideology are mainly Muslims. Although AQ claims to be attacking Western interests and military forces, the group kills far more Muslims in their attempts than Western soldiers. Whereas American and NATO forces that have been fighting in Iraq and Afghanistan seek to minimize civilian casualties, they often fail and civilians are killed. But AQ *never* seeks to minimize civilian deaths but maximizes them in order to gain a sensational media effect, as they often videotape the attacks and post them on the Internet. If civilians are killed in AQ attacks, it is not considered a planning priority to ensure that they are not harmed but to effect it in such a way as to cause much more harm to them. In war civilians are often the greatest number of killed or injured, but in AQ's terrorist version of war no one is safe and killing civilians multiplies the terror effect that Takfiris see as pleasing to God.

In Iraq, Abu Mussab al-Zarqawi saw to it that no Muslim apart from the Sunnah insurgents and their families could be counted as innocent. Shia Muslims were Rafidah, or rejectionists, and he saw no problem mass-murdering them. Al-Zarqawi also saw no difference between the intended victims and the innocent. To him the Qur'an's warnings did not apply. He said:

There is no doubt that God has commanded us to target the unbelievers, and to kill them and fight them with every means that can accomplish this goal. Even if the means does not distinguish between the intended warring unbelievers and unintended women and children, as well as those among the unbelievers whose intentional killing is not permitted.[15]

Let us pose a simple test of questions to those who carry out these acts against humanity: Was the woman in Afghanistan killed for the sake of God or for political control of a village? Why did the terrorists need to invoke God's name in order to live with themselves and the result of their handiwork? Were the fifty women and children killed in a rest tent in Iraq doing more than resting and drinking tea? Were five pounds of plastic explosives and hundreds of ball bearings on a human bomb necessary to please God? The terrorists who manifest the fringe religious movement are deeply rooted in the philosophy of historically extremist writings well outside the norm of traditional Islamic practices.

It can be said by believers in Islam that God prescribed them to die on that specific day, but was the instrument of their deaths, a woman said to be a Muslim, working for good or for evil that day? Where did she assume the right to be God's executioner and take the role of the angel of death? What justice can al-Qaeda or their allies say befell her? What was the real crime they were exposing by piercing a woman's breast with bullets and strangling her son? Is it not more likely that the Taliban just needed someone that day to play the spy, so that they could continue the campaign to make decisions unto themselves and eliminate the power of the tribal leaders in that region?

The goals of the terrorists who fought in Algeria, Morocco, Egypt, Somalia, Yemen, Pakistan, Saudi Arabia, Afghanistan, Bangladesh, Indonesia, and other places are to exercise personal control over the lives of men as long as they live on earth. The terrorists mask their political avarice with the words of religion and execute their policy against their coreligionists.

The behaviors of al-Qaeda and their franchise organizations around the world are far from the true meanings and practices of Islam. It would take a corrupting philosophy of one man, misinterpreting many scholars and employing his own belief system, to imagine that Islam itself was designed by God to be a guidance system of an unlimited number of human-powered weapons and that to purify Islam he had to create a philosophy that encouraged Muslims to kill other innocent practicing Muslims as well as any and all non-believers—and that they must be killed in large numbers simultaneously, in order to ensure that God was pleased.

CONTRADICT THE QUR'AN ON SUICIDE

MANY SCHOLARS AND Islamic jurists will commonly note that *shaheed* is a death not performed for ego, respect, or vengeance. It must come purely for the sake of God and not because one was instructed to perform suicide in lieu of real martyrdom in face-to-face battle. These bin Ladenist interpretations are true heretical innovations that belie all of the heroic battles that were performed in the birth of Islam against the Prophet Mohammed's enemies. To sully that religious reputation with mass murder is unacceptable and should cause all Muslims to wonder if these men and women are Muslims at all. Even the doctrinaire Pakistani terrorist group Harakat al-Mujahideen wrote a correct reading of the Quran, that "to die as a Shaheed is an honor. Some people desire this title if they must die because of the great reward. Other people can achieve equal reward as a Shaheed: those who die from terminal illnesses like cancer, the woman who dies as a result of childbirth or those who are murdered."[16] It should be especially noted that the victims of Takfiri terrorists are the true *shaheeds*, not those who violate their own religious principles to commit those murders.

Suicide is strictly forbidden in Islam. It is considered one of the greatest wrongdoings. The Qur'an notes:

> Allah says: "Do not kill yourselves. Allah is merciful to you, but he that does that through wickedness and injustice shall be burnt in fire. That is easy enough for Allah."[17]

An incentive to be a *shaheed* is found in the hadiths that state:

> No one who enters Paradise will want to come back to the world and have anything on the earth except the "Shaheed." He will wish to return to the world and be killed ten times because of the honor he sees.[18]

Often as justification some stories of the hadith are used to illustrate their action, which they view correctly as missions with long odds and virtually no chance of survival. An article in the terrorist magazine *Nida'ul Islam* stated:

> In Nayl Al Awtar, Al-Shawkani comments: "When ten Muslims under the leadership of Asem Bin Thabet were sent by the prophet (s.a.w.) to a tribe to invite them to Islam, in the road they were surrounded by a hundred of the unbelievers. They fought strongly, seven of them killed, one of the three captive survivors, feeling their deception, said: 'By Allah I will not guide you to Muslims and I have a wonderful example in front of me' (meaning his killed brothers), they tried to force him guiding them, when they failed they killed him." This Hadith proves that, it is legitimate for a Muslim to fight the many enemies to death. On the other hand, it is permissible to accept to be a captive.[19]

Al-Shawkani is completely wrong when he attempts to equate the historical example with a suicide mission. The mission described in the hadith is one of extreme risk, from which there was little chance of escape, but it differs dramatically from modern-day suicide missions, as Takfiris expect to kill themselves first in order to possibly kill their enemies. They have a complete disregard for collateral deaths of anyone, Muslim or non-Muslim, in the vicinity. However, they try to reverse the interpretation to cover their explosive method of suicide bombing, which is not facing the enemy and dying at his hands but, in fact, is just the bomber killing himself. This is the heart of the problem with Takfiris: they take historical accounts of Islam, interpret them literally, and then use the heretical justifications as proofs.

Romanticizing the Takfiri Warrior Ethos: The "Salafi Raider"

IN 2005, BRITISH police raided an AQ safe house in Manchester, England. There they found a computer copy of an al-Qaeda operatives manual for the waging of terror war against the West. The introductory section had a tribute that characterizes the AQ combat philosophy with regard to its enemies:

> To those champions who avowed the truth day and night . . . And wrote with their blood and sufferings these phrases . . . The confrontation that we are calling for with the apostate regimes does not know Socratic debates . . . , Platonic ideals . . . , nor Aristotelian diplomacy. But it knows the dialogue of bullets, the ideals of assassination, bombing, and destruction, and the diplomacy of the cannon and machine-gun . . . Islamic governments have never and will never be established through peaceful solutions and cooperative councils. They are established as they [always] have been by pen and gun; by word and bullet; by tongue and teeth; in the name of Allah, the merciful and compassionate.[20]

The dialogue of bullets, the ideals of assassination . . . this was the new way that the extremist fringe would come to terms with the West. Acts of terror was going to be the deeds to drive the West out of the Muslim world. OBL would apply indiscriminate and wanton destruction against all who were non-believers, or anyone who accepted their ways of living. Essentially the task was enormous; the world outside of his Emirate in Afghanistan was now Dar al-Harb, the land of War, and only the Emirate of Afghanistan, perhaps better labeled Takfiristan, was the Dar al-Islam, the land of Islam . . . for Salafist warriors and their families. OBL said:

> "Fight in the path of Allah, you are not charged with the responsibility except for yourself, and urge the believers, lest Allah restrain the

might of the rejectors, and Allah is stronger in might and stronger in inflicting punishment," and His words: "And what is it with you that you do not fight in the path of Allah, whilst the weak amongst the men, and the women, and the children who say: 'Our Lord take us out of this town the people of which are oppressive, and make for us from You a protecting friend and make for us from You a succourer,'" and His words: "So if you meet those who reject, then strike the necks . . ." We have given an oath to Allah to continue in the struggle as long as we have blood pumping in our veins or a seeing eye, and we beg of Allah to accept and to grant a good ending for us and for all the Muslims.[21]

The world was now his target. He had to get working.

Forging the "New" Neo-Salafist Muslim

IN THE WORDS of al-Qahtani the new Takfiri would be a harder person. He or she would reject the ease of the world and all associated with it except the love of God and the mission of jihad: "Islam is actively concerned with the sincerity of devotion to Allah; it requires the absolute renunciation of whatever else one may long for or wish to follow; it seeks to bind the heart to its Lord in hope and fear, in humility and trust." OBL believes that Muslims should accept this or join the infidels.

M. J. Akbar notes that the modern Takfiri terrorists are a completely different model of Muslim. They go to war or into madrassas that cultivate this mind-set. They return only to compliant homes or they stay away on Hijrah. They will not tolerate a fat society; they will question and rebel against rulers they feel are corrupt and will openly criticize their lifestyle; they will publicly contradict the traditional religious leadership. Most important, the neo-Salafists will redefine the Qur'an literally and in their own manner, while proudly ignoring centuries of jurisprudence. Neo-Salafist Takfiris justify their attitude toward the Muslim world with the verse from the Qur'an that says:

Verily, those who deny Our Ayât [proofs, evidences, verses, lessons, signs, revelations, et cetera] and treat them with arrogance, for them the gates of heaven will not be opened, and they will not enter Paradise until the camel goes through the eye of the needle (which is impossible). Thus do We response of the Ka'bah and eat and drink but waste not by extravagance, certainly He (Allâh) likes not *Al-Musrifûn* (those who were by extravagance).[22]

The Old Muslim: Early Al-Qaeda Description of the Corruption of Muslim Youth

IN THE BIN Ladenist world the old image of the Muslim man as a fat, lazy, and indulgent slacker who lives off of the state and strives to live the lifestyle of the princes is one bin Laden seeks to dissolve permanently. The Takfiri Hijrah, or voluntarily emigrating away from all of those who are un-Islamic or not Islamic enough, is the principal method of brainwashing the neo-Salafists use. The recruit is brought into a world where striving for the moment of death and reaching Paradise is the ultimate quest. Not dying is failure to please God, and patience is paradise delayed.

OBL blames the Kingdom of Saudi Arabia for working hand in hand with the West to deliberately produce generations of lazy and slothful Saudis. All oil-rich Arabs disgust him, be they Kuwaiti, Emirati, Qatari, Bahraini, or other. To OBL, they work for the colonialists. In his alternate universe, Western colonialists "aimed at producing a wasted generation that pursued everything that is Western and produced rulers, ministers, leaders, physicians, engineers, businessmen, politicians, journalists, and information specialists. [Qur'anic verse:] "And Allah's enemies plotted and planned, and Allah too planned, and the best of planners is Allah."[23]

> They [the rulers] tried, using every means and [kind of] seduction, to produce a generation of young men that did not know [anything] except what they [the rulers] want, did not say except what they [the rulers] think about, did not live except according to their [the rulers'] way, and did not dress except in their [the rulers'] clothes. However, majestic Allah turned their deception back on them, as a large group of those young men who were raised by them [the rulers] woke up from their sleep and returned to Allah, regretting and repenting. The young men returning to Allah realized that Islam is not just performing rituals but a complete system: Religion and government, worship and Jihad [holy war], ethics and dealing with people, and the Koran and sword. The bitter situation that the nation has reached is a result of its divergence from Allah's course and his righteous law for all places and times. That [bitter situation] came about as a result of its children's love for the

world, their loathing of death, and their abandonment of Jihad [holy war].[24]

British classified documents on militant recruitment report the process of "'Culturing' people in their way of thinking." Among Takfiris recruiting was necessary, particularly among friends and in prayer or study groups, as a way to "propagate the revival of the Caliphate as the way to salvation." They then should "Publicly" oppose non-Muslims and Muslims who they claim have "strayed from the true path of Islam."[25]

Characteristics of the Salafist "Raider"

Terrorist killing machine: The AQ mind-set is illustrated perfectly in this recruiting prequalification found in the Manchester, England, terrorist manual: "[The member] should have a calm personality that allows him to endure psychological traumas such as those involving bloodshed, murder, arrest, imprisonment, and reverse psychological traumas such as killing one or all of his Organization's comrades. [He should be able] to carry out the work."[26]

The Takfiris believe that they must mobilize the Ummah from the bottom up, but in their combat ideology they adhere to the same view they ascribe to the Western military: that Muslim lives don't count for much. When Takfiris produce collateral damage, every Muslim they kill can be considered a *kufir* or an accidental martyr to their cause—which is God's cause. Since God caused the death, it must be looked on with God's approval.

Militant literature and videos often talk of the calmness and serenity in the faces of martyrs after death. They focus on the near-mystical effect the suicide bombing or death in combat has on the corpse. They describe faces with smiles, bodies warm to the touch, and claims of smelling rose or musk scents ("I could smell perfume from the blood of those martyrs!").

Dr. Khaled Abou El Fadl categorizes this rationalization for murder as follows: ". . . the image is as they believe like a teenager who thinks 'I'm not angry for myself. I'm angry for God. I am not speaking because I want X or I want Y. No, no, no, no. It's because God wants [it].' . . . You basically take your own emotions and you . . . project these emotions upon God. You pretend as if God is basically a frustrated, highly angry teenager. That's how you start imagining God. . . ."[27]

Loves and adores death: A senior South Asian diplomat with personal experience with the Afghan mujahideen and who was personally acquainted with OBL commented that the mind-set of the Takfiri extremist militant is a form of personal intoxication with warfare and death. He calls it Jusbah-E-Jihad, or the "Emotion of Jihad Intoxication."

An example of this comes from a wounded militant injured at the Zawar Kili al-Badr terrorist training camp who survived the 1998 cruise missile attack. What he stated from his hospital bed illustrates the mind-set of continual combat: "Yesterday, we witnessed the disintegration of the Soviet Union and now we will witness America burning . . . We are not afraid of anybody. Mujahideen come for the battle of Islam with coffins."[28]

Speaking on the matter of dying, OBL endlessly emphasizes that the new Takfiri terrorist does not fear for life but desires Paradise.

As for fearing for one's life, it is difficult to explain to you how we think of ourselves, unless you have full belief. We believe that no one could take out one breath of our written life as ordained by Allah. We see that getting killed in the cause of Allah is a great honor wished for by our Prophet (PBUH). He said in his Hadith: "I swear to Allah, I wish to fight for Allah's cause and be killed, I'll do it again and be killed, and I'll do it again and be killed." Being killed for Allah's cause is a great honor achieved by only those who are the elite of the nation. We love this kind of death for Allah's cause as much as you like to live. We have nothing to fear for. It is something we wish for.[29]

A good example of the fundamentality of personal sacrifice, even by suicide, is noted in this translation from an interview with an Afghani Takfiri:

My name is Mohammad Yar Afghani . . . One day I went to my friend Haq Nawaz Bhai and he told me that this world is finite and everyone must die, life after death is infinite, therefore let us train for and join jihad. So I joined madressah Syed Ahmed Shaheed for training and am now going to Kashmir. If I am martyred, I have recorded a cassette of my poems, please give that to my friend Haq Nawaz so that he remains in touch with the holy war.[30]

This power of devotion to death is based on their literal belief that in Paradise there is a special place for fighters who face the enemy and die. It is said in the hadiths that the Prophet Mohammed said:

The best of the shuhada' [martyrs] are those who fight in the first rank, and do not turn their faces away until they are killed. They will have the pleasure of occupying the highest dwellings in Paradise. Your Lord will smile at them, and whenever your Lord smiles upon any of his slaves, that person will not be brought to account.[31]

This is an accurate belief in Islam, but it is contradicted by trying to become a martyr through sinful, wicked acts of murder.

Forgiven of all sins: In Islam, Muslims believe it is God alone who calls the shots. No man or woman can judge or determine what will happen to others. If a man is killed, it is God's will. If Osama bin Laden has been taken up by evil and is under the influence of Satan, that, too, is God's will. OBL knows this all too well, and in his mind he sees all acts that are allowed to happen as God's will and a sign of goodness and acceptance. Islam is a very forgiving religion, and OBL and his compatriots know that whatever they do, they can claim it is God's will. Granted, one cannot know the intent behind every religious thought and that the ulemic jurisprudence is detailed and that this can be debated until Judgment Day. Perhaps AQ can feel solace and blessing from their evil in Qur'an 39:53, which may allow them to believe that God will cleanse and forgive their sins:

O, Ibadi [my slaves] who have transgressed against themselves [by committing evil deeds and sins]! Despair not of the Mercy of Allah: Verily, Allah forgives all sins. Truly, He is oft Forgiving, Most-Merciful.[32]

With passionate devotion to worship and equal rejection of all things non-Islamic, bin Laden and his followers have an unparalleled belief in the mercy of a God whom they fear and claim to serve. With this concept in hand and believing this verse, they know there is virtually nothing they can do that will not be forgiven.

Will join the Companions of the Prophet as reward: So revered are the Companions that the Takfiri devotion to them seems to violate the

Wahabist dictum of not worshiping saints or asking for God's intercession through others.

Many of the names of AQ terrorist cells and subgroups reflect the true names of these original Muslims or the Salafist belief system. For example: Battalions of the Companions of the Prophet and Salafist Jihad battalions. Direct names of the Companions have adorned terrorist cells, including the Al Zubayr bin al Awwam Brigade, Abu al-Yaman al Madani Brigade, al-Hassan al-Basri Brigade, and Al Baraa Bin Malik Martyrdom Brigade. Though it could be said that they name these suicide units and terror cells in honor of the Companions, not in beseeching them, the ideology of AQ members makes one question that belief.

Examples of Cleansing Islam

THE FOLLOWING ARE a few examples that typify al-Qaeda's style of field campaign and are indicative of the type of victims targeted by this extremist ideology:

- In 2001 in the Algerian city of Annaba, the al-Qaeda-supported Armed Islamic Group (Groupe Islamique Armé, or GIA) stormed a nightclub during a musical performance. They rushed the stage and seized a singer named Sihem Echaouiya. Her cries to God were ignored as she was thrown face-down by two of the terrorists, her hair pulled back by a third while a fourth came up and slashed a sword through her throat.[33] Her offense in the ideology of GIA was being a Muslima who was singing.

- In 2001 in New York City a Bangladeshi emigrant named Mohammed Salahuddin Chowdhury left home on the morning of September 11, 2001. His wife, Baraheen, at the time was nine months pregnant. He had a six-year-old daughter. Baraheen and her husband prayed before he went to work at the Windows on the World restaurant at the top of the World Trade Center Tower One.[34] Two hours later he was burned alive and then turned to dust when the top of the building where he worked fell 107 stories to the street below. His child Farqad was born without his father forty-eight hours later. Mohammed's offense in the ideology of al-Qaeda? He was working in the West serving food for infidels.

- In 2009 near Karbala, Iraq, a woman suicide bomber entered the women's and children's tent at a pilgrim's rest stop near the city, mingled among the crowd, and detonated her belt of plastic explosives.[35] She killed forty women and children who died in the blast, and eighty-nine others were wounded. Their offense in the ideology of al-Qaeda was being Shiite Muslims walking to mosque and resting.

Is any of this truly representative of justice? More to the point, does the God of Abraham, the same God that Islam, Judaism, and Christianity all worship, view this as pleasing to his eyes? Do any of the millennia of teaching reveal that murder is what man must to do in order to please Him? No matter what your confession, there is scant evidence of that.

A threat is defined as an entity with the intent, capability, and means to carry out an attack. OBL and his allies constitute a threat to all of Islam, both with the sword and with the tongue. More lethal than the bombs he trained the young men to explode themselves with were the words that would move them to do so. To effect this a clever reading of Islam was tied with absolute, unswerving commitment to what al-Wala' Wa al-Bara' asked of them and unquestioning loyalty to their Emir al Mujahideen.

As noted before, the America bin Laden needed was a rampaging rhino destroying all in its path. OBL had this America under George W. Bush, so now would need to ratchet up the stakes to achieve his most important ideological goal, establishing the NIC.

6.

Afghanistan-Pakistan:
The New Takfiri Emirate
of Osama bin Laden

WHEN AFGHANISTAN'S PRESIDENT Mohammad Daoud Khan and his family were shot to death on April 28, 1978, during a coup d'état by the communist People's Democratic Party of Afghanistan (PDPA), no one expected that it would lead to more than thirty years of non-stop strife for the people of that country. After their bodies were dumped into a mass grave in the Pul-e-Charkhi area of Kabul they would be unearthed after three wars had killed tens of thousands of others, including Khan's killers.

The Soviet army rolled into Afghanistan in December 1979, almost a year after the President of the republic was murdered. At the time, the Islamic-borne tribal resistance to the Russian and Afghan communists was nascent. After two centuries of toying between the empire of Great Britain and Czarist Russia in the "Great Game" of influence in Central Asia, Afghanistan was thrust into the communist sphere through armed force. The Soviet Russians quickly installed Babrak Karmal as their puppet President and established a Soviet client state. The Afghan tribes rose in rebellion to this invasion and sought assistance from those who saw the Russian invasion as an affliction that only those loyal to God could defeat.

Five million Afghans fled to Pakistan and organized guerrilla groups and, with Pakistani assistance, started armed incursions across the Pakistani-Afghan border from their sanctuaries in Pakistan. At first President Jimmy Carter offered military assistance to Pakistan's President, Muhammad Zia ul-Haq. Zia deemed it insufficient and turned it down. Soon a new U.S. president would take power and with his wily director of the Central Intelligence

Agency, William J. Casey, would offer billions to fund the mujahideen. This time Zia accepted. Other nations were encouraged to join the American covert effort to damage the Russians. Saudi Arabia encouraged young men to fight under the flag of Islamic resistance to a godless communist regime. The resources for this armed resistance started to flow after President Ronald Reagan authorized billions of dollars and large quantities of advanced weapons to go to the mujahideen.

At the urging of President Reagan, the Saudi government called upon young men to go and help in the new defensive "jihad" that was being waged in assistance of their Afghan coreligionists. Osama bin Laden, twenty-two at the time, was one of the thousands of young, educated Arab men who took up the call to arms. Using the millions of dollars of resources of his family business, the Bin Laden Group, a large multibillion-dollar construction company, he moved heavy equipment to Pakistan for Arab mujahideen camps and helped establish the logistics pipeline in weapons, equipment, and manpower. Bin Laden was first known not as a combat commander but as a logistician for humanitarian aid. He led the International Islamic Relief Organization, an agency that assisted more than six million Afghan refugees in Pakistan. Bin Laden proved to be an inspiring personality who lived by the words of the Prophet Mohammed, who stated, "He who equips a Ghazi (raider or fighter) in the way of Allah is as if he has taken part in the fighting himself, and he who looks after the dependents of a Ghazi in his absence, is as if he has taken part in the fighting himself"[1] and will receive a reward and status of the jihadist in the afterlife. Bin Laden's quiet but intense style of speaking made many swear themselves to the cause. He also proved a phenomenal fund-raiser, who managed to draw millions to his "charity" to arm and feed the Arab guerrillas.

In the early 1980s OBL joined forces with his former university professor, the powerful mujahideen leader Abdullah Azzam. Bin Laden was organizing the logistics of the jihad and the financial aspects of bringing in weapons and equipment for the Arab mujahideen. Food and charity shipments often covered for the importation of mines, explosives, and weapons for the Afghan-Arab forces. Between 1984 and 1987 OBL would lead the way in bringing critical material support to these disparate groups. In 1987 he transformed himself from logistician to combat commander by participating in the battle against the Soviet garrison at Jaji, and then at Jalālābād Airport. He was wounded in the encounter but gained great respect for his enthusiasm in battle despite being a novice. In 1986 bin Laden met Dr. Ayman al-Zawahiri, a radicalized member of the

Egyptian Islamic Jihad (Gihad al-Islamiyyah) terrorist group. Born in Cairo, Egypt, in 1951, al-Zawahiri was involved in jihadist activities from as early as age fourteen. He was formally educated as a surgeon and medical doctor. Al-Zawahiri was imprisoned and tortured in Egypt for his association with Muhammad 'Abdus Salaam Faraj, the leader of the group that dispatched Lt. Khaled Islambouli, the Egyptian army officer, to lead the assassination attack that killed Egyptian Pres. Anwar Sadat in 1981.

After being imprisoned, then acquitted and released, al-Zawahiri left Egypt and soon joined with bin Laden in Pakistan. Another devotee of Dr. Abdullah Azzam, al-Zawahiri came to Afghanistan in 1986 to work as a doctor and quickly became a supporter of the jihad movement and opened the Islamic Jihad Bureau and met Osama bin Laden. By 1988 bin Laden was in private conflict with Abdullah Azzam. The Soviets had withdrawn from Afghanistan and OBL saw a new phase of work for his jihadists. Azzam advocated for the jihad to end and for the insurgents to return home—just in time for Azzam to be vaporized by Dr. Ayman al-Zawahiri.

In 1989 an unknown assassin planted plastic explosives under the seat of Abdullah Azzam's car in Peshawar, Pakistan, as he left for the mosque with his sons. They were instantly killed. The murder of the spiritual godfather of the internationalist jihad against the West was surprisingly convenient. The usual accusations were levied against Russia, America, and Pakistan, but his death benefited only OBL. Azzam's mujahideen who did not return to their homelands were quickly folded into bin Laden's group.

By this time bin Laden had started to espouse his philosophy based on Sayyid Qutb's writings, which asserted that apostate rulers must be overthrown by force, Arab lands with Western-backed dictators and kings would be liberated and formed into an NIC, and the West's hostility to Islam would be confronted directly. To meet his aims OBL secretly established a new organization to supersede the Azzam-less MSB. It was known as al-Qaeda.

After the Soviet withdrawal, bin Laden returned to Saudi Arabia a triumphant hero with the battle scars to prove his worth as a fighter. The image of the pious warrior allowed him great latitude in an otherwise well-controlled political environment. OBL lectured the Saudi people about his desire to spread the story and fame of the brave and outnumbered mujahideen in Afghanistan and how, like the Prophet Mohammed, he and his companions overcame all for their God.

The story takes an abrupt turn after the 1990 invasion of Kuwait by Iraq. The King's invitation of America into the Kingdom was considered a betrayal of his faith. The Americans were no better than the Russians, and if anyone could defeat a highly mechanized army in Kuwait it was bin Laden's Afghan-Arab mujahideen veterans. Disgusted, bin Laden moved first to Afghanistan and then on to Sudan. His veterans went out and started creating the movements within their home countries in order to carry out a strategic plan that received scant attention until later in the decade. OBL turned on his former sponsors in the Kingdom and swore that he would cleanse Islam, but first he would have to remove the greatest obstacle to Muslim advancement in the world, America. OBL believed that a few humiliating strikes would suffice to make America leave the stage in the Islamic world. When the Taliban, a group of armed student theologians, retook Afghanistan from squabbling warlords, he moved back and assisted in helping them create a perfect Islamic Emirate in Central Asia. In a 1996 interview he discussed how the Taliban movement and their Emir Mullah Omar fulfilled a dream for him.

All gratitude to Allah, our relationship with our brother Mujahideen in Afghanistan is a deep and broad relationship where blood and sweat have mixed as have the links over long years of struggle against the Soviets, it is not a passing relationship, nor one based on personal interests. They are committed to support the religion approved by Allah, and that country remains as the Muslims have known it, a strong fort for Islam, and its people are amongst the most protective of the religion approved by Allah, and the keenest to fulfill His laws and to establish an Islamic state.[2]

Once safely entrenched and after dabbling in a few terror strikes, bin Laden trusted his heart and the guidance he was supposedly receiving from God and openly declared war on America and the West. By 2001 all was in place for him to launch his greatest plan, and in his eyes it worked magnificently.

The Holy Sanctuary

THE TERROR MISSION bin Laden called the Holy Tuesday Operation was supposed to bring America to Afghanistan and let the Taliban, AQ's 055 Arab mujahideen brigade, and Pashtun Pakistanis break its thin logistic back through daring guerrilla attacks. OBL had a vision. U.S. forces would meet a coalition of religious fighters that would dog their every step until their army and foreign policy in the Muslim world were left in tatters. Like the nineteenth-century British forces in Afghanistan and the twentieth-century Russians the Americans would find their army besieged as they struggled to maintain their bases and roads at the beginning of the twenty-first century. They would succumb to the incessant attacks. Eventually America would tire and finally surrender to the mujahideen, just like the British, just like the Russians. It would be a perfect victory and it needed a catalyst and demonstration to reveal to the world that bin Laden was ready. Holy Tuesday, September 11, 2001, would be the fire to light the fuse. But before that could happen, some basic groundwork needed to precede it.

On September 9, 2001, two bin Laden–dispatched suicide bombers, Dahmane Abd al-Sattar and Bouraoui el-Ouaer, dressed as a Belgian news team of Moroccan origin. They made an appointment to interview Ahmed Shah Masoud, the famous "Lion of Panjshir," who was one of the most effective combat commanders against the Soviets. Masoud was the only Afghan warlord who could truly rally the nation to the Americans' cause and help defeat the Taliban Emirate in the coming war with America. He had to be eliminated. Once el-Ouaer was seated in Masoud's presence, the camera he carried blew up. Now that Masoud was dead the plan could proceed. Less than forty-eight hours later the nineteen hijackers struck in America.

OBL, knowing the Americans would be coming, called out to Pakistani tribes to assist him: "We exhort our Muslim brothers in Pakistan to fight with all their might to prevent the American Crusader forces from conquering Pakistan and Afghanistan."[3] It was a noble call, but before they joined forces major disaster struck—the Americans openly purchased the loyalty of most Afghan warlords and unleashed them on the Taliban.

On October 20, 2001, the American forces performed a combat parachute jump into Qandahar, Afghanistan. All went according to OBL's plan until the American-backed Northern Alliance invasion in late October pushed OBL and AQ into Tora Bora. Tora Bora was a snow-covered complex of caves in the Hindu Kush mountaintop stronghold overlooking Jalālābād. Under withering American firepower and facing imminent collapse of his forces to the Americans, he decided that God wished him to fight another day. OBL simply walked off Tora Bora and down into his Pakistani sanctuary with his men and escaped.

The tactical victory at Tora Bora was ballyhooed by President Bush, who would incessantly claim that two-thirds of AQ leadership were captured or killed. OBL knew the sanctuary was critical and that in the coming years he would need to bring his Pakistani brethren along into the jihad.

One hundred days after 9/11, I traveled to Pakistan and Afghanistan to research a single question. Where was Osama bin Laden? I wanted to resolve the issue as to where the leadership of AQ could have dispersed. I made my way to the newly liberated Jalālābād. After a meeting with the newfound American ally Haji Qadir and his lieutenants, I was taken up to the Tora Bora battle site. It took not more than an hour to see the trail of footprints heading down the other side of the Tora Bora mountain and realize that al-Qaeda did not vanish. They simply walked off the Afghanistan side of the mountain down into the sanctuary of Pakistan, just as they had done for the ten-year-long Soviet-Afghan war.

Answers to the question of what happened to the AQ organization since 9/11 have been filled with a wide range of punditry, analysis, braggadocio, propaganda, and what the intelligence calls SWAGs, or Serious Wild-Assed Guesstimation. Within days of the end of the battle at Tora Bora the word on the political street was that AQ was finished and that bin Laden walking down off the mountain and into Pakistan's FATA was a mistake that would lead to his immediate capture or killing.

I returned to Pakistan. I could have left, but I wanted to know what was on the other side of the mountain. Where were they going to gain sanctuary and would their ties to the FATA be enough to sustain them? Every day the truth was becoming patently more obvious. For some reason, the Bush administration did not see their cross-mountain escape as important to the overall Afghanistan mission. Perhaps Bush trusted that Musharraf was waiting to finish the job. Maybe the White House staff believed that only a few hundred hardliners would be no problem for Pakistan and that bin Laden in a cave was now isolated and without support. It was widely reported that the administration shifted their thoughts to prepare for an invasion of Iraq. No matter what the rationale, the escape of al-Qaeda was a strategic mistake quite possibly unparalleled in American history. It was akin to stopping World War II after D-Day and ordering an invasion of Mexico.

The Historic Province:
The Dream of the Islamic Emirate of Iraq

WITHIN WEEKS OF the Tora Bora escape, the Americans rapidly withdrew numerous combat, intelligence, and support units from the hunt for the 9/11 killers. President Bush and his administration had decided, on no evidence but their own imagination and "gut" feelings, that AQ was in league with Saddam Hussein. No matter how fundamentally foolish this decision was, it was to be acted upon at the expense of killing OBL. To the neoconservatives in the Bush White House, letting AQ escape from Tora Bora into Pakistan meant that they were no longer a significant threat, so the neoconservatives moved all of the American army's manpower and equipment to invade Iraq.

It was as ludicrous as it sounded. A rabid religious extremist to join forces with a brutal dictator who executed religious extremists at first sight? In the intelligence community it was not only unfeasible but also improbable. No matter; America abandoned much of its pressure in Afghanistan and turned its full force to destroying Iraq. For a man who was supposed to be wanted "dead or alive" it could never be better than this. America was actually going to position itself *closer* to the recruiting base of AQ in the Middle East. Like manna from heaven, it was wholly unexpected and made OBL grateful to God.

A New al-Qaeda

A FEW WEEKS before Saddam Hussein's army was eliminated in a blitzkrieg invasion, Abu Mussab al-Zarqawi, the leader of the Jordanian terrorist group Tawhid wal Jihad, entered Iraq with his men and volunteered to fight for the Ba'athists. They moved to the town of Fallujah, west of Baghdad. They found houses deep in the city and made contacts with other Salafist groups that were forming there. Instead of going to the battlefront to fight the Americans, the Salafists sat out the combat and let the Ba'ath Party get slaughtered. They were waiting for the post-war insurgency, where they could practice guerrilla warfare in the American rear and force them out, just like the Soviets in Afghanistan.

By August 2003 al-Qaeda launched their first suicide strikes in Iraq. First they hit the Jordanian embassy and then the UN Canal Road headquarters. A myriad of small Salafist Takfiri groups soon collected themselves and formed the Tanzim Qaidat al-Jihad fi Bilad al-Rafidayn (al-Qaeda in the Land of Mesopotamia al-Qaida in Iraq, AQI for short). In 2005 they would declare an Islamic Emirate of Iraq.

Bin Laden, not quite in touch with the reality on the ground, harbored a great image of a fully entrenched insurgency that created the "Islamic State of Iraq." After four years of brutal fighting it was clear they would fail miserably. But in 2008 he still believed that it was so effective that it could bring his now-dead jihadists closer to assisting in Palestine. He said, "Iraq is the perfect base to set up the jihad to liberate Palestine,"[4] not seeming to be aware of just how bad his losses in Iraq were.

But by 2009 the overwhelming preponderance of the AQI force was slaughtered by the very people who had asked them to come into Iraq in the first place—the ex-Ba'athist Sunnah insurgents. The Iraqi Sunnah insurgents maintained a combat force of over forty thousand men and supporters. They used AQI as a precision terror group to strike selective and hard targets. They controlled the Emir of the jihad Abu Mussab al-Zarqawi's logistics and weapons and his forces' movements in Iraq. Bin Laden had less control than he believed, because without kissing the ring of the tribal Iraqis, most of whom were beholden to Hussein for survival, his men could not flourish.

AQI immediately made two critical missteps that eventually eliminated their effort. First, they practiced an unrelenting brutality that shocked even some of their most ardent supporters. The situation grew so bad that Ayman al-Zawahiri had to write al-Zarqawi and ask him to desist from televising his beheadings and mutilations lest they lose the support of the Muslim world:

Among the things which the feelings of the Muslim populace who love and support you [al-Zarqawi] will never find palatable—also—are the scenes of slaughtering the hostages. You shouldn't be deceived by the praise of some of the zealous young men and their description of you as the shaykh of the slaughterers, etc. They do not express the general view of the admirer and the supporter of the resistance in Iraq, and of you in particular by the favor and blessing of God. And your response, while true, might be: Why shouldn't we sow terror in the hearts of the Crusaders and their helpers? And isn't the destruction of the villages and the cities on the heads of their inhabitants more cruel than slaughtering? And aren't the cluster bombs and the seven-ton bombs and the depleted uranium bombs crueler than slaughtering? And isn't killing by torture crueler than slaughtering? And isn't violating the honor of men and women more painful and more destructive than slaughtering? All of these questions and more might be asked, and you are justified. However this does not change the reality at all, which is that the general opinion of our supporter does not comprehend that, and that this general opinion falls under a campaign by the malicious, perfidious, and fallacious campaign by the deceptive and fabricated media. And we would spare the people from the effect of questions about the usefulness of our actions in the hearts and minds of the general opinion that is essentially sympathetic to us.

Interestingly, to al-Zawahiri, slitting throats off-camera and committing mass murder by suicide car bomb or gunfire was just fine. He finished:

And we can kill the captives by bullet. That would achieve that which is sought after without exposing ourselves to the questions and answering to doubts. We don't need this.[5]

Second, AQI attempted to impose an absolute neo-Salafist rule on a community of 5 million that had enjoyed wealth, status, and prosperity under Saddam. Being asked to sacrifice their country and to revert to the archaic neo-Salafism was just asking too much. The tactic that had worked so well in the Pakistan FATA, forced intermarriages with tribal women, had not gone over well at all in Iraq. So when the ex–Ba'athist insurgents resisted, AQI started to execute their leaders. By late 2006 the tribes had gone into open rebellion against AQI. Worse, they had told the Americans to stay out of the way while they slaughtered AQI. The Iraqi Sunnah community had turned on them, and by 2008 they had openly joined the Americans to root them out of their tribal belt.

The Iraq war was the prize that bin Laden wished had occurred in Afghanistan. The delay and loss of the "Mesopotamian Knights" who fought and died there allowed him breathing room. America had split its forces, and with just a few dozen veteran terrorists his deputy, Abu Mussab al-Zarqawi, managed to make good on his promise to bring a full-scale terrorist resistance operation into the heart of the Middle East. Al-Zarqawi was killed in due time, but not before he had created a wing of AQ that had never before existed and the Americans had given the Muslim world a reason to completely mistrust them. By 2007 the local Iraqi Ba'athists, never the most reliable of allies, turned on al-Zarqawi's terrorist forces and the war started winding down.

Perhaps OBL considered Iraq not a loss but a beginning. Even though it was clearly lost by 2008 and only some indigenous Takfiri extremists continued operations there, AQ was on the cusp of building something bigger. It was time to establish not one but two Islamic Emirates: the Islamic Emirate of Afghanistan and the Islamic Emirate of Western Pakistan. From the winter of

2006 through the fall of 2008, military offensives by the Taliban and the Tarik-e-Taliban resulted in at least two provinces declaring that they were the first new Islamic Emirate. Together with Mullah Omar of the Afghan Taliban and the new allies from the Tarik-e-Taliban of Pakistan, they envisaged a trans-border nation right between the two countries, protected by the Hindu Kush. The establishment of the NIC and the men to fight for the liberation of both Afghanistan and Pakistan would destabilize both governments in such a way as to help AQ reach the Takfiri alliances' strategic goals perhaps more rapidly than imagined.

Pakistan's Tribal Agencies— Province of Greater Takfiristan

THE TALIBAN, WHO operated from the North-West Frontier, and their al-Qaeda brethren in 2001 impressed me. That they were eventually going to be eliminated from the face of the earth one at a time mattered not to them. In fact, they impressed everyone who was inclined to be impressed, and in the North-West Frontier Province (NWFP) of the tribal regions of Pakistan, that was nearly everyone. They wore only thin cotton shirts and pants (called *shalwar khamees*), wool Pakhool hats, and wool blankets wrapped around their shoulders. The only other items they wore regularly were Kalashnikov rifles and canvas Chinese ammunition bandoleers. They could traverse a ten-thousand-foot mountain pass wearing this or maybe a cheap Chinese jacket or Karachi leather coat. But that was generally all that the men we were fighting would be using for their mission to spoil a rapid victory. This was the garb of the global guerilla—the Vietcong of our past dressed similarly, as did the modern Abu Sayyaf guerrillas in the Philippines, the Tamil Tigers in Sri Lanka, and the Interahamwe in Rwanda. Like all small warriors they fought and moved like Alpine-style mountain climbers—superlight, superfast, and with only the necessary tools to get the job done.

The regions that directly border Afghanistan are the NWFP, the FATA, and the province of Baluchistan. The FATA covers seven areas or agencies along the Afghan border; from north to south they are Bajur, Mohmand, Khyber, Kurram, Orakzai, North Waziristan, and South Waziristan. Altogether the three regions encompass almost one-third of Pakistan. The men who live here are natives of a centuries-old tradition of resistance, religious piety, and honor. They had spent centuries, in particular the last three decades, showing their mettle as tough guerilla warriors in combat, deeply religious Muslims in Islam, and hard-living tribesmen who hated uninvited outsiders.

The Arabs who led al-Qaeda were the internationalist allies and strategic thinkers who lived in these regions by the leave of the local tribes according to the tribal law of Pashtunwali, or honor code. It is Pashtunwali that forbade them to give up a guest even unto death. The terrorists had come from different parts of the world to fight for what they believe is the defense of a threatened Islamic regime and an opportunity to create a new Islam. They were told to thrive despite the difficulty of the terrain, the lack of food, ammunition, water, and rest, as a form of sacrifice. Like fasting during Ramadan, it was a sign of deep piety and love of God to come kill infidels. They believed they were living as the first Companions of the Prophet Mohammed had, and so they are.

From 2001 until 2006 the Afghan war continued. To the Americans progress was slower than they desired, but it plodded on as America became embroiled in Iraq.

But by 2006 something had changed in the political dynamic in the nation that safely endured the Pashtun harboring of AQ. The Pakistani dictator, President Pervez Musharraf, was growing weaker and his dictatorial missteps were being challenged by the FATA guerrillas. George Bush and his acrimonious way of segregating peoples into fully compliant friends or death enemies were so unpopular that OBL had a far higher approval rating in Pakistan for over five years, and Musharraf's support was seen as sycophantic at worst and puppetry at best. By the end of the year his forces would lose a campaign in the FATA against AQ-backed tribal insurgents.

Musharraf would allow his generals to cut deals to keep casualties low. These deals essentially were self-defeating because they strengthened the community stranglehold of the Taliban and al-Qaeda when their terrorist demands were met. Usually they started benignly, demanding Islamic law be implemented and run by the Taliban; then once the army had gone, the killings began.

Soon the Pakistani ideological guerrillas of the TTP, advised by AQ, decided to confront Musharraf directly. They seized the Red Mosque (the Lal Masjid) in Islamabad and filled it with women and children in an effort to confront Musharraf with a purely Islamic face and see if he would spit in it. Like all good dictators, who are often myopic to the subtleties of their own doom, Musharraf did spit in the face of the Islamic community, and with such fury and vengeance that he effectively separated himself from the word "Islam" in Pakistan. He then changed laws, suspended the Supreme Court, and placed the nation in a state of emergency. Musharraf was then quickly besieged with the dilemma of the return of former Prime Minister Benazir Bhutto to challenge him. If the chaos of Pakistani politics was food for the tribal extremists, then Bhutto's return was the icing on the cake for the FATA Islamic alliance.

The former Prime Minister Benazir Bhutto may have been attractive to much of old Pakistan, but to the Pakistani Taliban and its allies there was to be a new, far more Islamic Pakistan. The country itself was having difficulty deciding on whether to lean toward a more Islamic political rule or liberalize itself with a woman whose husband, Ali Asif Zadari, was widely reported to have taken 10 percent off the top of all contracts his wife issued. For men who routinely decapitated women and children for slight offenses, the question of whether this woman should survive her return did not remain unanswered for long. After two failed attempts on her life, Bhutto was killed when first a gunman first shot her in the head and then a suicide bomber blew himself up alongside Bhutto's car. She died instantly. Musharraf was forced out of power and Bhutto's weak husband, Zadari, took the reins. By 2009 his government would be seeking deals with the FATA guerrilla tribesmen and their AQ allies. The scenic Swat Valley was besieged by a three-thousand-man guerrilla unit and the government was forced to declare that Sharia law would be the method of administration. The movement was in the hands of the FATA/AQ alliance and the politics of Pakistan were changing to support greater political acceptance of Sharia law in large swaths of the country. This changed somewhat by TTP overreaching in 2009 when the Pakistani army took back the Swat agency.

The players in the destabilization of Pakistan include the Pakistani version of the Taliban, comprised of the Movement for the Enforcement of Islamic Laws (Tehreek-e-Nafaz-e-Shariat-e-Mohammadi, or TNSM), the Pakistani Taliban Movement (TTP), and the Army of Islam (Lashkar-e-Islam, or LeI). These groups working with OBL and the Afghan Taliban could see a different strategy playing out. Though combat against the Americans would be a high priority, the destabilization and "rescue" of Pakistan by the Pakistani guerillas in the FATA/NWFP/Baluchistan regions would give them the political leverage to go for a greater prize—their extremist ideology being respected and given greater political influence in Pakistan. AQ has solidified their refuge in Pakistan and is well on their way to developing a state within a state. Until then the sanctuary in the FATA needs to be stabilized, weapons replenished, manpower inspired, recruited, and trained. This region has now become to al-Qaeda what Cambodia and Laos were to the North Vietnamese army in the 1960s—it is a sanctuary of unprecedented difficulty to enter and an anvil that has broken armies on its mountainous peaks. OBL and his allies now hide in what has been alternately called Talibanistan, Jihadistan, or al-Qaedastan, what *Newsweek* called "an autonomous quasi state of religious radicals, mostly belonging to Pashtun tribes who don't recognize the Afghan-Pakistan frontier—an arbitrary line drawn by the British colonialists in 1893."[6] Add to that the Takfiri groups' new image of themselves and the nation that they are carving out.

A better description would be that the al-Qaeda central leadership, the Afghan Taliban, the Pakistani Taliban, and the Pashtun tribes are forming the Emirate of Greater Takfiristan. Takfiristan is an emirate whose resident forces intend to solidify their military capability, project guerrilla power in both Afghanistan and Pakistan, plan terror missions worldwide, and greatly influence the political balance in Pakistan with the hope of someday acquiring nuclear materials or, worse yet, weapons. To do this they need to spread and impose their variant of Islam across the ideological mainstream of the Muslim world in order to influence a new generation of potential recruits and sustain their ability to project terror.

If they continue to apply enough pressure, then the existing power structures in Pakistan, AQ, and the Pakistani Taliban most likely will attempt to negotiate concessions that may be granted in the face of populist and political pressure. Each time the political shift occurs within the national government to negotiate, the militants will invoke the furies in defense of their faith and await another concession. The intent of this step-by-step pressure is to erode the basis of religious support for the government. Once a settlement is achieved through violence, the militants will pause, then violently escalate again and again. The internal pressure through violence will continue until they reach a tipping point where the majority of the population is completely on their side. With a highly motivated and more devout populace they believe that the existing power structure could be toppled quickly. This model is being played out in Pakistan.

On Nuclear Weapons and Other Weapons of Mass Destruction

IN AUGUST 2001 OBL and al-Zawahiri are said to have met with Bashir-ud-Din Mahmood, a Pakistani nuclear engineer with a Ph.D. from Manchester University.[7] A man forced from his position as a top nuclear scientist, designer of Lahore's Khushab nuclear power plant, and director general of

Nuclear Power of the Pakistan Atomic Energy Commission, he was also highly sympathetic to the Taliban in Afghanistan. After his retirement he became an Islamic scholar and started a non-profit charity called Ummah Tameer-e-Nau (UTN), which was designated by the U.S. Department of the Treasury as having provided direct material support to terrorist groups, the Taliban and al-Qaeda.[8] The second guest was Abdul Majid, his deputy at the charity. After news of this meeting was revealed, the Pakistani intelligence agency, ISI, picked them both up and they revealed that they had met with AQSL and outlined the international pipeline for acquiring nuclear materials. They also discussed various types of nuclear weapon designs that were "simply structured, transportable and effective. Bin Laden and Zawahiri pressed him with how-to questions."[9] After being told that enriched uranium was expensive and time-consuming, OBL asked Mahmood, "What if you already have enriched uranium?" This is not the sort of question that a global terrorist leader should be asking. Did bin Laden mean to hint that he may have a faster pathway to achieving his goal of gaining control of the ultimate weapon? The answer remains unknown.

Nuclear arms are hard to come by, and perhaps OBL's question was that of an engineer thinking ahead. With effort, smaller mass-effect weapons could be acquired. The Japanese religious cult Aum Shinrikyo managed to develop their own sarin nerve gas and experimented with mustard and phosgene gas as well as the less lethal and hard-to-disperse poison ricin. America had been attacked by someone within the country by relatively ineffectual anthrax attacks, but the terror it produced was impressive.

After the seizure of Afghanistan, the Department of Defense, in a report to Congress, testified that AQ had indeed been looking to acquire chemical and biological weapons. They wrote:

In 2004, we received multiple disparate reports that *mujahidin* and insurgents in rural areas along the Pakistan-Afghanistan border were attempting to conduct attacks using "anthrax." The description of the substance allegedly in possession of these individuals was generally more consistent with a chemical-based contact poison than anthrax, and it appeared that many *mujahidin* in the region used the term "anthrax" as a catch-all phrase to describe any poison, chemical, or biological agent.[10]

Surprisingly good information came from the journalists at CNN who found some convincing and incriminating documents addressed to Abu

Khabbab, a man believed to have been Osama bin Laden's top chemical and biological weapons expert.[11] The documents outlined some of the information that may have been passed on by Dr. Mahmood of the Pakistani nuclear program.

OBL had a firm opinion about the criticality of acquiring atomic weapons. He saw them as an absolute must for his vision of the Muslim world. He thought the Pakistani program was a boon to Islam. Bin Laden once remarked:

> . . . when Israel is stocking up on hundreds of nuclear warheads and atomic bombs, and when the Christian controls a vast proportion of these weapons, this is not an accusation but a fact. We cannot accept that anyone accuse us of this. How can it be claimed that a man is a brave warrior when the claimant is backward and stupid? We supported and congratulated the Pakistani people when God blessed them with possession of a nuclear weapon, because we consider it the Muslim's right to have it, and we will not pay any attention to these shabby American accusations.[12]

Well in line with his desire to further his ideological campaign, he saw no harm in marrying this urge for WMDs with the call for permanent and offensive jihad. He continued:

> . . . there is a duty on Muslims to acquire them, and America knows today that Muslims are in possession of such a weapon, by the grace of God Almighty.[13]

There is a fierce debate about the potential for AQ to attain nuclear materials, but no question is more serious than that of whether they could acquire or construct an entire nuclear weapon. That is simply a matter of technical expertise meeting the right resources. More important, AQ believes they now have religious justification to commit genocide via atomic weaponry. In one statement, bin Laden claimed that AQ was justified in killing as many as 10 million Westerners. On May 21, 2003, a thirty-six-year-old Saudi imam, Naser bin Hamad al-Fahd, released a fatwa, or religious ruling, claiming that it was acceptable for AQ to acquire and use nuclear weapons:

> This is the case of the United States in our times. The attack against it by WMD is accepted, since Allah said: "If you are attacked you should

attack your aggressor by identical force." Whoever looks at the American aggression against the Muslims and their lands in recent decades concludes that it is permissible. They have killed about ten million Muslims, and destroyed countless lands. If they would be bombed in a way that would kill ten million of them and destroy their lands it is obviously permitted, with no need for evidence.[14]

Al-Qaeda and Taliban Threaten
Pakistan's Arsenal

THE PAKISTANI PROGRAM for the development of nuclear weapons was designed to be a balance against India. It increased dramatically after India's first atomic test in 1974. The father of the Pakistani program, Dr. Abdul Qadeer Khan, arrived in Pakistan in 1975 to head up the process. He was a German-trained metallurgist who brought with him knowledge of the gas centrifuge technologies needed to enrich uranium to weapons grade. He was in charge of building and operating the Kahuta nuclear research facility (now named the A. Q. Khan Research Laboratories). This was done in relative secrecy until Pakistan itself tested up to three weapons on the same date, May 30, 1998, in Baluchistan.[15] A. Q. Khan was arrested after he was found selling nuclear technology to Libya, North Korea, and Iran. It was his deputy Mahmood who is alleged to have held a meeting with OBL and the Taliban.

Could the global Takfiri jihad, particularly since it appears to have a base of popular support in South Asia, eventually destabilize Pakistan in five years, ten years? Twenty years? It is too early to tell if the ideological shifts within the Pakistani tribal areas and incited by AQ have had any impact on the military and security forces of Pakistan. It is the hope and dream of OBL that this will happen and that the personalities, safeguards, and security of the program will fall into the hands of brothers in the Pakistani nuclear establishment that could carry out his fervent wish to arm the New Islamic Caliphate with the ability to destroy Saudi Arabia, Israel, and America.

Many assume that if AQ were to acquire a nuclear weapon it would be an American city that would first taste the wrath of Islam. In my assessment it would be much closer to home. It would be Riyadh that would be vaporized. And with it bin Laden would be ridding Islam of the Saudi royal family and create such panic that his organization would allow a new emir to take custodianship of the Land of the Two Holy Shrines.

Thoughts from a Cave: Tilting at Crucifixes

ESTABLISHING A NEW Islamic Caliphate appears to start with ignoring history. In OBL's quest to acquire the weapons, manpower, and ideology for a new dawn of Islam, his ideology appears to completely ignore virtually all Islamic expansion, though fragmented and fractious. In the eight hundred years since the Crusades, he, Ibn Taymaiyya, 'Abd al-Wahab, Sayyid Qutb, Faraj, and others have viewed the Islamic era before the Mongol invasion as the last period of pure historical Islam. To the ideologues, all since the Mongol reign has been a false enlightenment—a state of war (Dar al-Harb) and in Jahiliyyah (the state of ignorance before true Islam). He completely discounts the conversion to Islam of the Mongols from Shamanism and Buddhism, which in many quarters has been seen as a second period of scientific, artistic, religious, and military enlightenment in Islam and a sign from God that the power is coming to the truth of Islam. As Prof. Khaled Abou El Fadl notes, "By emphasizing a presumed 'Golden Age' in Islam, the adherents of Salafism idealized a time of the Prophet and His Companions, and ignored or were uninterested in the balance of Islamic history."[16]

OBL rhetorically seizes on British, French, and Italian colonialism and lumps it into conspiracy theories about how the United Nations formed Israel and how America uses the Jews as its hammer to pound down Muslim nails when it does not use its own direct power to corrupt the youth of Islam with technology and sex. It's a far-ranging, interwoven conspiracy theory that originates with Pope Urban II and is brought to light by the actions of George Bush. Bin Laden notes in his own words soon after the fall of Afghanistan to U.S.-backed forces:

> Look at this war that began some days ago against Afghanistan. Is it a single, unrelated event, or is it part of a long series of Crusader wars against the Islamic world? Since World War I, which ended over 83 years ago, the entire Islamic world has fallen under the Crusader banners, under the British, French and Italian governments. They divided up the whole world between them, and Palestine fell into the hands of the British. From that day to this, more than 83 years later, our brothers and sons have been tortured in Palestine. Hundreds of thousands of them have been killed, hundreds of thousands of them detained.

OBL relies on the ignorance of history and on the Muslim world understanding and accepting his Western conspiracy theory, religious ultraorthodoxy, and suicide Puritanism. With the invasion of the Near East and establishment of European cantons in Palestine and Syria, the Crusaders attempted to re-create Christian feudal states of their home countries and failed miserably.

When his forces were soundly defeated in Afghanistan he blamed the Crusades:

> The Crusader nations went forward. What is the concern of the Arab nations in this Crusader's war? They involve themselves with it openly, without disguise, in broad daylight. They have accepted the rule of the cross.[17]

OBL somehow connects even the smallest and most benign Western social center to colonialism or the Crusades. For example, in his statement after a suicide bomber destroyed an amateur British theater in Qatar he claimed it was a "Crusader outpost." When he could not enjoin the Muslims to remove the Americans from the Arabian Peninsula he reminded them of the Crusades and nineteenth-century colonialism at the same time:

> Colonialism and its followers, the apostate rulers, then started to openly erect Crusader centers, societies, and organizations like Masonic Lodges, Lions and Rotary clubs, and foreign schools.[18]

By seizing on Crusader imagery and his striking targets, which would seem innocent to rational people but could be transformed into Crusader colonies, he plays to virtually every audience from Morocco to the Philippines. It is a prime example of how the Bin Ladenist Victory Ideology seizes virtually any code word and equates it to danger to Islam. For all of the effort, it has only had marginal effect.

As I have noted before, the Crusades were less than the disaster that had befell Islam. They were a victory that OBL seems to have completely missed. Scholar Bernard Lewis categorizes the Crusades this way:

> I would not wish to defend the behavior of the Crusaders, which was in many respects atrocious. But let us have a little sense of proportion. We are now expected to believe that the Crusades were an unwarranted act of aggression against a peaceful Muslim world. Hardly. The

first papal call for a crusade occurred in 846 C.E., when an Arab expedition from Sicily sailed up the Tiber and sacked St. Peter's Rome. A synod in France issued an appeal to Christian sovereigns to rally against "the enemies of Christ," and the Pope, Leo IV, offered a heavenly reward to those who died fighting the Muslims. A century and a half and many battles later, in 1096, the Crusaders actually arrived in the Middle East. The Crusades were a late, limited, and unsuccessful imitation of the jihad—an attempt to recover by holy war what had been lost by holy war. It failed, and it was not followed up.[19]

No matter, as OBL quickly characterized the war on terrorism as the newest iteration of the Crusades, in an interview after the invasion of Iraq he said:

> This is a war which, like previous wars, is reviving the Crusades. Richard the Lion heart, Barbarossa from Germany, and Louis from France—the case is similar today, when they all immediately went forward the day Bush lifted the cross."[20]

There is only one missing component to the thought behind the Long War strategy as spelled out by OBL. His dream and Qutbist education make it clear why he views Afghanistan-Pakistan FATA as the launching base of the NIC. It meets all of his goals for a perfect place to start the Takfir, Hijra, and jihad on a pan-Islamic scale. But more interesting is that he may have come up with the idea that he needed to launch a cleansing war of liberation similar to the very Crusades that he despises. Some say he sees his Islamic jihad as more akin to the *ghazwahs* or raids made against the enemies of the Prophet Mohammed. But bin Laden's expedition to create a new Islam within the existing Muslim world is almost an exact replica of a Christian Crusade—a failed last thrust at recovering something that did not belong to it.

If Bernard Lewis is correct in his description of the Crusades as a limited, belated, and ineffectual response to the expansion of Islam, it offers a conundrum—who is using the Crusader here? There is much evidence to suggest it is bin Laden himself who intends to replicate the Crusades. OBL is establishing an Islamic-cultist variant of the Christian Crusades. Like Pope Urban II, OBL has issued a non-binding religious ruling for men to go to a designated holy land in a war in God's name and to cleanse it of his religious opponents. He gathered religious men who saw themselves as knights, from across a broad geographic spectrum, who penetrated infidel lands.

Did OBL decide to mimic the Christian Crusades? That era's misguided objective, laced in the burning hatred and devotion to the warrior ethos, is similar in scope and zeal to OBL's jihad, which most likely will suffer the same end results. If the Crusades are too far a projection for OBL's intentions, historically speaking, AQ are on the verge of making the Islamic sects of the Khawarij and the Qaramita look mild.

The Triumphalist Vision
of the Victorious Denomination

THERE IS NO doubt that OBL is attempting to re-create an Islamic feudal state on the Afghanistan-Pakistan border. He seeks to acquire the power to bring down Islam, through the destruction of his enemy's capital, Riyadh, and then march triumphantly into Mecca.

It could be supposed to be a warrior-based attempt to create a Sunnah Islamic Revolution on par with the 1979 Iranian Revolution. But, unlike the first *fitna* between Ali and Mu'awiyah, there will not be a parlay because of Qur'an pages stuck to a bayonet or sword. To OBL this is a war of waste. The revolution is armed with the spiritual belief that anyone in its way will accept bin Ladenism or die. It is also prescribed that the men and women of the revolution should die until Islam is restored.

OBL views this as a long, multigenerational war but believes he and his Takfiris will ultimately win, with or without Pakistani atomic weapons. He does not care if he sees this in his lifetime, and he won't, but he has started the path. He hopes to achieve glory as the theologian and ideologue who set the ball in motion, the ideological spread of a Takfiri utopian nation-state, the NIC. In this next phase, he fully intends to succeed by creating the heart of the NIC in the countries of both Pakistan and Afghanistan. He adopts a sometimes realistic and often fatalistic view that has sometimes been lacking in the West. In 1998, after nearly being killed in a cruise missile attack and witnessing the physical destruction of his global headquarters, he said, "War has its ups and downs, sometimes it goes our way, sometimes not."[21]

One can only hope on this point it goes against him. For the rest of the Takfiri militants, only breaking their link to Islam will crush them completely.

Part III

═══

Coup d'arrêt:
Launching Counter-Ideological
Warfare Against al-Qaeda

7.
Rallying to the Defense of Islam

Muslims cannot be defeated by others.
We Muslims are not defeated by our enemies,
but instead, we are defeated by our own selves.
—ABDULLAH AZZAM[1]

"We Ask God to Accept This Offer"

MAY 29, 2004, was a clear blue day. It was 7:25 A.M. that Saturday when Michael Hamilton, a British citizen living in Khobar, Saudi Arabia, was walking to his car at the gated compound of the Arab Petroleum Investments Corporation (APICORP).[2] He heard the automatic weapons gunfire at the front gate where terrorist members of al-Qaeda of the Arabian Peninsula (AQAP) were shooting the two Saudi security guards to death. A senior manager in the finance and trade department and a father of two, Hamilton had worked in Saudi Arabia for over fifteen years when the leader of the "Al-Quds" (Jerusalem) Brigade of AQAP, Fawwaz bin Muhammad al-Nashmi, and his men stormed the compound. Hamilton was headed from his residence to pick up his wife at the British embassy and was in his car when the terrorists sprayed it with gunfire. When he was incapacitated they came over and rejoiced at killing a *kufir*. Not content with letting the dead man lie, they dragged his wounded body out and tied it to the bumper of their car. Al-Nashmi, in an interview with a Takfiri militant magazine, praised God for allowing him to kill this man:

> We got into our vehicle [after tying] the infidel by one of his feet [to the car] and we left the company premises and saw the patrols. The first to arrive was a Jeep with one soldier, whom we killed . . . The clothing of the infidel [tied behind the vehicle] had been ripped off, and he had become naked in the street. The street was full of people

because this was during work hours, and everybody saw the corpse of the infidel dragged behind the vehicle, praise to God.[3]

The terrorists made their way to a nearby business park named the Petroleum Center, where they asked the Saudis present to identify the Westerners and stated their intentions: "We are jihad fighters and we want the Americans. We did not come to raise our weapons in the faces of Muslims. We came to purify the Arabian Peninsula from infidels and polytheists who kill our brethren in Afghanistan and Iraq, in accordance with the will of our Prophet, Muhammad, peace and blessings upon him. We want you to lead us to them." They then stormed an office and killed an American and South African. Al-Nashmi bragged, "When he looked at me, I shot him in the head, which exploded." Engaged in a running gun battle with Saudi police and military, the terrorists then stormed the heavily guarded Oasis compound and managed to shoot their way in. Their first act was to capture a Swedish man, behead him, and leave his decapitated body with the head on his chest as a warning to the security forces. The terrorists then entered the compound buildings and systematically proceeded to slaughter eight Indians ("Hindu Dogs"), two Sri Lankans, and three Filipino Christians: "so we cut their throats and dedicated them to our brothers, the jihad fighters of the Philippines." Al-Nashmi gloats, "We purified the land of Muhammad from many Christians and polytheists on that day."

Afterward the terrorists found an Italian man working in the restaurant of the hotel. They held him hostage and forced him to call Al Jazeera:

We called Al-Jazeera and asked the anchor to speak to him, so he did. The anchor asked me whether the Italian spoke English. I asked the anchor whether he had any Italian translators. He said yes. I said: "Then let him speak in his own language," so he talked for a few minutes. Then I asked the anchor: "Did you record?" He said yes, so the heroic Nimr cut [the Italian's] throat. Highly impressed, the interviewer from *Voice of Jihad* begged, "We ask God to accept this offering."[4]

War for the Land of the Two Holy Shrines

WHEN OBL STARTED his global insurgency, initially the overt strategy was oriented to secure the withdrawal of U.S. forces from Saudi Arabia in the run-up to the first Gulf war and liberation of Kuwait. At the invitation of the King, American forces staged at Saudi Arabian bases and forced Iraq out of Kuwait. I noted earlier that OBL wanted this honor and desired to use his Afghan-Arabs to eject Iraq by guerilla warfare. The King had good reason to be suspicious of OBL. The outspoken Saudi extremists had started to organize under the returning jihadists and had managed to secure the support of many influential jurists. The rhetoric of the Takfiris was now entrenched in destroying the Kingdom, removing the Saudi royal family from the face of the earth, and installing an NIC. Two clerics, called the Awakening Sheiks, distributed audiocassette speeches demanding that the Americans get out. A group of clerics forwarded a letter to King Fahd called "The Letter of Demands" insisting on Islamic reforms including "unquestioned primacy of Islamic law, equal distribution of public wealth, more funding of Islamic institutions, religious control of the media and a consultative assembly independent of the royal family."[5] This form of heresy was kept quiet in the typical Saudi fashion, but after the invasion of Kuwait and the war called Desert Storm OBL had agitated enough.

The Saudis had a limit, and in 1991 it was reached. With the advocacy of the CIA, Saudi intelligence expelled bin Laden, claiming it was because of an American plot to assassinate him. He left the Kingdom for Afghanistan and never returned.

As early as 1992 it became apparent to the Muslim world that the United States would continue to use Saudi air bases, where their reconnaissance and fighter aircraft were watching Iraqi airspace. This led to a temporary shift in the OBL strategy to attack both the Kingdom and the United States with a Near *and* Far Enemy (N-F) Strategy simultaneously. Ayman al-Zawahiri, bin Laden's Egyptian companion, however, had been assured in 1988 that the near enemy would be the Egyptian regime, not Saudi Arabia and the Americans. The Egyptian militants had suffered since the time of Hassan al-Banna and were being so decimated that al-Zawahiri himself had to leave for Afghanistan and fold his Egyptian Islamic Jihad terrorist group under AQ. Now OBL wanted to shift this to his immediate enemies.

OBL never misses an opportunity to directly confront the Islamic traditional leadership. He declared the al-Saud leadership, and in effect the mainstream Muslim world, as believers who had abandoned Islam, "apostate." He carefully uses these words with the intent to cut a black-and-white line of hatred by Muslims who may not realize that this is a political ploy to drive them into

apostasy themselves. OBL's choice of language is not rhetoric; it is carefully designed to incite rebellion against Islam by using Islamic terms. For example:

> The so-called "Custodian of the Two Holy Mosques," King Fahd bin
> Abdul-Aziz, has once again proved that he is in fact the "Traitor of the
> Two Holy Mosques." Not only do the puppet governments of the Mus-
> lim countries fail to fight the enemies of Islam themselves, but they
> are actually the first obstacle in the way of the Muslims that do want
> to fight the enemies of Allah.[6]

However, bin Laden referred to acts against America as a reaction to both
American and Saudi foreign policies in Palestine, Egypt, Iraq, Pakistan, and
Afghanistan. In a March 1997 interview, bin Laden told CNN's Peter Arnett
the exact strategic nature of his anti-American campaign, which was based
on a global jihadist support structure.

> . . . the effect of jihad has been great not only at the level of the Islamic
> movement but rather at the level of the Muslim nation in the whole
> world . . . Of this, the acme of this religion is jihad. The nation has had a
> strong conviction that there is no way to obtain faithful strength but by
> returning to this jihad. The influence of the Afghan jihad on the Islamic
> world was so great and it necessitates that people should rise above many
> of their differences and unite their efforts against their enemy.[7]

Bin Laden made it clear that his jihad was about not just driving America
away from Saudi Arabia but also creating and supporting a broad-ranging
campaign against America on a global scale. In the end the effect of this
would be to eventually topple the Saudi regime and allow him to create a
new Caliphate based on his interpretation of Islam. The basic ideological
thought about why and how this could be done was answered by an interpretation from al-Qurtubi, a thirteenth-century classical scholar, who said:

> The command to denounce disbelief is from Allah, even when the
> disbelievers are fathers or sons. They may not be taken as protectors
> once they have chosen disbelief over faith.[8]

To the Takfiris, Saudi Arabia had done just that, and the sentence from OBL
was death.

The Raids on the Kingdom

TO BIN LADEN the Kingdom of Saudi Arabia (KSA) and the United States were the same nation, both despoiling the shrines of the Prophet. From the time of bin Laden's expulsion forward, the Kingdom would be the heart of his ire. The new anti-KSA/anti-USA strategy became a major pillar in AQ political and combat operations for the next decade. For all of his support and bluster for attacking Israel, he would support other jihads as best he could with terrorist strikes, such as those in Somalia, Europe, and Asia. But the two devils he needed brought low were America and Saudi Arabia. The Americans would suffer—that was in the works and all stops were removed from the most devilish and clever methods of attacking them globally.

In the meantime, al-Qaeda militants would start to slowly squeeze from within. Their *ghazwahs*, or raids, were designed to bring attention to the people of the Ummah, that men of courage were striking out against the Kingdom.

On November 13, 1995, the building housing the U.S. Office of Personnel Management for the Saudi National Guard was stuck with a truck bomb that killed five Americans and two Indians. It was the first attack of its type in the Kingdom. The Saudis, on the one hand, were stunned, and in typical fashion they clamped down on news and the case of finding the perpetrators. Once they were found, the regime would not let the Americans interrogate the four Saudis involved. They promptly beheaded them.[9] The Americans, on the other hand, assumed all terrorism originated from Iran or Syria and blamed the attack on members of Hezbollah Syria.

At 9:55 A.M. on June 25, 1996, a large water tanker truck pulled up next to the U.S. Air Force high-rise in Khobar, Saudi Arabia. Two men jumped from the truck, abandoned it, and fled in an awaiting sedan, which peeled out. A U.S. Air Force security policeman on the top of the ten-story building knew what was coming . . . it was a bomb delivery. Before he could sound a complete alarm, the truck blew up, immediately killing 11 and injuring more than 160 personnel, including more than 60 seriously.[10] It was clearer this time that the killers were also Saudi, but the threat was still not focused on the Afghan-Arabs who fought under bin Laden.

Bin Laden was proud of his operations. He stated:

All that has been proved is our joy at the killing of the American Soldiers in Riyadh and Khobar, and these are the sentiments of every Muslim. Our encouragement and call to Muslims to enter Jihad against the American and the Israeli occupiers are actions which we are engaging in as religious obligations. Allah Most High has commanded us in many verses of the Qur'an to fight in His path and to urge the believers to do so. Of these are His words: "Fight in the path of Allah, you are not charged with the responsibility except for yourself, and urge the believers, lest Allah restrain the might of the rejectors, and Allah is stronger in might and stronger in inflicting punishment."

Ironically, bin Laden's public claims of awareness and possible involvement in the Riyadh attacks went unheeded in Washington. In November 1996 bin Laden himself addressed this oversight and took claim for the operation in the jihadist magazine *Nida'ul Islam* (Call to Islam):

A result of the increasing reaction of the people against the American occupation and the great sympathy with the Jihad missions against the Americans is the eagerness of the Americans and the Saudis to propagate false information to disperse these sympathies. This can be witnessed in their statements that some of the countries in the region were behind the Jihad missions inside the country of the two sacred mosques, however the people are aware that this is an internal Islamic movement against the American occupation which is revealing itself in the most clear picture after the killing of the four champions who performed the Riyadh operation, the ones concerning whom we ask Allah to accept amongst the martyrs.[11]

OBL, who had bounced between Afghanistan and Sudan, made clear the intention of the attacks from his new sanctuary in Taliban-controlled Afghanistan:

There were important effects to the two explosions in Riyadh on both the internal and external aspects. Most important amongst these is the awareness of the people to the significance of the American occupation of the country of the two sacred mosques, and that the original decrees of the regime are a reflection of the wishes of the American occupiers.[12]

He explained in his interview why they naturally occurred in the Kingdom. As far as OBL was concerned, the Kingdom of Saudi Arabia was equal to America and Great Britain:

The external policy of the Saud regime towards Islamic issues is a policy which is tied to the British outlook from the establishment of Saudi Arabia until 1364 ah (1945 ac), then it became attached to the American outlook after America gained prominence as a major power in the world after the Second World War. It is well known that the policies of these two countries bear the greatest enmity towards the Islamic world.[13]

The next few years saw a gradual shift to lower-level tactics among the neo-Salafist Takfiris operating within the Kingdom. Al-Qaeda's brigades were not yet formed the way they would be a few years hence. However, the long proselytizing of the Salafists within the more extreme elements of the Kingdom and the large number of Afghan-Arabs made a low-level campaign of individual attacks to be possible. Starting in November 2000 a four-year-long anti-Western campaign took place in the Kingdom. The campaign started simply when a small bomb attached by a magnet, known as a soap-dish bomb (or also known as a sticky bomb), blew up a British national and injured his wife. Several other bombings of this type occurred in quick succession. More than a dozen individuals from Western nations were killed or injured.

The fly in the ointment of managing the Takfiri insurgency was that the Kingdom's investigations were handled by the Saudi Interior Ministry Investigations Division, the Mubahith. Almost instantly they were determined to hide the truth. After two years of investigating, they denied there were attacks conducted by terrorists and claimed the bombings were part of an "illegal alcohol smuggling ring."[14] They arrested two British citizens, sentenced them to death, and exchanged them for Saudi nationals detained in Guantánamo Bay prison camp. It was odd behavior, as the Saudis would soon be locked in a death struggle with AQ bombers. Saudi hopes that blaming outsiders for deaths of non-believers would encourage the more militant Salafists to refrain from terrorism. It did not work, but it did manage to make the Saudis look even more craven and weak to the extremists.

After the arrests of the British the bombs continued and soon became more personal. A British national received a letter bomb in a manila envelope that blew off his hand.[15] On October 6, 2001, a suicide bomber, the first ever in the Kingdom, attacked and killed American Michael Martin, a thirty-three-year old engineer working for Halliburton and living in Khobar.[16] The bomber was seen following Martin and other Westerners and then entered the Al-Mushiri Trading Establishment and blew up. The bomber, a Palestin-ian dentist living in the Kingdom, was decimated. Saudis, however, looking for an answer that did not involve Salafist militants, ignored the method and sophistication of the devices. The bombs were military-style IEDs seen in Afghanistan. This was yet another oversight that would come back to bite them. Again the Saudis tried to blame the suicide bombing on alcohol smug-glers. A search of the bomber's flat found explosive residue, as well as valid Indian and Egyptian passports. It was too apparent that these attacks were starting to be related to a covert terrorist insurgency. AQ knew the strength of the security forces on the Arabian Peninsula required longer-term infiltra-tion and terror operations. By 2003 their attacks would stun the Kingdom but result in a massive backlash from the monarchy.

Al-Qaeda in the Arabian Peninsula

THE SITUATION IN the Kingdom was deteriorating. On May 12, 2003, nine suicide attackers drove three car bombs into a Western residential com-pound in Riyadh. The gun battle and suicide bombs killed all of the attackers and twenty-six Saudis and Europeans. OBL's campaign for inciting revolu-tion in Saudi Arabia had arrived, and his men would force a referendum by the gun on the monarchy.

To incite the population to change the regime, bin Laden had a plan. He would capitalize on the unpopular and remora-like relationship between the Kingdom of Saudi Arabia and the United States. He would use the special af-fection of the al-Sauds for America as a fulcrum to show they were apostate. Any Saudi actions favoring America would only prove to the Muslim world that the Saudis were *kufir*, apostates who had turned their backs upon Islam for the promise of earthly riches in oil sales to America. The punishment for this transgression was death.

When bin Laden struck America, the animosity of the attacks peeled away popular support in both countries. 9/11 created a firm wedge between the two nations. Now he thought Saudi Arabia vulnerable enough to be taken back by his knights. He would establish a new guerrilla system in the Kingdom called al-Qaeda in the Arabian Peninsula.

The American invasion of Iraq had been a fantastic boon to the Takfiris throughout the Muslim world. Iraq helped AQ organize their men, supplied them with an unbelievably large quantity of weapons, and sent back leaders with combat skills. Until now most weapons had been coming from Yemen, but

Iraq gave al-Qaeda quantities that could not be imagined any other way. Thousands of Kalashnikovs were being smuggled. Hundreds of tons of explosives were making their way into the Kingdom. With the weapons came an attitude of armed revolution. The attacks on the Kingdom increased. However, what al-Qaeda needed most was loyal volunteers. Hundreds of Saudi youths were going to Syria and then on to die in suicide bombings in Iraq. AQAP needed them in the Kingdom, as it was considered a greater sphere of insurgency. Iraq was proving a drain to keeping up the demands for newer members and attacks. The problem became so acute that the leader of AQAP Saleh al-Oufi called for Saudis to fight at home:

> Your country, the Peninsula, is in greater need of your services. There are several borderlines here to protect. The enemy that you want to go to, those who are defaming the honors in Afghanistan, in Iraq, and in Palestine, that enemy is here, amongst you. He is on your land, pillaging your religion and your treasures. It is the lawful duty of a Muslim to close the hole that is nearest to him. Clerics have agreed that, if an enemy occupies one of the Muslim countries, he needs to be pushed away from the nearest point, then the one after that.[17]

The leader of AQAP Sa'ud Bin Hamoud al-Utaybi declared 2004 a banner year:

> Jihad fighters everywhere! This month of Jihad (Ramadan) has come with all its blessings and with the double reward [granted to Jihad fighters] in its course. Come closer to Allah through the blood of infidels, do not relent in spilling [their blood], and through [this blood] wipe out humiliation and disgrace from among your Muslim nation! Make this month like the month of the Battle of Badr, the conquest of Mecca, [the conquest] of Shaqhab, and other Islamic victories.[18]

In 2004, attacks on individual Westerners continued with sticky bombs, shootings, kidnappings, and suicide bombings. The Khobar massacre at the Oasis compound occurred. A BBC cameraman, Simon Cumbers, was shot and killed while filming a background shot with reporter Frank Gardner. Gardner survived the shooting but with severe injuries. Terrorists with valid security passes massacred six Westerners at a petrochemical plant in Yanbu. American Paul Johnson was kidnapped from a fake police security checkpoint, killed, and beheaded. The American consulate in Jeddah was attacked and six of its expatriate staff were gunned down. Saudi Arabia was spinning out of control, and it would take two years of mass arrests, running gun battles, and more terror attacks to quell the insurgency.

Men fighting within the Kingdom, like al-Utaybi, were speaking directly to the people of Saudi Arabia and harnessing the power of traditional Islam and tying it to the social ills they believed would bring the average Muslim to bin Laden's neo-Salafist ideology. Speaking of the Kingdom, al-Utaybi said:

> These tyrants try to seduce you, [claiming] that you will be martyrs on behalf of the homeland after your death and that the governor of the region will pray over you and will promote you after death, after the grave has been closed on you and your ribs have been mangled [by the torments of the grave]. You will then receive [the consequences] of your evil deeds, namely, fighting to defend the cross and to protect the [Arab] tyrants. The gate to Hell will be opened to you, because Hell is your abode. What do you say then? [That] perhaps the Day of Judgment will not come? Or the Day of Resurrection? . . .
>
> Oh, men of Jihad everywhere! There are two types of Jihad in Ramadan: The diurnal Jihad [expressed by] fasting and the nocturnal Jihad [expressed by] prayer. Perform the Jihad against your enemies with your [own two] hands, sacrifice your souls and your property in fighting your enemy, as an imitation of [the acts of] your Prophet [Mohammed] in the month of Ramadan [and in order to] enrage your enemies.
>
> Oh, men of Jihad, the victory of Allah's religion will be as [Allah] said: "Fight them until there is no civil strife [fitna] in the country, and God's religion shall reign supreme" [Qur'an 8:39]. For the country is full of civil strife and unbelief.[19]

Al-Utaybi was correct, there was a fitna (civil war) occurring in the Kingdom, and OBL was pleased at its initiation. This was the heart of the jihad for the future NIC. The Kingdom had to be transformed or the struggle would operate at the periphery in perpetuity.

Always pragmatic, bin Laden would accept a long, slow ending of the regime. If this could happen in a century, it would be moving quickly. A year after the two bombing attacks in Riyadh, OBL gave an interview to the magazine of the militant movement Nida'ul Islam and made this statement about the priority of attacking the Kingdom of Saudi Arabia:

The regime in the land of the two sacred mosques has given a very high priority to this organization, and has been able to enlarge its position in the estimation of the people until it made of it an idol to be worshipped aside from God amongst some of the common people, and without the will of the members of this organization.[20]

Alas, there was a chink in the AQ revolutionary armor. For all of the indifference Saudis paid to the attacks on the Westerners, they did not appreciate the mass murder of Muslims in the Kingdom, even if they were from other nations. The first error occurred in 2005 in the attack on the al-Mohaya compound at Laban Valley. Members of AQAP converged on the compound, which housed Western workers from the United States and Britain as well as others from Arab countries. The terrorists from AQAP brought with them four vehicles, two of which contained suicide car bombs. As they approached, one of the car bombs exploded prematurely. The rest of the terrorists attacked and died in the onslaught. The Laban Valley attack ended in the deaths of all twelve terrorists. Unfortunately, it also ended the lives of eleven Muslims. Killing Christians was one thing in the Land of the Two Holy Shrines, but killing innocent Muslims left the average Saudi outraged.

As far as AQ was concerned they had one mission in the Kingdom—bringing it low enough to effect revolution. Bin Laden had been harboring this in his heart since 1996, when he stated in an interview his ultimate goal:

> . . . this is a very difficult and dangerous one for the regime, and this involves an escalation in the confrontation between the Muslim people and the American occupiers and to confront the economic hemorrhage. Its most important goal would be to change the current regime, with the permission of Allah.[21]

At the street level the appeal to fight in the Kingdom was based on the presence of the Americans. By the end of 2004 al-Oufi again requested that Saudis fight in Saudi Arabia, not in Iraq:

> I categorically refuse that I or my "wanted" brothers go to Iraq. Besides, our enemies, the Crusaders, have invaded Iraq through this land. They do not run Iraq's affairs from there, rather they do it here. The enemies are effectively abundantly present in this Peninsula.

Why go follow the Crusaders' tails when their heads and bases and supports are on this blessed land.[22]

However, the pressure was truly on. The Saudi army took these attacks personally and fought with their own brand of religious zeal, their men fighting with the belief that AQ members were "evil criminals" and "bandits" and operating under the orders of a corrupt Muslim. The Saudi commando and security forces, trained by the American Special Forces, grew exponentially more effective. In a nationwide manhunt the AQAP was tracked down relentlessly. Terror attacks ended almost immediately after the Saudis decided to kill off anyone else found to have used violence. In rapid succession, AQAP lost one commander after another—Muqdisi was killed in 2004, al-Oufi was killed in 2005 in a shoot-out with Saudi security forces in Medina, and the rest were forced to flee to Yemen by 2008.[23]

For now the Kingdom is secured by way of land, sea, and air, but the ideological battle continues. Over the next decade, should AQ not be broken operationally, the blitz to inspire, recruit, and push for the dissolution of the Kingdom will continue to grow from their bastion of Pakistan.

Islam Is Truly Under Attack

THE FRAME OF Islam under attack and that the world needs to rally to its defense is not limited to the neo-Salafist Takfiris. This line of rhetoric has long been used successfully, from the time of the Prophet and by other Islamic theorists and ideologues right up to today by OBL, to rally the resources of the Muslim world.

On this point I find myself in agreement with al-Qaeda. Islam is under attack and the Muslim world must expend all resources to combat the threat to the Ummah. However, the case to be made is that the threat to Islam is the neo-Salafist Takfiri bin Ladenists espousing the armed religious ideology of Sayyid Qutb and Abdullah Azzam. They follow a man who is a cult leader, not the words or actions of God.

For al-Qaeda, their worldwide base of support has been to capitalize on their stated love and devotion to Islam and to return it to the pure state as in the era of the Prophet Mohammed. Yet OBL has many times stated his goal to destroy that entity and reform Islam. America and Israel are just red meat for the terrorist base.

Who can resist a billionaire who rejects his wealth and status to become a pious fighter? One who gives his life for his people, no matter where they are or how they are oppressed? This "Robin Hood" analogy is highly respected in the emerging world as well as the Muslim one. Yet in the war against Islam, this Hiraba he has been waging secretly veils his true intentions.

Al-Qaeda's terminal strategic goal is simple: bin Laden seeks, and has always sought, to create an alternative to the present-day Islamic power structure and the way Islam is practiced. He wants to take control of the guardianship of the two holy shrines and thereby become the ideological dictator of how 1.5 billion people will practice Islam . . . his variant of Islam. That is all.

The bin Ladenist threat is a real, existential danger to the 1.5 billion Muslims in the world. Like Juhayman al-'Uteybi, the leader of the seizure of the Grand Mosque in 1979, bin Laden interprets Islam based entirely on Bid'ah of Takfir, al-Wala Wa al-Bara', and mass murder. This Bid'ah desires absolute elimination of the way Islam is practiced today. "What of the al-Saud's family stewardship of the shrines and practices of Islam?" one may ask. Is there not something to the claims of corruption? That is not relevant, say Islamic scholars. In the hadith of *Muslim* the Prophet said: "There will be appointed over you rulers, some of whom you will like and others whom you will dislike. The one who dislikes what they do will be free of blame, the one who denounces that will be safe, but the one who approves of that and follows them will be in peril." They said, "O' Messenger of Allah, should we not fight them?" He said, "No, not so long as they pray."

Few in the Muslim world, or the rest of the world, for that matter, actually support any of the truly revolutionary goals of al-Qaeda. Though some polls in a strongly militant nation such as Pakistan gave as much as 64 percent approval to al-Qaeda after September 11, it had dropped markedly, to as low as 13 percent, by 2008. Most realized that bin Laden is a practitioner of politics, not Islam. If individuals in the Muslim world did support AQ it was usually based on political disgruntlement, not religious motivation. However, al-Qaeda bases their call for support from the Muslim community, the Ummah, on the ideological argument that they are and have been fighting invaders of Muslim nations in the name of Allah for over twenty years. They claim to be fighting jihad for the sake of their oppressed people.

There is as much concern in the Muslim world about extremism as there is in the West. After 9/11 the opinions about the core Islamic values may not have changed much, but the worry about the Islamic extremism of AQ had many countries, even those with high approval ratings of OBL, worried about the spread of militancy. In 2005 the Pew Poll of Islamic Attitudes on Extremism found that respondents in Morocco had a 73 percent fear of unleashed extremism. This came immediately after a series of suicide bombings in Casablanca, an event unheard of before in the Maghreb. Even in Pakistan, a nation that supports AQ and the Taliban, 52 percent worried about the trend. It continued in Turkey (47 percent) and Indonesia (45 percent) and tapered off in Lebanon (26 percent) and Jordan (10 percent). It should be noted this poll occurred before both Jordan and Lebanon were struck by terrorists.[24]

Even more surprising was a 2007 BBC poll where Egypt, a new conservative bulwark of support for militant causes, revealed a split between those who saw a difference between armed resistance in Iraq and those who saw the AQ terror war as acceptable. The Egyptian majority (54 percent) believed that Muslim and Western cultures can find common ground. Although 43 percent believed a clash of Western and Islamic civilizations is inevitable, 57 percent believed it would be based on political power and national interests. These opinions trumped differences between religion and culture as the basis of a clash. More to the point, Egyptians overwhelmingly (59 percent) blamed "intolerant minorities from both sides."[25]

In the same poll they found that even during the Bush years Americans were highly optimistic about working and understanding Islam, despite the terrific setbacks in Iraq and Afghanistan. Although 64 percent of Americans felt the two cultures could find agreement, only 31 percent viewed violence as inevitable. It should be noted that this same number corresponds to the minority that consistently supported George W. Bush's actions over eight years no matter how flawed. While 73 percent of Americans blamed intolerant minorities for the trouble, only 17 percent said the fundamental differences between Islam and Christianity were to blame.[26]

From where does OBL acquire his gut feeling that all Muslims will side with him? We should be warned: American law professor Dr. Khaled Abou El Fadl identifies OBL as having a potential audience that is receptive to his ideology:

> The issue is how marginal is bin Laden or what does bin Laden really represent . . . There are few that are as arrogant or self-righteous as bin Laden within the Muslim world—but the most dangerous is a type of thinking that would allow a person to think they speak authoritatively and decisively for God. And that type of thinking is more widespread in contemporary Islam than bin Laden.[27]

If this is in fact a potential stepping-stone for bin Ladenism to take root in the Muslim world, then the depth of the rift between what is mainstream Islam and the terrorists needs to be exposed. The neo-Salafist Takfiris could best be described as a modest terror threat to democracy, but they are an even greater spiritual and cultural threat to Islam.

Recall that AQ views the Muslim world after the Mongol invasion as completely apostate. In such a light, the members of al-Qaeda cannot be considered in any but the most extreme political terms. Religion is a smoke screen to justify their political objectives. Their pious guise masks a dangerous armed cult that seeks earthly power.

Although bin Laden expounds on parts of this multigenerational plan to demolish the fourteen-hundred-year traditions of Islam openly—principally by complaining about the wantonness of the Saudi Arabian monarchy—he almost never openly states that he desires that bin Ladenism first burn across the other nations of the Muslim world. He rarely reminds people that his men will be the judge, jury, and executioner concerning who is a proper Muslim and who is not. In fact, when the evidence is laid out to Muslims on the street, they cannot believe the audacity that someone would dare challenge the word of Allah and seek to overturn the traditions of the Prophet Mohammed.

Islam Was Warned by the Prophet

THERE HAVE BEEN warnings about the emergence of splinter groups from within Islam. At the Battle of Hittin, the Prophet warned the dissenters who were angry about his partial distribution of the spoils that "at the end of my ummah there will be people who will tell you things of which you and your fathers have never heard; beware of them and avoid them."[28]

Many believe that this was in relation to a continuing Khawarij threat, which in fact did emerge. Most likely the Prophet was warning of schisms and reinterpretations of the Qur'an. On this point he was again right when the Qaramita rampaged across the Arabian Peninsula and when al-Qaeda sought to reinterpret and rewrite Islam. All of these were and are Bid'ah (innovation or heresy).

It was Ibn Taymaiyya himself, the jurist most revered by neo-Salafist Takfiris for his warnings about the invasion of Genghis Khan and who called for jihad against the Mongol adoption of Islam, who passed a warning on OBL's intentions with establishing a new Islamic caliphate.

The Religion of the Muslims is built upon following the Book of Allah, the Sunnah of His Prophet (sallallaahu 'alayhi wa sallam) and that which the Ummah has agreed upon. So these are the three infallible usool (fundamentals). So whatever the Ummah differs in, then it is referred back to Allah and His Messenger. Thus, it is not for anyone to set up a person for the Ummah, and to call to his way and form walaa' (love, loyalty and allegiance) and 'adaa (enmity and hatred) based upon that, except for the Prophet (sallallaahu 'alayhi wa sallam). Nor is any speech set up for them based upon which they form walaa' and 'adaa except for the Speech of Allah, and that of His Messenger, and that which the Ummah has agreed upon. Rather, this is that practice of the people of innovation, who set up a person or a saying, with which they cause splits in the Ummah; forming walaa' and 'adaa based upon that saying or ascription.[29]

OBL is a man with no Islamic standing to declare jihad. However, the members of AQ are more loyal to OBL and his lieutenants, human personalities, than to the word of God Himself. AQ has clearly set up a person, OBL, which has caused a split within Islam. As Ibn Taymaiyya said, these are the "people of innovation."

The main argument against bin Laden's legitimacy is that he has absolutely no authority to issue fatwas or declare wars. He is not a selected or elected Islamic authority. He bases his claim to leadership on the religious authority to be prayer leader. He boldly extended even this illegitimate claim to be a Prince of the Jihadists (Emir al Mujahideen). Islamic scholar Dr. Abdal Hakim Murad describes bin Laden's lack of authority this way:

Certainly, neither bin Laden nor his principal associate, Ayman al-Zawahiri, are graduates of Islamic universities or seminaries. And so their proclamations ignore 14 centuries of Muslim scholarship, and instead take the form of lists of anti-American grievances and of Quranic quotations referring to early Muslim wars against Arab idolaters. These are followed by the conclusion that all Americans, civilian and military, are to be wiped off the face of the Earth. All this amounts to an odd and extreme violation of the normal methods of Islamic scholarship.[30]

None of this has been missed by the highest religious leaders in Islam. In 2008 Shaikh Saleh Al Laheedan, chairman of the Saudi Arabian Supreme Judiciary Council, said:

Osama is a preacher of evil and destruction while Al Zawahiri is an eccentric, who left for turbulent regions when his country was not accommodative [to] his evil designs.[31]

They Corrupt the Meaning of Jihad

IN CAIRO'S AL-AZHAR University, the Oxford of Muslim scholarship, sits the Islamic Religious Research Center. It is the heart of all Islamic jurisprudence and rulings. It is there, soon after September 11, 2001, that it was ruled there was no legitimate jihad to be carried out against America and the West. In fact, the Grand Mufti of al-Azhar, Sheikh Abdul Aziz al-Ashaikh, the highest religious authority in Islam, profoundly and vigorously rejected all association between Islam and the 9/11 attackers. The Grand Mufti's statement read:

> Hijacking planes, terrorizing innocent people and shedding blood constitute a form of injustice that cannot be tolerated by Islam, which views them as gross crimes and sinful acts.[32]

In Islam a legitimate jihad must meet several specific requirements. A Muslim must never be the aggressor; a Muslim must fight only those who fight him; and women, children, and the elderly should be spared the duress of war. Jihad is chivalric to the extreme. It has set rules.

OBL has even evinced a stunning hypocrisy on the authority to call jihad. One minute he calls it the right of every Muslim, even though the rules are clear that an authority must declare jihad, then the next he reverses himself and states that only a worldly person, such as himself, should ignore those authorities:

> . . . who defines what the right conditions are? Should it be those who have relied on the world, or those who have taken no share in legal knowledge?[33]

OBL, in the same interview, contradicts himself when he states that the entire basis for declaring jihad is invested in one with legal authority and knowledge:

> The Sheikh of Islam Ibn Taymaiyya makes it clear in this regard that he who issues a judicial decree regarding jihad is he who has knowledge of

184/ AN END TO AL-QAEDA

the legal aspects of religion, who has knowledge of jihad and when it should be waged. In other words he should wage jihad himself.[34]

By Ibn Taymaiyya's own words, neither OBL, a man with education in marketing and civil engineering, nor Dr. Ayman al-Zawahiri, the medical doctor turned terrorist, has the knowledge or Islamic scholarship to issue a judicial decree or the religious standing to declare jihad.

The Debate: What Are They?
Khawarij, Qaramita, or Just a Cult?

SPIRITUALLY SPEAKING, IS the corruption of AQ not a part of God's plan? It may be, but perhaps we could also see it more clearly as a test of the truly faithful. The Khawarij were a test to the Companions of the Prophet, and it was finally passed after they were eliminated, but it caused the great rift between Shite and Sunnah Islam. The Qaramita, a group that literally destroyed the holiest sites of Islam and desecrated Mecca, were fought by the Muslims and equilibrium was restored.

After the 9/11 attacks a council of Islamic scholars, just six of the thousands who condemned the attacks, called the attacks Hiraba, or war on society, the Islamic version of a crime against humanity.

Scholar Bernard P. Lewis, in remarking on the 1997 declaration of war by OBL, noted:

To most Americans the declaration is a travesty, a gross distortion of the nature and purpose of the American presence in Arabia. They should also know that for many—perhaps most—Muslims, the declaration is an equally grotesque travesty of the nature of Islam and even its doctrine of Jihad.[35]

Sheikh Mohammed Sayyid al-Tantawi, the imam of the al-Azhar Mosque in Cairo, called it more plainly:

Attacking innocent people is not courageous, it is stupid and will be punished on the day of judgment . . . It is not courageous to attack innocent children, women and civilians. It is courageous to protect freedom, it is courageous to defend oneself and not to attack.[36]

Worse than Hypocrites: Al-Qaeda Is a Cult

AL-QAEDA IS A cult of the highest magnitude. AQ is a militant heretical organization, with bin Laden more akin to other cultists such as the leader Jim Jones, who manipulated more than one thousand people to commit mass suicide, than to past leaders of resistance/insurgent groups. Although bin Laden has transitioned from using terrorism to fighting "resistance" operations in open combat against the Western armies in Iraq and Afghanistan, he remains illegitimate.

Al-Qaeda is no different from those who have used religion before to sanctify death, to extol themselves and glorify causes that have no ground in this life or the next.

Why is AQ a cult and not just misguided sons of a religious body? Because like all mass murder, AQ's acts of cruelty have no religious force or support. They are human cruelty wrapped in the thin guise of representing and speaking for God.

Bin Laden has companions, not those Companions of the Prophet but David Koresh, the American charlatan who claimed he was the reincarnation of Jesus Christ. Koresh also exhibited a variant of al-Wala' Wa al-Bara' when he forced his followers to swear loyalty to him and their love for God and hatred of all those outside of his cult compound. They stored an arsenal of hundreds of automatic weapons with tens of thousands of rounds of ammunition. When the police forces came to disarm them, they killed four and wounded eighteen agents. After a month-long siege, they set themselves aflame and conducted mass murder/suicide.

Another companion of bin Laden is the cult leader of the Buddhist cult Aum Shinrikyo, Matsumoto Chuizo, better known as Soko Asahara. Aum Shinrikyo, which stood for "Aum Supreme Truth," arguably was a terrorist organization with a global reach capability on parity with the al-Qaeda organization. Like OBL, Asahara created an international organization with tens of thousands of followers from Asia, Russia, and Europe. Based in Japan, he called for the destruction of Japanese society and the creation of a new world government and social order with him as its leader. His ideology of mass murder was also in line with OBL when Asahara preached a philosophy that killing people who had committed "sins" was an act done for their own "salvation." He came to apply this to all people living in the modern world and extolled mass murder as a cleansing of souls.

Collecting tens of millions of dollars from donations, Aum created a secret compound outside of Tokyo filled with scientific laboratories. Aahara attempted to cultivate weapons of mass destruction in order to kill the entire population of Japan. Under his orders his supporters, many of them the brightest scientific minds in Japan, developed sarin nerve gas, mustard gas, and phosgene and experimented with harvesting biological diseases including anthrax, Q fever, and botullism. Aum sent medical teams to Africa during an Ebola virus outbreak with the intent to harvest the disease and weaponize it for release into the air. Aum purchased helicopters and radio-controlled unmanned drone aircraft to spray nerve agents over cities, manufactured vehicles with large blowers, and successfully poisoned the air with the improvised poison-blowing trucks. That incident in June 1994 was when he managed to release quantities of sarin gas at night, killing 7 and sickening 253 in Matsumoto, Japan. Somehow Japanese authorities did not attribute this to terrorism. No one considered religious groups capable of producing chemical weapons. All came to light after Aum members attacked the Tokyo subway with sarin nerve gas, killing 12 people and injuring 5,510.

One of the world's foremost experts in terror psychology is Jerrold Post, professor of political psychology. When given an al-Qaeda manual to interpret he noted:

> . . . above all, the manual is a good example how a cult mentality can hijack and manipulate legitimate religious beliefs and turn them into fanatical tenets. The text reveals an organization that follows a very peculiar and extreme kind of Islam and that does not hesitate one bit to depart from Islamic teachings to pursue its own interests.[37]

FOR ALL OF the complaints by OBL about the embargo and its effects on the Iraqi and Palestinian children, it is by his encouragement that these very acts occur in Pakistan and Afghanistan, just as they did when he was advising the Taliban in the 1990s. By his own voice he denied women the right to education and medications.

In Afghanistan the stories are legion. Children, particularly girls, are pulled out of schools. Education and medicine have little part in their world. Always ready to spread a conspiracy theory, in March 2009 in the Swat Valley AQ pushed the Tarik-e-Taliban to stop the vaccinating of over three hundred thousand children by the World Health Organization. OBL spoke of his personal hatred for the United Nations as betraying Palestine and ordered that they never be trusted:

> Aren't our tragedies actually a result of the United Nations' actions? Who issued the decision to partition Palestine in 1947 and gave Islamic lands to the Jews? It was the United Nations. Those who maintain that they are the leaders of the Arabs and are still part of the United Nations are contravening what was revealed to Mohammed. Those who refer to international legitimacy have contravened the legitimacy of the Quran and the teachings of the Prophet. For it is at the hands of this same United Nations that we have suffered so much. No Muslim nor anyone in his right mind should appeal to it under any circumstances. It is merely an agent of this crime by which we are massacred daily, and which it does nothing to stop.[38]

With that the militants have blocked almost all non-governmental organization operations in their areas, with the exception of Islamic charities that have been groomed by them and that support their terrorist operations. When queried about the WHO ban on vaccinations, Muslim Khan, the spokesman for the Tehrik-e-Taliban Pakistan (TTP), said, "The TTP is against polio vaccination because it causes infertility." When pressed, he argued that it is also against Islam. "It's a U.S. tool to cut the population of the Muslims. It is against Islam that you take a medicine before the disease,"[39] he said. In a final justification he argued that his own health situation was a model for the others: "I'm forty-five and have never had one drop of the vaccine and I am still alive."[40]

Al-Qaeda has a religious and political ideology that has been discredited by the Muslim world. Since its inception, this organization has killed or caused the deaths of more Muslims than the United States has in the entire Global War on Terrorism. In fact, until September 11, al-Qaeda had targeted almost exclusively Muslims within the Middle East for suicide bombing, mutilation, and execution, a staggering thought that is rarely pondered in the Arab media.

The number of people killed and directly caused to be killed by al-Qaeda's actions around the world over the last twenty years is well over one hundred thousand. Thousands were children. One sheikh put it this way:

> This is more like the actions of the Qarāmiṭah (a severely violent, misguided sect). They are more like the Qarāmiṭah because the actions of

the Qarāmiṭah are secret, based on secrecy and underhandedness, and what these people today do is also based on secrecy. The former Khawārij—their actions were not kept hidden and secret; they would make themselves and their objectives known, publicly announcing them. So, these people are even worse than Khawārij.[41]

Islam Is Not Terrorism

THE OVERWHELMING MAJORITY of Muslims are culturally pious. However, even though they lead simple lives, they are less insular regarding the activities of nations in foreign policy than their American counterparts. They are aware of the militias in Afghanistan, the pirates off Somalia, and what the imam in India said about the attackers in Mumbai. They read and absorb the day-to-day punishments the Israelis inflict on the Palestinians. They have a deep knowledge of the injustices suffered since the British Empire first discussed its plans for Palestine. They know more about the Middle East movements of our secretary of state than the majority of educated Americans do. They are in tune with their regional politics on the international stage. Most have cogent, fact-based views about what affects the Muslim community and their lives.

Far too long, and often in the words of Western politicians and pundits, Takfiris have been given the legitimacy of an actual military, political, and social movement that has been equated with the mainstream religious populism of Islam. In fact, not one of those factors equates even the more radically conservative readings of Islam to the apocalyptic mind-set of the Takfiris. The Takfiris are not a military organization, though they have weapons and training. They are terrorists and have no religious authority or standing.

The Takfiris do not represent Islam. I will say it again, the terrorists do not represent Islam and Islam is *not* terrorism. The neo-Salafist Takfiris' numbers are minuscule. Their foot soldiers are a fraction of a fraction of a percent of even the extreme wing of the Saudi Salafist movement. If we allow that forty thousand militants graduated from all of the terrorist and militant training camps over the last twenty years, these militants still number less than one three-thousandth of a percent of all Muslims.

The Takfiris occupy the furthest right wing of the fringe hoping that Western missteps and rhetoric catapult them into the position of being the only alternative for mainstream Islam. In this way they will choose and use terrorism as their principal way to voice dissent and insinuate themselves into the mainstream. Once a fixture in the mainstream debate, no matter how illegitimate their philosophy, they will move to change Islam as they see fit.

Since 9/11 and the rise of AQ in particular, there still stands an enormous ideological rift between the peaceful 1.5 billion Muslims and the few thousand AQ terrorists, Taliban gunmen, and other religious militants. Until Western society comes to understand that this is not Islam the terrorists will continue to capitalize on this error.

Al-Qaeda, the irreconcilable Taliban, and all of their followers worldwide are not what they appear to be despite what they say. They are not Salafists, followers of a traditionally pure and ultraconservative philosophy. Neither are they truly Wahabis, followers of another ultra orthodox interpretation of Islamic practices as described by the eighteenth-century Islamic scholar Mohammed ibn 'Abd al-Wahab. Although al-Qaeda followers love the ultra-orthodox and rigid sacrifice 'Abd al-Wahab calls for in his teachings, they readily reject the core tenets of Islam: peace, love, and adherence to the words of God as written by the Prophet Mohammed in the Qur'an. Most of all they reject the fourteen hundred years of traditional Islamic jurisprudence and interpretations.

Al-Qaeda's cultlike movement has so far been a relatively minor threat to Middle Eastern democracies. Even unstable democracies such as Algeria, which underwent a ten-year civil war with the AQ-inspired Groupe Islamique Armé (GIA) extremists, managed to hold on and defeat the terrorists because the GIA quickly lost support among the population. Many could support the ideology of an Islamist government, but the massacre of almost one hundred thousand by cutting their throats was too much for any population.

Happily the cult-based philosophy has yet to spread significantly. But its message is viral. It works slowly, insidiously, and corrupts from within at the weakest elements, often among the disadvantaged and the politically dissident but educated. So long as the West ignores its chance to stop this virus in its tracks, al-Qaeda will continue capitalizing on their core strength—inspiration by mass murder. No matter that this action involves massacring Muslims by the thousands, al-Qaeda's using the cover of Islam to justify their deeds could be their greatest weakness if the right anti-radicalization strategy was mobilized.

Islam Is About Incrementalism, Moderation, and Tolerance

ISLAM, FOR ALL of the white noise in the Western media, is in fact a religion that constantly preaches tolerance. The Qur'an, for all of its fiery speech and messages of war and mobilization for the Prophet Mohammed to reclaim Mecca and Medina and fight the first fights against dissenting tribes, invariably follows such speech with words of caution and respect.

In the Qur'an God says of good Muslims: "They reconcile between people, because this is one of the greatest means of doing good and it is the pinnacle of that which is good and proper, and because reconciling between people foils the plots of the Shaytan and his aim to spread enmity and hatred among the Muslims."

Clearly the Qur'an spells out that those who fight this reconciliation are acting in the hands of Satan. These admonitions lent caution to very few of their most militant ideologues, including Abdullah Azzam. He must have had, on occasion, to recognize that God's word, as seen here in Surah At-Taubah, verse 36, must reflect the accurate intentions of the Prophet: "And fight the pagans all together as they fight you all together *but know that Allah is with those who restrain themselves.*"[42]

Islam is not represented by Takfir or al-Wala' Wa al-Bara'. Most Muslims would reject those out of hand and stress the principle of *irja*, which means tolerance or, more specifically, the suspension of judgment. Under this concept, the issue of who is and who is not a Muslim is left to Allah. More generally, many Muslims would oppose Takfir on the basis of *taqarub* or *tasamuh* (rapprochement or toleration).

Even at the height of animosity between the Prophet and those pagans, Jews, and Christians who fought against him, he gave explicit instructions that those who are even the most strict Islamic constructionists cannot avoid:

> But when the forbidden months are passed then fight and slay the pagans wherever you find them and seize them, beleaguer them and lie in wait in every stratagem (in war) but if they repent, establish regular prayers and pay Zakat (alms to the poor) then open the way for them, for Allah is oft-forgiving, most merciful.[43]

In bin Ladenism, the restraint cautioned in that statement, as in many others is routinely removed.

The only people to ignore that Islam constantly presses for restraint, tolerance, and respect are the Takfiri terrorists and those who seek to place the false label of a religion based on "Conversion by the Sword" on Islam for their own limited personal or religious purposes. That is not at issue here. For Jews and Christians who bear enmity toward Muslims the day has come to set aside the hatred and prejudice. Islam is in need of allies, and this day is the day to lend them our camaraderie.

Modernization does not hinder Islam. Even the militant theorist Sayyid Qutb admired the technological advancements of the West and encouraged Muslims to use them. Western values or technologies aren't forced on peoples that do not want them. Indonesia is the most populous Muslim country in the world and shows the balance of an advanced society where Islam is not compromised for advancement.

Not all ideologies in the modern world were opened by democracy. Our largest trading partner, China, remains a communist nation by strength of arms, but from the inside out the natural desires of all men and women come to the surface. There was no need to invade with weapons and bring democracy by force. China's modernization and changes to communism came about due to the need for them to join the rest of the modern world. Islam is no different. There is no prohibition for Islam to avoid modern society and embrace technology.

Will the Islamic world change? It already has, incrementally in some ways and dramatically in others. Never before has there been such interest in the religion. The fastest route for a man or woman to learn about Islam is to type the word into Google or Yahoo! What comes out is a discussion of Islam. History has shown that near absolutism on personal behavior, economics, theology, and personal liberty has gradually lost its foundations. Islam is compatible with a twenty-first-century world and ideas, but Islam itself must be respected from within and without. Above all, Islam must be purified of the lethal virus that is bin Laden's terror.

The Qur'an supports this thesis:

O' you who believe! Eat not up your property among yourselves in vanities; but let there be amongst you traffic and trade by mutual good will. Nor kill [or destroy] yourselves, for verily Allah has been to you All-Merciful. If any do that in rancor and injustice, soon shall We cast him into the Fire, and easy is it for Allah.[44]

Confronting the Takfir Ideology

THE DEFENSE OF Islam, which is centered around the ideological battle to maintain the purity of traditional thought and the physical battle to protect the Kingdom of the Two Holy Shrines, cannot be effected with just guns. The single best way for us to ensure bin Ladenism and AQ die on the vine is to make certain that their operational philosophy be clearly shown as so repugnant that it offends the listener. It must be challenged so readily and with authoritative and credible resources. AQ must be forced to expose themselves to a public image debate. Drowning out the words and images of AQ is of equal strategic importance to stopping their terrorist attacks. Damaging their ideology requires that we attempt to remove ourselves past the illogical Bush administration policies (or, as one observer put it, "words from the devil himself") and offer a new image of America ready to help empower the 99 percent of the Muslim world to speak for themselves about defending their faith and future from militant extremists.

Senator John Kerry, speaking out about Saudi Arabia's stand against AQ, praised the Saudi capability:

> So the question is, how did they do it? The answer: they were smart. They thought outside the box and, with their backs against the wall, the Saudis transitioned from a narrow approach—focused primarily on using force—to a broader campaign to win the people away from extremism. Saudi security thinkers understood that for every terrorist killed, ten more were created. They realized they were fighting an ideological battle—a war of ideas—a war that could not be won with guns and bombs alone.[45]

What is needed is to move the errors of OBL front and center to a debate within Islam. Over 84 percent of Muslims reject the methods OBL uses. Explain the details of his strategy to effect an NIC by toppling the fourteen centuries of Islamic traditions and converting Islam into the Dar al-Harb, where all Muslims must take his test of loyalty to his version of what he believes is God's wishes, there would be a wellspring of rejection.

The Muslim world must stand in defense of Islam by shaming anyone who believes the false perception that AQ members and their families will be honored in heaven for their deeds on earth: murdering women and children, beheading Muslims, mutilating the bodies of the dead, playing games with human corpses, hanging children, sentencing mothers to death for no reason, banning music and songs but playing music and songs in videos of their men beheading people of the book, and claiming to speak for God in the way of the Prophet is too much. In Islam, only God can make the final judgment of what happens to OBL and his followers spiritually. Yet their acts are so repugnant and a direct assault on the foundations of Islam that the only way to defend the faith is to expose the true objectives behind their ideology to the rest of the Muslim world and call al-Qaeda what they are—a cult. We must work together to eliminate them and squash all their attempts to justify their fighting as being for the people and done in a way that pleases God.

Fundamentally, destroying AQ is about defeating the linkages between Islam, al-Qaeda, and the fraction of active supporters within the Muslim world. This must be done from within the Ummah and with the world's full support.

If al-Qaeda were to be universally seen as they truly are—apostate, heretical, and mass murderers of Muslims (as opposed to the frame they have made for themselves as heroes and knights fighting for Islam)—they would be forced to terminate their operations almost overnight in fear of being publicly reviled. The nature of the organization is that they will resort to even more violence and murder to instill fear among the Ummah . . . that is reason enough to end this outrage.

Perhaps it was in a minute of guilt, Osama himself gave the clearest explanation of what he has done to the Muslim world and how in the name of God he himself veered away from Islam. In an interview with Al Jazeera he said, "Praise be to God. We beseech Him for help and forgiveness. We seek refuge for God from the evil of our souls and our bad deeds. He whom God guides will not go astray, and he whom he leads astray can have no guide."[46] Clearly, Osama bin Laden has no guide.

8.
Reframing America, Reframing al-Qaeda

THE FAMILIES OF the bride and the groom were riding in a convoy with two hundred guests. The men, women, and children rode in the busses and vans to celebrate a wedding feast. As they rode, some sent rifle shots from their Kalashnikov rifles into the air. The shots flashed in the dark for a brief second and faded. From a distance the revelers could barely be seen in the dark. Celebratory rifle fire is an Asian and Middle Eastern tradition over four hundred years old, and the night in the Deh Bala district of Nangarhar Province was one for celebration.

The American AC-130 gunship hovered over the mountains at ten thousand feet watching the spectacle. Onboard infrared sensors detected the movement of the convoy. Zooming in with the high-powered cameras, the sensor operators detected the sparks of gunfire emanating from the convoy. Assuming they were firing at the hum of the AC-130, which would have been nearly inaudible from the ground on a moving vehicle, the crew of the "Spooky" decided that the target was viable and requested permission to decimate the convoy of what they assumed were al-Qaeda or Taliban operatives. When the crew received permission, the sensor operator designated the trucks and the four weapons system operators locked the massive armament of twelve 20mm cannon barrels, a 40mm anti-aircraft cannon, and a computer-driven 105mm artillery piece onto the vehicles and opened fire.

The hundreds of 20mm depleted uranium bullets from the two six-barreled M61 Vulcan Gatling guns and the artillery rounds of the cannons tore through the bodies and skulls of the wedding party and guests. Thousands of rounds of ammunition were fired. When the sensor operators detected only dead and wounded they broke off the attack and chalked up another mission success against what they assumed were the perpetrators of the 9/11 attacks.

In fact, the 47 dead and 117 wounded were nothing of the sort. They were the very people the U.S.-led NATO coalition forces were sent to safeguard and peel away from supporting the Taliban in that province. Of the dead, 39 were said to be women and children. It would take months for the coalition forces to acknowledge that there may have been an error. The mistaken massacre of civilians in Deh Bala was the sixth of seven large-scale combat actions against Afghan and Iraqi wedding parties over six years. In that time U.S. forces erroneously killed more than 247 civilians who made the choice to attend a celebration in a time of war.

The corpses of the villagers burned brightly before disintegrating from the blasts of the aerial artillery shells. Skulls were opened and brains scooped out by the 20mm projectiles that split heads in half, despite the fact that everyone assumed that firing a rifle into the dark sky at night was harmless and a ritual of every wedding party. What they could not know was that to the coalition air forces any gunfire detected from air was assumed as hostile. Traditional celebratory rifle fire has been seen thousands of times by coalition forces for more than eight years and noted in intelligence briefs, pre-flight briefings, and turn-over manuals from the first days of the war, but many assume it is always hostile and always aimed at them, no matter how stealthy or out of reach their aerial platforms. On this day it was another gift to Osama bin Laden. The seeming American indifference to Afghani and Arab lives would be broadcast in horrific, shocking detail, one child's burned body after another.

Crusader War: Right Now
bin Laden Defines America

INFORMATION WARFARE IS the art of using truth, intelligence, propaganda, psychological warfare, and media in a unified effort to control the way an enemy's own ideology or policies are perceived by the global public. It reached near perfection in World War II. Considering the trillions spent since 9/11 on warfare with al-Qaeda, one would think this was an arena where America's technological dominance would be yielding dramatic results and badly damaging a crude enemy. Nothing could be further from the truth. Arguably, the greatest failure of the Bush years, in an administration beset with failures, has been assisting al-Qaeda's success in defining for the Muslim world what America stands for. This is called framing.

Framing is the act of characterizing a subject, through words or visual media, in a such a way that may or may not be true but appears or feels to the target audience to be emotively true. Simply put, it is what comic Stephen Colbert calls truthiness. It is a feeling and perception of how a subject wants to be seen or made to be seen. In the political sphere it either positively or negatively defines a subject or event. It could bolster, diminish, or deflect a person's or incident's strengths or weaknesses by fostering a perception or point of view that becomes the dominant narrative for the discussion.

For almost two decades AQ has encouraged and mastered the distribution of unconventional media to spread their hatred of America. Their information war has been as asymmetric as their terrorism. In the 1980s and 1990s, with global media dominated by television, they distributed their ideology by audiotape and local radio broadcasts. It was a logical choice, as the FM radio/cassette player was the most common medium in South Asia and the emerging world. Audio lectures could be listened to over and over and shared with others for debate. By 1996, with satellite television widely available, AQ chose to go viral again—they chose the Internet. They were early masters of the digital video downloaded onto a compact disk that was sold for pennies or distributed for free from Morocco to Manila. They were adopting a minimalist credo. Al-Qaeda's media machine, As-Sahaab, transformed the organization from a terrorist public affairs office into a consultant's template for radicalizing supporters of the extremist jihad. Almost all is now done on the Internet. Al-Qaeda-supporting media have been online for well over ten years. Where mainstream media would not allow them access they created their own distribution system.

AQ's strategic message is always simple, "truthy," and easily supported by half-truths, conspiracy theory, and lies. The message is: "We are martyrs dedicated to giving up our lives for you. We avenge America's attacks on Islam and those who corrupted our religion and values." It is an effective deception. When framed in the simplistic, religious-based way it is reasonable and almost justifiable for the man on the Muslim street. It is an almost unstoppable message.

A measurement of the effectiveness of their campaign is that there are dozens of pro-jihadist Web sites and thousands of videos popping up and down virally on the Internet. AQ no longer controls the spread of it. It is their active supporters on the Web who allow them to communicate, motivate, and explain to the world why they fight. They prove their word by dramatic combat footage of themselves in action. Again, the Web messages are simple, clear, and easily consumed. The videos they produce are designed to inspire and thrill an audience from semi-literate peasants to university-educated people. Al-Qaeda supporters blanket their acts with quotes from the Qur'an and manage to synchronize the images of violence with the seemingly appropriate authority from God.

Dr. Khaled Abou El Fadl, speaking on the public TV show *Frontline*, shows he understands how this occurs but notes that despite the commonalities between AQ's positions and the opinion of the Muslim world, AQ does not speak for Islam, nor does this mean that the Muslim world embraces extremism:

> . . . That doesn't mean that the majority of Muslims are extremists. It doesn't even mean that a sizeable minority are extremist. However, what it does mean is that certain of the attitudes of the school of thought have had a considerable amount of influence, particularly the attitudes that don't celebrate moral thinking, don't celebrate humanism, consider history to be unnecessary, an aberration, something that you don't really study or analyze . . . What it has done is that it created fertile grounds for the immersions of the type of extremism that bin Laden represents.[1]

The constituency of AQ's messaging system is brought into an understanding with the terrorists that God is the goal and they could also join the terrorists through "good deeds" and an obligation to defend God's faith. At the street level, the religious justification for their acts is extremely effective, even if the tactics are abhorrent. The fatalistic attitude of many in the Muslim world allows that if these acts are permitted, it must be God's will. This passive buy-in means that few actually will publicly reject al-Qaeda as anything but slightly misguided Muslims who are frustrated and took action when action needed to be taken. Many Muslims also respect the terrorists for being exceptionally pious and supremely motivated. This link of support to the terrorists is the center of gravity for all of their global terrorist operations. Break it and the organization crumbles quickly.

The Avenging Knights:
How We Enabled al-Qaeda's Frame

AQ'S ENTIRE TERROR existence is founded on the old anarchist dictum of Propaganda by Deed. In bin Laden's world, actions are proof. To AQ's target audience it is no matter that bin Laden speaks in truths, half-truths, and deliberate misinterpretations. He shows himself as a man who can back up his rhetoric with action, deeds, and sacrifice. This is something to which his target audience can relate. We call it terror and suicide bombings . . . but he calls it Justice and Vengeance. OBL just tells his story to the audience of more than 1 billion Muslims much better than we can tell ours to the global audience of 6 billion. OBL openly states what he intends to do and challenges the listener to watch the actions not only of his men but also of his enemy. He dares the observer to see which party sticks to their true selves and which acts hypocritically.

OBL did not do all of this on his own. He had help from his enemy in the form of the Bush administration. On the surface it may not be apparent, but American actions since bin Laden escaped from Tora Bora have driven the AQ narrative so exceptionally well it was almost impossible for America to keep up. When bin Laden wishes to make a point he just waits for America to perform as he had just predicted—never mind the subtleties of foreign policy, OBL speaks to his potential and continuing supporters, not to the United Nations or statesmen. When it came to the actions versus rhetoric of George W. Bush's administration OBL was rarely disappointed. With Bush OBL managed to make simple American statecraft look devious. When it was devious, in instances such as the invasion of Iraq, torture at Abu Ghraieb, the negative symbology of Guantánamo Bay, and the numerous false terror alerts during the 2004 election cycle, Osama's word gained strength in the Muslim world. OBL's skill at verbal judo made him appear to be a truth teller and Bush the hypocritical liar.

The reason we failed to keep up was that the administration's arrogance and surety enabled their very enemy with credibility. They ignored what AQ said, what AQ did, what AQ was going to do, and what they would push us to do to hurt our image abroad. The arrogance of the Bush administration was revealed through George Bush's absolute unwavering certainty that he could do whatever he wanted and only his actions mattered. AQ was dismissed as a player in Bush's world. This fundamental lack of understanding that one's terrorist nemesis has a say in what occurs gave AQ a winning formula in the global perception battle that they never should have had. The American "Say-Do" gap was wide enough that you could drive a nation the size of Iraq through it. American strategic messaging is so ineffective that the American government remains befuddled at why they even have to try to defend against any frame AQ puts into the media. The reason al-Qaeda has had such an easy ride has been because the image of them as bloodthirsty terrorists has been replaced by the world's perception of an American "Global War on Terrorism" gone amok. The travesty is that the nation with the greatest communications architecture in the world, which practically invented mass-media advertising, appears inept at communicating honestly. Yes, sadly, America's message was so hypocritical and so inept that it was lost to that of a mass murderer living in a cave.

Whether their religious-based story is true or not, AQ plays well in the media and tells it in such a way that many reasonable people would agree with them, even if they reject al-Qaeda's methods. For example, when President Bush made a statement early on in the war he referred to it as a "Crusade." AQ was quick to pounce. OBL, speaking to his core constituency and potential recruits and the Muslim world in general, "explained" what Bush meant:

> Bush left no room for the doubts or media opinion. He stated clearly that this war is a Crusader war. He said this in front of the whole world so as to emphasize this fact. Those who maintain that this war is against terrorism, what is this terrorism that they talk about at a time when people of the ummah have been slaughtered for decades, in response to which we do not hear a single voice or action of resistance?[2]

In AQ's framing, America and its allies are like characters in children's fairy tales: the better-armed and wealthy (Christian) Kings, who use their black knights (the military), to oppress the people (Muslims) and attempt to dishonor (invade) a beloved maiden (Iraq). To defeat this the AQ militants are the white knights who sacrifice their lives for the good of their religion. The story inspires a deep awe of the heroes and hatred of the villains. It worked for William Shakespeare, the Brothers Grimm, Scheherazade, and Walt Disney—it works for OBL, too.

The AQ viral media campaign was made dramatically effective not only by videos of suicide bombings but by America's own strategic political errors. The photos and testimony of the abuse at Iraq's Abu Ghraieb prison, the hypocrisy of the judicial black hole called Guantánamo Bay, and the public defense and use of torture made bin Laden's 1988 frame of a cruel America that needed to be punished a reality for many Muslims.

According to the World Opinion Poll of 2009 an overwhelming majority, more than six out of ten Muslims, believes the United States tries to promote international laws on other countries but is hypocritical because it often does not follow the rules itself.[3] OBL was again quick to point this out.

You have claimed to be the vanguards of Human Rights, and your Ministry of Foreign Affairs issues annual reports containing statistics of those countries that violate any Human Rights. However, all these values vanished when the mujahidin hit you [on 9/11], and you then implemented the methods of the same documented governments that you used to curse. In America, you arrested thousands of Muslims and Arabs, took them into custody with no reason, court trial, nor did you disclose their names. You issued newer, harsher laws.[4]

Faulty News Media Narratives

ANOTHER FAILURE WAS that the administration convinced the American media that there were always two sides to every story. In the Bush years the media emphasized that "balance" was crucial to understanding any political action.

In the global media, if everything about Bush's intentions was debatable, then often bin Laden's intent was debatable. AQ saw this argument as another critical opening. Although OBL is a heartless mass murderer, the media balance inadvertently gave him a foggy lens through which he could be supported as something other than the obvious. Like the American-initiated debate about what is or is not torture, whether Iraq was invaded for oil or weapons of mass destruction, or if American-killed civilians were dead or just collateral damage, AQ could now rely on a fog shadowing the meaning of "terrorist" and "terrorism." Maybe he was a terrorist, maybe a freedom fighter. It was all considered debatable. For OBL, this American media method of framing everything as "debatable" was a communications narrative he could live with.

The information war against bin Laden has been essentially one of luck. The moment to create a damaging frame in the Muslim world necessary to destroy al-Qaeda came and went within the first 180 days after the attack on the Twin Towers. In fact, any negative perceptions the world has about AQ came from their own murderous excess, not by any integrated effort to frame them as the cult of mass murderers they truly are. This is where we are missing the chance to break them.

The narrative of an honest and justified war against a small band of determined but cruel religious cultists rapidly gave way to the American neoconservative brand of stunning arrogance. America didn't seek help; it was demanding it. America didn't want war against al-Qaeda; it wanted a global campaign against anyone who could even think of choosing the tactic of terrorism. Al-Qaeda wasn't the main target—Iran, North Korea, Iraq, Somalia, Lebanon, Palestine, and Syria were all going to be recalibrated into democracies, so they were all targeted. While the world reeled from the shock of such talk, the administration's media machine was turned into a domestic propaganda operation aimed at winning support for unrelated legislation and political longevity. What this "narrative" did not do was hurt al-Qaeda. They were having tea in a safe sanctuary, plotting to overthrow Islamic governments and gain nuclear weapons.

Challenging Conspiracy Theory

AQ AND THEIR allies have not only mastered the simple storytelling narrative for their target audience. AQ's street-level information campaign also capitalizes on what would best be called global conspiracy theories, like the anti-Semitic "Protocols of the Learned Elders of Zion," the unlimited ideas of the powerful Red Mercury, and the insane 9/11 truth movement. Do not dismiss the fact that conspiracies such as these have a ready ear in the emerging world. They are widespread and widely believed.

OBL himself ties the clash of civilization conspiracy to his success on 9/11. Additionally, he spent a few minutes rubbing America's face in the First Amendment:

> But I mention that there are also other events that took place, bigger, greater, and more dangerous than the collapse of the towers. It is that this western civilization, which is backed by America, has lost its values and appeal. The immense materialistic towers, which preach freedom, human rights, and equality, were destroyed. These values were revealed as a total mockery, as was made clear when the U.S. government interfered and banned the media outlets from airing our words (which don't exceed a few minutes, because they felt that the truth started to appear to the American people, and that we aren't really terrorists in the way they want to define the term . . .[5]

In 2003 the Anti-Defamation League, an American organization that fights anti-Semitism, issued a report on the large volume of anti-Semitic conspiracy theories about the 9/11 attacks promulgated on the Internet and in books and media. These conspiracies often originated in the United States itself, within the heart of the anti-government racist groups such as the American Neo-Nazis and white supremacists pumping out anti-Jewish statements on the Internet within hours of the attacks. These concoctions and a broad range of other "America did it" theories were broadly believed in the Middle East.

In the Middle East even highly educated people, from academics to high-ranking military officers, are susceptible to conspiracy theory. Another challenge to American strategic communications is to make a massive effort to publicly overcome those misguided perceptions about what happened.

Conspiracy theory has legs in the militant world and among their supporters. Inferences from militants like bin Laden are that America itself or, more bizarrely, Israel perpetrated the attacks that morning in order to complete a conquest of the Islamic world. For many in the Muslim world these street-level conspiracies fulfill an informational niche to explain what they will not believe or cannot believe themselves. In one instance I sat with a high-ranking Gulf states diplomat to a large NATO country. He was completely doubtful of the veracity of the 9/11 attacks, though he was educated in Europe and saw the events play out on television. I told him I was a witness and rescuer at the attack on the Pentagon. It took ten minutes to convince him that I saw the Pentagon attack with my own eyes and that it was indeed an airplane. Once I told him the story of the heroism, pain, and suffering of the attack he was apologetic and near tears. Yet until he was given a concrete example, a personal witness, he was convinced it was an American-delivered bomb, as written by a French journalist.

Al-Qaeda Frames of a Weak and Divided Islam

AS I NOTED in earlier chapters, the AQ senior leadership are extremely in tune with the Muslim street. OBL can reliably capitalize on public disgruntlement and popular opinion polls in the Muslim world whereby he can craft an appropriate response that brings sympathy and acceptance of AQ's fantastical desires. AQ manages to work its strategic communications system to attain regional goals when opportunities arise. In July 2007 when Pakistan's President, Pervez Musharraf, was confronted by Taliban militants who seized the Lal Masjid in Islamabad, he acted with typical dictatorial brutality and wiped out the armed terrorists. He also did not spare women and children brought in to shield them. That this was a trap designed to elicit such a response did not appear to occur to Musharraf. No sooner was it complete than AQ called for revolution in Pakistan and overthrowing the government so Pakistan could become an Islamic state. AQ's second in command, Dr. al-Zawahiri, spoke via audiotape to Al Jazeera and Pakistani television for the entire militant movement:

> Pakistan, your salvation is only through jihad . . . This crime can only be washed away by repentance or blood . . . If you do not revolt, Musharraf will annihilate you. Musharraf will not stop until he uproots Islam from Pakistan.[6]

The message was powerful, clear, and virtually unanswerable, as Musharraf had just killed eighty-three people, including women and children. This was a clear victory for the Takfiris' efforts within Pakistan. The loss of lives did not matter—it was crucial to the plan.

By 2008 the BBC and Pew opinion polls noted that overwhelming majorities believe the United States wants to weaken and divide Islam. The 2009 World Opinion Poll respondents claimed almost eight out of ten Muslims believe that this is the military objective of the U.S. government in the Middle East. This was followed by the same percentage saying that the United States wants to spread Christianity and gain control of Middle Eastern oil. AQ often claims these very opinions as their own and, despite the radical nature of their military activities, are well in line with the mainstream opinion. OBL even manages to link the various Christian denominations together into one wide-ranging conspiracy to cause mass genocide. He connects the Crusades, English anti-Muslim imperialism, American energy policy, and the two centuries of Russian warfare in Chechnya as another component of the Christian war to eliminate Islam. Bin Laden says:

> Then look at recent events, for example in Chechnya. This Muslim nation has been attacked by the Russian Predator, which believes in the Orthodox Christian creed. The Russians have exterminated an entire people and forced them into the mountains, where they have been devoured by disease and freezing winter, and yet no one has done anything about it.[7]

AQ is always quick on the mark to meet the negative public expectations in the Muslim world. When they responded to the Middle East peace conference held in Annapolis in 2007 they claimed that this was like the post–World War I and World War II plans to carve up the world and divide Palestine.

Speaking for bin Laden, Dr. Ayman al-Zawahiri claimed, "The Arab states and governments were present as false witnesses to the latest of the treacherous deals to sell Palestine."[8]

Polls reveal that Muslims believe American activities are designed to expand Israel's borders. Again, the perception of this is strong in the Muslim world and AQ just enunciates it. The polls support them: "Egypt 86%, Indonesia 47%, Pakistan 52%, Morocco 64%, Palestine 90%, Jordan 84%, Turkey 78%."[9] When presented with questions about military activity to prevent rule by extremist groups, only one in three respondents said that was the real U.S. mission.[10] Worse than this, the polls show there is virtually no confidence that the United States seeks to create a Palestinian state.

AQ's propaganda strength is that they make continuous half-true assertions to an audience that hears their own opinions played back to them. They watch what America does and conclude that America cannot be trusted, wants the Middle East's natural resources, and attributes no value to the lives of Arab people. The invasion of Iraq and the grievous casualties inflicted by the response to Iraq's insurgency validated fifteen years of speeches OBL made calling America an aggressor seeking Arab oil riches.

Bin Laden's greatest goal was to fight a jihad similar to the one he fought against the Russians. OBL knew America would go to Afghanistan but was shocked and delighted America also invaded Iraq. The proximity of Iraq to the heart of the Muslim world meant volunteers from all over the Middle East and Europe could travel relatively short distances to join the Iraqi Sunnah resistance. Thus was born al-Qaeda in Iraq. This jihad deep inside the heart of the historic Muslim world could not have been better planned by AQ themselves.

The invasion of Iraq also jump-started failing terror operations in Yemen, Saudi Arabia, Somalia, Algeria, Morocco, and Europe. The al-Qaeda narrative no longer had to justify the "Holy Tuesday" operation in America. To the Muslim world, the invasion of Iraq explained America more clearly than all other actions. Al-Qaeda just had to shift to offering their lives for defense of brother Arabs by use of suicide bombs in Iraq and Afghanistan.

AQ's pioneering use of viral video on platforms such as YouTube and Facebook and Web forums made these operations attractive to their target audience: young Arab men and women looking for a more pious way to resolve the injustices to the Muslim world. It was made effective not by anything specific al-Qaeda did (apart from the daily suicide bombings) but often by America's own actions and reactions to these incidents.

America Must Set a New Master Frame

FRAMING IS A "schemata of interpretation"[11] that sets or fosters a perception or renders perceived meaning to an event that can become the dominant narrative. Clearly in order to take advantage of the opportunity to defeat AQ in any sphere we must restart any counter-ideological warfare campaign by reframing the true nature of AQ and their leadership to the constituency they seek to impress. Then we must reframe ourselves.

The true image of AQ's revolutionary cultism must be reengineered into a "master frame." This is an all-encompassing frame that brings together all individual frames into a unified perception.

Counter-terrorism ideology experts such as Joas Wagemakers, lecturer in the Department of Arabic and Islam of Radboud University in Nijmegen, Holland, believe that AQ currently operates under a master frame of "defending Islam on a religious and political scale." This frame is centered on the concept of al-Wala' Wa al-Bara' (affiliation and disavowal) and generally limited to the Muslim world.[12] In short, AQ does not care what we think of their acts, only what their target audience perceives.

AQ's vulnerability is that this master frame of Muslim perception is susceptible to being recalibrated into a stronger frame, and should be. The world, with assistance from the West, must reframe al-Qaeda and identify the characteristics that make them not only a military threat to Islam but a spiritual one as well. The master frame we must seek to use as a template is of al-Qaeda as an exceptionally dangerous armed militant cult that seeks to completely transform Islam and create a cultist state from which to control Muslims because of the religious dreams of a single man.

To extend our master frame we must work to achieve what sociologists call Frame Amplification. This is the ability to open up the megaphone in our strategic communications arsenal and reach peoples who have not been hearing our message, stress the relevance of it to their own values, and show AQ as a moral threat to those values.

We also want to broaden our strategic message to reach people who do not agree with us and who may agree with many facets of AQ's ideology. Here we seek as our result Frame Transformation, where the active constituency and passive supporters may transform their beliefs from the ones they hold now (AQ = Some good, some bad) into a position where they may reject the AQ message (AQ = Evil + a threat to spiritual welfare).

Concerning our own projected image in the Muslim world, until the master frame of the "American Cowboys Unleashed" is realigned to "Yes, Westerners, but Well-Meaning Ones Who Want to Help Us," many Muslims will not consider America's problem with AQ as their problem.

Because of this negative perception, America has yet to defeat the al-Qaeda-driven narratives and has repeatedly failed to secure one globally acceptable definition of what AQ is and why they must be utterly defeated.

In the face of a global economic meltdown and the hubris of the Bush administration's wild lashing out using force, the Muslim world has a poor mental image of the United States. Propagating new frames, transforming old ones without suspicion, will be difficult but achievable depending on the commitments to amplifying and concentrating the information in our megaphone. It is even more important who is doing the talking.

Damage Control: The Reset Button

THE OBAMA ADMINISTRATION started off well by tacking in the opposite direction of the Bush administration. Choosing Al Arabiya for the first major media interview and speaking directly to the Muslim world was an excellent start. Some argue that it doesn't matter what we do, as al-Qaeda is more viral and widely disbursed. However, this new opportunity with a new President who shares a Muslim heritage lets American actions speak loudly and with an attentive audience. America must reorient its strategic communications system to capitalize on the good intentions behind future actions and support a truthful, highly credible narrative.

By breaking the mythical narrative al-Qaeda has created and reframing ourselves as finally returning to our historical level of compassion and charity, we find a more ready audience looking for assistance to resolve the corruption of their religion. The Muslim world would generally not have a problem with America lending a hand in striking where bin Laden fears it the most—at the links between his foot soldiers and Muslim society. What the Muslim world fears is that that hand will then turn and strike them.

President Obama took the biggest step in starting the pushback against twenty years of al-Qaeda ideological indoctrination about what is and is not America. In his speech before the Turkish parliament he clarified the position of America in the twenty-first century with regards to Islam:

The United States is not, and will never be, at war with Islam. In fact, our partnership with the Muslim world is critical not just in rolling back the violent ideologies that people of all faiths reject, but also to strengthen opportunity for all its people."[13]

The atmospherics are now right. The narrative can now be reset: Americans are an aggrieved people seeking justice. The murderers of our people are now seeking to topple Islam. Al-Qaeda and their allies are willing to kill as many Muslims as necessary to do so. We must all join together in this fight.

America needs to project a new image to the Muslim world that will reassure them that we will become a fair broker in matters outside of counter-terror war against the Takfiris. America needs the support and understanding of the world Islamic community far more than it needs Predator drones, cruise missiles, and air strikes. The war in which we must engage is 95 percent counter-ideological and 5 percent combat. AQ and its Takfiri allies have morphed from a small radical group of armed militants into an emotionally based cultist lifestyle that will commit genocide if we refuse to challenge the intellectual and religious basis of their core operating philosophy. The murderous values of the Takfiris must be spelled out to the people who will suffer the most should the ideology take root in five to ten years.

Americans must also recognize that we have delivered fear for eight years to the very people whose assistance we most desperately need. In this regard the world watches our errors in horror. If the insurgency in Iraq has taught us anything, it is that though the terrorists led the way in brutality, we often followed with crushing blows that smashed all in their path. The terrorist relies on this and gains a little more sympathy and support from the local populace. Unfortunately, the terrorist enemy has been far more adept at framing our errors for his propaganda network to be consumed by the local population that was just brutalized. BBC journalist John Simpson notes:

> Al-Qaeda speaks to the disaffected, the people who feel that the empty materialism of life has nothing to offer them, who are affronted by what they see as the arrogance of the United States and Britain. And it encourages them to hit back. The ideology is a beguiling one, and it is more likely to attract the educated and semi-educated than the poor and down-trodden.[14]

Despite what many Western pundits and anti-Muslim bigots in the global media say, there is no need for a "reform" within Islam. Like all world religions, it has its own pace and its own extremists. If Reynauld de Châtillon, the murderous French Christian Crusader who pillaged hajj caravans, could be justly dispatched by Salahudin al-Ayyubi without the blink of an eye in Christendom or if Adolf Hitler with the complicity of the Vatican could be stopped by an alliance of Christian nations from committing genocide on 6 million Jews, then perhaps the modern Islamic world can be allowed to defend itself from miscreants like OBL without demands for restructuring. The pot-meet-kettle dilemma the Western world often finds itself in needs to be suspended until the strategic issue of eliminating al-Qaeda is resolved.

To the untrained eye it would appear that there is no end in sight to OBL's "Long War," bin Laden's term for the multidimensional, multicultural challenge that al-Qaeda has established for itself to create the New Islamic Caliphate. Since 9/11 the organization has appeared to project an impressive array of terror firepower, particularly in Iraq. Al-Qaeda has proven that as a covert terrorist force they should be taken seriously. In the fight against al-Qaeda, the indirect enabling of bin Laden by American errors in judgment and policy has allowed the Takfiris to win several decisive ideological engagements. The most significant was the massive flow of fighters to Iraq and Afghanistan after the revelations of the torture and abuse at the Abu Ghraieb prison in Iraq. Their desire to acquire nuclear weapons to meet their goals and the claim that they will use such weapons if they arrive in their hands should make the most jaded observer pause and take note. We are at a historic crossroads.

The world is engaged in a global insurgency that is being performed by a stateless command cell of terrorists and insurgent supporters huddled in the FATA region of Pakistan and sprinkled throughout the Muslim world. They recruit young men from all across Islam to emigrate and join their insurgency or any insurgency nearby. They exhort those who are in remote or isolated regions of the Western world to individually radicalize and do whatever they can to meet their obligation as Muslims and fight in the "jihad" wherever they are and with whatever they have.

That Islam needs to defend itself is wholly rooted in the fundamental definition of jihad in the Qur'an. When the Prophet met with resistance on the Hijaz he had to fight a war of necessity. When forces outside of the first Muslims came to destroy the new religion he organized and bound his followers with their obligation to the community and God. Had the Prophet Mohammed not had a compelling reason for his call to defend the earliest group of Muslims, Islam might not exist today.

Today, like a patient with a malignant cancer, Islam is faced with a lethal internal threat. It is embroiled in an insurgency where Baghy meets Hiraba and where Islam itself is considered illegitimate and, at the same time, its reinterpretation the goal for the neo-Salafist terrorists. In the ideology of AQ the entire world outside of the Afghanistan-Pakistan NIC is now Dar al-Harb . . . the land of war.

It was the Chinese communist leader Mao Tse-tung who wrote in his book *Aspects of China's Anti-Japanese Struggle* that "the people are like water and the [guerilla] army is like fish." Mao's now famous allusion to the guerrilla and terrorist swimming undetected in the lush support of the sea of people meant that a steady network of supporters will sustain the adept guerrillas' travels, feed their operatives, provide intelligence, and lend moral support. That is, if there is a sea to swim in. On the one hand, in any insurgency or guerrilla war goodwill and support of the population are critical. It provides intelligence and cooperation while denying the enemy supplies and information. On the other hand, any area where a population is hostile to the insurgents will become one where they will eventually be forced to remove themselves or overreach and push the populace into a decision about which evil is the lesser one.

Our counter-insurgency effort must remove the strings of commonality that tie Takfiris to the mainstream Muslim community on a strategic scale. A strategic counter-ideological communications narrative must be set to reframe and neutralize AQ's messaging. This structure and the messages it projects must speak to the goatherd in Uzbekistan as clearly as it does to the President of the United States. Any counter-ideological strategic communications operations must be executed flawlessly and in such a way as to be seen and regarded publicly as an honorable, right, and just response to corrupt and brutal criminality.

Why should this effort take front and center from military operations? Because our hard power message since 9/11 has been corrupted by stumbling and incompetence. Any resulting political successes, if it ever comes to that, in Iraq and Afghanistan will be eclipsed and removed from the psyche of the Muslim world because of the way that the wars came about. A post-9/11 Afghanistan invasion was far easier to justify, but after the disaster of invading Iraq all American intentions are seen as suspect. The Muslim world cannot see a benefit of any American presence in fighting AQ because our own missteps have blinded them to seeing any. This blindness is the corner from which AQ operates and thrives.

For all of the pain and murder there is a bright hope. Al-Qaeda is diminishing in their capacity to strike outside of their bastion in Afghanistan. It has suffered major defeats in Iraq, Saudi Arabia, Yemen, Somalia, and Algeria. Pakistan is forcefully pushing back. AQ is finding it near impossible to perform all but the most perfunctory attacks in the West. Their banner infecting Islam with the virus of the Victorious Denomination has been halted, their foot soldiers forced to defend them as the forces that could obliterate them look for the right opening. Any faltering on the part of AQ's enemies would only see their strength grow and their resolve stiffen, and would inspire others to join their caravan of hatred. The opportunity has arrived to strike this cult's colors forever.

To bring the Muslim world to see the upside of eliminating Islam of the anathema that is AQ there must first be an aggressive global counter-ideological campaign. This campaign must be almost entirely based on strategic communications and focused on the specific link between mainstream Islam and al-Qaeda's variant of neo-Salafist Islam.

Al-Qaeda Has Already Lost a Major Counter-intelligence Battle: The Anbar "Awakening"

WHEN AMERICAN TANKS entered Firdous Square in Baghdad in April 2003, there was already a tiny but energized band of al-Qaeda-associated cells creeping into Iraq. The Jordanian terrorist group Tawhid wal Jihad was working to attack the Americans in postwar Mesopotamia and to establish what they could not under Saddam Hussein: a centralized Sunnah province within the NIC. Within six months they would operate within a massive and purely Iraqi insurgency made up of the ex–Ba'athist Party military and intelligence forces. The Sunnah Insurgency was based within the tribal homelands of the Sunnah Triangle, a roughly triangular area of land from Hilla, south of Baghdad, to Mosul in the north and from all points to the Syrian border. When I arrived in Baghdad that summer I found that this was a popularly based insurgency and that the Sunnah population supported the desire of both groups of terrorists to kill me and any other American in the country.

A common thread to the insurgency repeated itself in both Iraq and Afghanistan. The ability of the terrorists to operate was enhanced because they could swim undetected within Mao's proverbial sea of supporters. The terrorists' social links to the community were the glue that bonded the network together and made them seem invisible and invulnerable.

Soon after I left Iraq a professional peer of mine in the U.S. Army, Capt. Travis Patriquin, a brilliant army intelligence officer and linguist who spoke Arabic, Dari, and Pashto, wrote the framework for the strategy that would help break the link between ex-Ba'athists and AQI. This tribal rebellion would be called the Awakening. As Travis saw it, the way to defeat insurgents was to simply remove the tribal support from them and watch them wither on the vine. He saw the immediate and immense value of co-opting the associates of al-Qaeda, the ex-Ba'athist Sunnah insurgents, the same men we had been fighting for years, to bring them back into the fold by empowering them with their own security and local control of power and enterprise. It was a plan to literally take the entire Sunnah insurgency away from the foreign fighters.

In my 2006 book on the insurgent strategy, *The Terrorists of Iraq*, I wrote a synopsis of our discussions where I summarized that the ex-Ba'athists needed an option to end their insurgency and get rid of AQI:

> As the American occupation of Iraq continues, U.S. forces have discovered that the former regime insurgents match the toughness of the al Qaeda martyrs. Given their brutality over the past fifteen years, the general Iraqi population harbors a deep hatred for the young guerrilla fighters from the former regime . . . What this means for American troops is simple: unless the insurgency is wholly destroyed (which is unlikely given the covert nature of their operations and depth of support), the Former Regime Loyalists (FRL) insurgents will fight until the Ba'ath are back in power or to the death. Especially if they believe those are the only two options. They need to be offered a third way. It has been said in many other forums and in different ways that they may reluctantly accept a negotiated settlement where they have a chance at earning revenue and control of their own commerce. I agree. They need to have an economic future that makes them competitive and to earn money for their families. That carrot has yet to be seriously dangled in front of them. All they see is the stick of the U.S. Army.[15]

I enunciated a belief that was growing among many combat commanders, that AQI and some former Ba'athists were to be considered irreconcilable, based on their own ideological beliefs. AQI has the popular support of the local former Ba'athists because they bring death and humiliation to the occupation forces.

On the other hand, AQI continues to fight us because we are within range of their strikes and they still have the tacit support of the local Iraqis in the Sunni provinces. But our presence in fueling the insurgency is beside the point. Al Qaeda is now deeply embedded and they intend to remain until the last of them goes to Paradise—full stop. . . . The only hope is to turn the future hopes of peace and prosperity of the Sunni insurgents into a weapon with which to destroy al Qaeda in Iraq. Once the political landscape has changed enough to give the Sunni community something to hope for, they will quickly turn against the foreign extremists in Iraq. All we can ask for is to get the Iraqi Sunni community to stop their insurgency in exchange for political rapprochement and cash. Additionally, we will need their assistance to halt any further expansion of al Qaeda and the Iraqi Islamic extremists. Once they have finished that task, then and only then can we say that our mission in Iraq is done.[16]

Surprisingly, it was the heavy-handedness of AQI themselves within the Iraqi community that created a hostile environment, which forced the mutiny by Sunnah insurgents. Al-Qaeda did themselves no favors in their brutal campaign to create an Islamic Emirate of Iraq. They started a strategy in Iraq that is being carried out today in the FATA of Pakistan. First they slowly started eroding the traditional tribal-based system of dispute resolution with an absolute Sharia law, but executed by their selected militants. They started to force marriages on members of families of select tribes in order to bind those tribes to their operational goals against the Americans and Shiites. They enforced the most strict interpretation of Islamic law and severely punished the local populace for minor infractions. Death was often the default choice for infractions, and immediate execution was al-Qaeda's hallmark.

By the summer of 2005 one tribe had had enough. U.S. Army forces were notified by local law enforcement that Sunnah tribesmen were going to carry out an armed action against AQI and to stay out of the way. Later that year the U.S. Army managed to convene secret, informal talks with Sunnah tribes in Anbar Province. Captain Patriquin was convinced this could be turned into a wave of support for the U.S. effort if the Sunnah tribes were brought out of the cold. In September 2006, with Captain Patriquin's influence, the army implemented the plan to increase support to the local tribes and let them finish the fight with AQ. In a group called the Anbar Salvation Council, the tribal leaders were led by Sheikh Abdul Sattar al-Rishawi al-Dulaimi, a young tribal leader whose father and three brothers were all killed by AQ suicide bombers. Many tribal leaders were recently the same insurgents of western Iraq who fought the Americans. Rejecting al-Qaeda's brand of militancy, al-Rishawi said, "If I had the tools, I could wipe al-Qaeda from Anbar within five months." Through negotiation these tribal leaders were enticed to work with the multinational forces in Iraq.

Unfortunately, both al-Rishawi and Captain Patriquin were killed before they saw the success of this plan. However, the linkage between the community supporter and the terrorist had been broken. The ideological bonds between the Sunnah insurgent groups and their former AQI subcontractors were damaged and their networks destroyed. Once this support was lost, suicide bomber violence and the threat of civil war with the Shiites was reduced to levels not seen since 2003.

The Iraq Awakening formula may not be applied in all of its aspects everywhere that AQ operates due to the nature of their culture and political history, but it does provide a framework to start and metrics for success. Progressive counter-ideological formulas with local twists must be drafted to hit AQ right at its point of greatest vulnerability—the link between the militants and the local community. Break this link and AQ dies a sudden death.

Part IV

════

*Coup lancé:
Ending al-Qaeda*

9.

Break the Links to Islam: Waging Counter-Ideological Warfare

Irregular warfare is far more intellectual than a bayonet charge.
—T.E. LAWRENCE (OF ARABIA)

IN RESPONSE TO 9/11, the Bush administration created an all-encompassing global war strategy. A key counter-ideological component of this strategy was that the AQ Muslim terrorists were to be placed on par with or said to be worse than major American adversaries of the past such as Nazi Germany and the Soviet Union. This validated the operational strategy of al-Qaeda's global resistance in a clash of civilizations. The prospect of seeing America place the West on the side of "good" and the Muslim world on the side of "evil" made a simple frame that fostered a new generation of terrorists to believe that perhaps OBL was telling the truth all along. From there AQ recruited thousands of men who had never before considered dying in a suicide bombing.

The frame worked equally well in the non-Muslim world. By 2003 the actions taken by the Bush administration seemed so rash, so arrogant, so precipitous, that to many people in the rest of the world (particularly in what Secretary of Defense Donald Rumsfeld called Old Europe) the tragedy and goodwill given to America after 9/11 was lost. The symbiosis of American action and AQ's viral ability to explain it to their potential recruits should not be ignored. "How will this play out on the streets of Peshawar or Cairo?" should be a consideration when making strategic messaging, if only to deny AQ the opportunity to frame us again and gain a few thousand more recruits.

OBL's own words describe the dilemma his organization poses to Muslims who want to take action but often question AQ's activities:

I say to the people who walk behind these rules, don't you have hearts? Don't you have faith? How can you declare faith while you are helping those fornicating disbelievers against the children of Islam?[1]

This message of being part of the Muslim world and helping defeat a perceived threat is powerful and can often overcome a lack of information. When faced with a "good"-intentioned Muslim who defends with the Kalashnikov or the invisible Western "fornicating disbeliever" who drops missiles down on weddings . . . the choice can be surprisingly easy for many. They will support the Muslim.

It is difficult for Muslims to choose an outsider over a coreligionist who appears to sacrifice all he owns, who speaks Arabic (the language of the Qur'an), and has come from the Land of the Two Holy Shrines to help stop what appears to be meaningless slaughter. It's a narrative that requires finesse to beat, but unless we play the game and jump into the war of words, ideas, and minds we will never be able to ultimately defeat the group with guns.

Counter-Ideological Operations and Warfare

"COUNTER-IDEOLOGICAL OPERATIONS and Warfare (CIDOW)" is the term for the strategy, activities, and programs dealing with AQ. It is the strategy of simultaneously challenging their standing and their support in strategic communications, ideological veracity, and influence management and religious authority. It encompasses all aspects of influence operations, from public diplomacy to psychological operations. Only this time the target will be the enemy's base of support and his fighters, not the American public. It can be done in a manner that is consistent with American values and laws.

There is a critical need to target AQ's potential base of support. That base is broad and varied; it is not just the lowest levels of the Muslim street. AQ manages to speak to the educated and uneducated, to men and women, young and old. They target people who feel politically and socially isolated and who seek spiritual fulfillment from a group of like-minded individuals.

A focused counter-ideological effort will help target both groups and support legitimate Muslim nations' own efforts toward de-radicalization by embracing traditional, mainstream beliefs. Most important, it will identify the danger of radical ideologies and spell out both the spiritual and personal consequences. Again, none of these efforts are designed for American domestic consumption, though passive identification and recognition are sure to occur.

Conceding the Battlefield
of the Mind to al-Qaeda

SINCE 9/11, THE game plan for fighting AQ has been the National Strategy for Combating Terrorism (NSCT). It has fully acknowledged that the battle against AQ was a pillar in the battle for the minds of Islam. The 2006 NSCT states:

> From the beginning, the War on Terror has been both a battle of arms and a battle of ideas—a fight against the terrorists and their murderous ideology. In the short run, the fight involves the application of all instruments of national power and influence to kill or capture the terrorists; deny them safe haven and control of any nation; prevent them from gaining access to WMD; render potential terrorist targets less attractive by strengthening security; and cut off their sources of funding and other resources they need to operate and survive. In the long run, winning the War on Terror means winning the battle of ideas. Ideas can transform the embittered and disillusioned either into murderers willing to kill innocents, or into free peoples living harmoniously in a diverse society.[2]

There are many organizations with some measure of responsibility for attacking and defeating AQ ideology. The National Counterterrorism Center was established by Presidential Executive Order 13354 in August 2004 and brought into law by the Intelligence Reform and Terrorism Prevention Act of 2004 (IRTPA). The mission of the National Counterterrorism Center is to "lead our nation's effort to combat terrorism at home and abroad by analyzing the threat, sharing that information with our partners, and integrating all instruments of national power to ensure unity of effort."[3] They have a specific unit for the mission of defeating the AQ messaging system called the Radicalization and Extremist Messaging Group. This organization is supposed to lead the intelligence community's efforts on radicalization issues.

American counter-ideological operations to date, if they could be called that, have been so inept as to actually strengthen the hand of AQ. The American presence on the battlefield of ideas was so limited that the terrorists virtually had free reign for eight years to speak as often and as loudly as they pleased to vilify America and recruit without any organized deterrent or re-buttal. Some of the tools and methodologies selected by the Bush administration left one to wonder if it was a joke or just rank incompetence. The latter choice was clearly the answer.

Almost immediately after 9/11 the Pentagon made preparations to seize the goodwill of the world and steer that sentiment to do its bidding. The Pentagon opened the Office of Strategic Influence (OSI) and publicly announced plans to change globally public sentiment, including plans to place false news stories in foreign public media. The Pentagon announced that the OSI would "... provide news items, possibly even false ones, to foreign media organizations as part of a new effort to influence public sentiment and policy makers in both friendly and unfriendly countries."[4] Needless to say, it caused immediate outrage.

The plans for that office were scrapped almost as fast as it was announced. The concept of the OSI was a good idea. The problem was the intentions of the people pulling the levers. The Bush defense and foreign policy team were experts in political manipulation who saw the target audience as first the U.S. voting population, then potential allies. There was scant evidence that they considered AQ their target at all. Eventually they would address the issue of balancing the megaphone of the terrorists, but in practice by 2005 they chose a deliberate strategy to ignore AQ. A document issued by the National Counterterrorism Center recommended that the White House and government officials "ignore" al-Qaeda in statements and press releases. This astoundingly dense assertion was taken seriously by the White House, and for months at a time President Bush stated that he was not thinking about Osama bin Laden and did not even mention his name. It was a shortsighted belief that if they refused to verbalize or respond to AQ propaganda then it would have no value in global media. OBL did not care—he was speaking to the thousands of recruits who heeded his call.

Somehow there was never an effort to create a unified, integrated strategy where every aspect of the U.S. government's power would be broadcast to defeat AQ's ideology on every level. For some the objective was too broad and it appeared that it was easier to to try to change the opinions of the American public and our allies. Rather than assisting our Muslim allies at crafting a singular message campaign appropriate for their locale and people, the few messages that did make it out to the information battlespace were crafted so clumsily that they appeared to have been done not to influence the target audience but to burn through money allocated for the task.

In 2004 the Defense Science Board (DSB) convened a special task force on strategic communications. In September of that year they released a comprehensive report on the desperate state of American global communications efforts. They stated that the American ability to project its message and to defeat the AQ message was "in crisis" and concluded that "U.S. strategic communications must be transformed with a strength of purpose that matches our commitment to diplomacy, defense, intelligence, law enforcement, and homeland security."[5] The board made a wide-ranging series of recommendations, but the most interesting was a plea for "leadership from the top." According to the report, the necessity of the White House to play a core role in ordering and implementing a unified strategic communications plan was crucial for buy-in by other agencies. The DSB made excellent recommendations, including putting a representative for strategic communications on the National Security Council (NSC) and creating a committee within the NSC and an independent center to guide strategic communications policy. Had these recommendations been implemented, it would have set the groundwork for a comprehensive long-term strategy to combat AQ's global message. Needless to say, they were not implemented.

The worst example, in my view, of harnessing strategic communications was the operations of the Lincoln Group in Iraq. A marketing company that was created to perform a "wide variety of advertising and public relations with a mix of strategic communication tools, advertising, marketing, training and specialty communications to influence the attitudes, perceptions and behaviors of key audiences in target countries," the Lincoln Group was reportedly paid nearly $100 million to place articles in Iraqi newspapers and provide unspecified information services to the U.S. Department of Defense. The placement was amateurish at best, and the articles could barely withstand the slightest scrutiny. Although it survived a Department of Defense investigation into the appropriateness of using such enormous resources for such clear propaganda purposes, the Lincoln Group continued operations in Iraq and supported the information operations task forces that were created to defeat the effective online viral campaign by al-Qaeda in Iraq. Their effectiveness, if any, has yet to be evaluated.

It appears that since the dismantling of the OSI virtually no operations of strategic impact have been performed at any level except information warfare support to the combat commanders in the field. If this is in error and there are operations, no matter how secret, it's a mystery how it is being done without anyone in the world noticing. If global "buy-in" is a measure of public diplomacy and strategic communications, then the Bush administration's efforts were for naught.

U.S. Military and Intelligence Strategic CIDOW Operations

A 2007 SENATE hearing on homeland security was attended by Michael Chertoff, secretary of the Department of Homeland Security; Admiral Michael Mullen, director of national intelligence; Robert S. Muller III, director of the FBI; and Vice Admiral Scott Redd, director of the National Counter-Terrorism Center (NCTC). They were delivering a report on the status of America's counter-terrorism effort when the issue of what these organizations have been doing in the counter-ideology effort came up. Senator Joseph Lieberman asked each of the witnesses what actions were being taken by the U.S. government to combat the war of ideas:

> There's another side to this prevention of acts of terrorism carried out by Islamist extremists and that is what has come to be called the battle of ideas—the battle for the hearts and minds of the Muslim world. I know there are some programs in the State Department that are directed toward entering that battle globally, but what about here at home?[6]

The director of the FBI reasonably stated that there was no responsibility for the FBI, as they dealt strictly in domestic criminal activities and had no role outside the United States Issuing propaganda and influencing operations outside the United States were prohibited by the U.S. Information and Educational Exchange Act of 1948, also known as the Smith-Mundt Act.

In questioning, Vice Admiral Redd responded that counter-ideology operations were a strategic planning issue and not an exciting point of discussion. Admiral Michael Mullen, the top U.S. intelligence officer, responded honestly that they were working the issue in foreign operations but had no capacity or legal mandate domestically. He never addressed the question of what America was doing overseas.

Secretary of Homeland Security Michael Chertoff noted that the DHS was working in outreach and enabling the Muslim community to respond from within the United States, but that the agency essentially was limited to doing that. Chertoff noted:

> And in the end, when you're trying to counteract radicalization that is directed at people within the Muslim community, the people who are best situated to counteract that is the community itself. They don't want to hear the government argue theology. What they want to hear are community imams and community leaders arguing theology. And so one of our big pushes is to get the community to step up and get more involved in the process of counter radicalization.[7]

Another ineffective reshuffling of the deck chairs came when the elements of the OSI and public affairs were organized under the Defense Department Office for Support to Public Diplomacy. It was formed in 2007 and immediately shut down after the inauguration of President Obama in 2009.[8] The office was accused of violating Pentagon policy on transparency and accuracy.

Non-Existent CIDOW in Public Diplomacy

AFTER THE DEFENSE Department closed the Office of Strategic Influence, the State Department took a stab at assuming the lead role in the influence operations arena. State took over public diplomacy when the U.S. Information Agency was folded into its bureaucracy in 1999. Unfortunately, this was not considered a career-enhancing field and it sputtered along until the upgrade in 2005.

Another organization that was closed in 1996, called the Counter-Misinformation Team, was also reopened. Headed by Todd Leventhal, the office sought to respond to AQ statements and claims but generally spent most of its time on the Internet debunking claims and urban legends about the President and U.S. foreign policy.

In 2005 State decided to add some pizazz to their attempt at explaining American foreign policy by promoting President Bush's campaign confidante and spokesperson, Karen Hughes (also known as "Hurricane Karen"), to the position of Under Secretary of State for Public Diplomacy and Public Affairs. Preceded by Charlotte Beers and Margaret Tutwiler, Hughes had limited experience at the job and in the end she presided over a spectacular globe-trotting flameout that drew the ridicule of the global media. John Brown, a journalist, wrote of her tenure in London's *Guardian* newspaper:

History is not compassionate, even to Texas conservatives. If it re-members Karen Hughes at all, it will be for her failures, not her achievements. . . . Hughes's third failure—and that of the administration she serves—is perhaps her worst. It is that American public diplomacy—at its best, an effort by the U.S. to show respect to the opinions of mankind and engage in a global dialogue—has become perceived worldwide as the basest form of propaganda. The educational exchange programmes and cultural presentations Hughes supported are all to the good, but with her public diplomacy justifying policies that much of the world finds appalling, she diminished whatever value public diplomacy can have in advancing U.S. national interests and international understanding.[9]

Hughes resigned in October 2007, after two years on the job. Soon afterward the Government Accounting Office, an investigative arm of Congress, stated in a report marking the deficiencies of the department in comparison to the Defense Department and U.S. Agency for International Development: "We found that State has generally not adopted a research-focused approach to implement its thematic communication efforts."[10] In other words, they did not use polling data or systematized research when producing messages intended to influence foreign audiences. In fact, the GAO found just the opposite; they used "ad hoc" methods with little scientific consistency:

U.S. government agencies conducting research on foreign audiences currently do not have systematic processes in place to assess end-user needs or satisfaction pertaining to research products, or to coordinate or share research. In the absence of systematic processes to understand the needs or level of satisfaction of policymakers, managers, and program staff, agencies generally rely on ad hoc feedback mechanisms, such as conversations with individual users and irregular e-mail submissions.[11]

This ad hoc methodology is fine for a kitchen table conversation—it gives one a gut feeling of what one thinks is the target audience's feelings. If we have learned anything from the Bush administration, it's that going on "gut" feelings produced the Iraq war.

In 2008 the final Bush appointee to State was confirmed. James K. Glassman seemed to be more pragmatic, but with less than a year in office he could do little about the U.S. image abroad apart from commenting on it using the words of the secretary of defense, Robert Gates:

> Over the long term, we cannot kill or capture our way to victory. Non-military efforts—tools of persuasion and inspiration—were indispensable to the outcome of the defining struggle of the 20th century. They are just as indispensable in the 21st century—and perhaps even more so.[12]

One month before the inauguration of Barack Obama, Glassman outlined a newer, Internet-centric "Public Diplomacy 2.0" strategy to the New America Foundation. He said that State was going to harness the power of the Internet and respond to AQ with Digital Outreach Teams and steer people to the State Department Web site www.America.gov, as well as inform the audience that the State had a Web presence on seemingly cool Web sites such as Second Life and Facebook. No one informed Osama bin Laden that he was to go to the Second Life Web site and confront American ideology. The Bush-era operations ended in 2009 an abysmal failure. Despite the excellent recommendations of the Defense Science Board task force, no one was in charge of anything relatively similar to their proposal for a National Security council seat on strategic communication. Since 2001 the battlefield of ideas has belonged to al-Qaeda.

Reversing the Anti-American Looking Glass

ALTHOUGH THERE HAS been a commitment to defeating AQ in the "battlefield of the mind" in each iteration of the National Strategy for Combating Terrorism, it is patently obvious that operations to defeat the AQ method of narrative framing were never taken seriously outside of the tactical level of military psychological operations. The failure of both State and Defense at influencing the Muslim world on our "good intentions" was masked by the horrific policies that led to one hundred thousand or more people dying. This cannot be reconciled with happy slogans or well-meaning spokespeople. It takes deeds as well as words. When Hisham Melham of the Middle East TV news network Al Arabiya interviewed Obama in January 2009 he summed up the entire frame that AQ pushed and won in two sentences:

Let me tell you, honestly, when I see certain things about America—in some parts, I don't want to exaggerate—there is a demonization of America. It's become like a new religion, and like a new religion it has new converts—like a new religion has its own high priests.[13]

This statement, which is entirely true, reveals that al-Qaeda's ability to frame America as evil is truly effective and frightening—it also reveals our incompetence at portraying who we really are and what our mission is. The good news is that this perception is completely reversible.

Abu Yahya al-Libi's Six Steps to Destroy al-Qaeda

THERE ARE PROPONENTS of breaking AQ's links to Islam. In fact, AQ themselves have given a rudimentary plan on how to limit their ideology push into the Muslim mainstream. In September 2007 a senior AQ leader, scholar, and strategist, Abu Yahya al-Libi, outlined to the West exactly what the organization feared the most in any counter-ideological war. Feeling comfortable that America would never achieve the ability to harm AQ by anything other than arms, he detailed six steps that he claimed would damage the movement and break the link between his group and Islam. Al-Libi claimed that these steps were denouncing AQ as heretics; discrediting the ideology and ideologues personally; publicizing AQ's atrocities; playing up former AQ members' renunciations of the group; backing Islamic political movements, particularly democratic movements; and, finally, playing up internal disputes. Al-Libi's extremely helpful recommendations and six additional ones are explored below.

I. RECOMMENDATION:
APPLY THESE TWELVE LINK-BREAKING TACTICS

THERE ARE MANY methodologies necessary to break the link between al-Qaeda and the Islamic world. These links need to have justification and a major strategic communications strategy and viral media campaign to work well enough that even the water seller in Quetta won't give the terrorists a cup. The Saudis were among the first to recognize that what was needed to combat AQ's rapid growth was a comprehensive and wide-ranging message campaign.

In announcing the all-encompassing campaign that the Saudis put into place in 2005, Crown Prince Abdullah's foreign affairs advisor Adel Al-Jubeir stated:

> The bottom line is that no Saudi citizen will be able to escape the clear message that intolerance, violence and extremism are not part of our Islamic faith or Saudi culture or traditions . . . We are using different forms of communication to send a clear and powerful message, and we are taking serious actions to undermine the strength of those that try to misguide our young people.[14]

Start a Social Epidemic of Rejection

Like any good viral medium, a social epidemic of personal revulsion against the "cult" could be seeded and spread to the point where supporting al-Qaeda's destruction would be seen by Muslims as not only reasonable but also critical to the purity of Islam. The single simplest method is to reveal and hammer into the public consciousness the ideological plan of the New Islamic Caliphate, which could better be called the Emirate of Alternative Islam.

Recall that AQ is attempting to rewrite the history of Islam. OBL seeks, and is being successful in the short run, to exceed all historical figures in Islamic history in terms of political and economic impact. Unless action is taken to counteract this frame, the lie that is AQ ideology could become a source of confusion. Children will study the Qur'an and then hear alternative heretical innovations on the Net and in viral propaganda.

Finally, the religious reputation AQ enjoys as devout Muslims and their continuous offering of a reasonable justification for why they generally kill more Muslims than those they declare infidels allows them access to the global social links that keep them in business. If al-Qaeda were properly framed as an illegitimate cult and anathema to Islam, only then would the global Muslim community adopt a hatred for the group through what one scholar calls a "social epidemic."

Identify the Criminality to al-Qaeda's Target Audience

In most societies, even those under Sharia law, people want the same things: good governance, stability in their lives and commerce, law and order, and justice. Criminals operate in all societies; calling AQ anything other than a criminal or terrorist organization validates their claim to be more than that.

Our name inflation is a component of the problem. When America brings common criminals the legitimacy in a "war" against "insurgents" who commit "martyrdom" it inadvertently validates the terrorists' frame, when, in fact, we should frame the argument that we are fighting criminal cultists who conduct mass murder on the population we need to protect.

No matter in what part of the world one lives, when a major terrorist group upsets the daily norm people will speak out. For example, when Saleh al-Oufi, the second commander of AQAP, was killed by Saudi security forces, the effect on the Saudi population was one of relief. It was notable in residents, one of whom said:

> I was happy and sad at the same time. Happy that finally a criminal was gunned down and sad that such an incident could happen in the peaceful city of the Prophet Muhammad (peace be upon him). These terrorists have no dignity and do not care about people and no one is sorry that they are dead.[15]

President Obama needs to take the strategic narrative out of the hands of the military and create an integral message of who Americans are and why we will bring justice to al-Qaeda . . . the right way. Our main goal is to bring everyone who was shocked by 9/11 back to the realization that this is a critical mission, which won't be fumbled again.

Although the media broadcast virtually every word and utterance of OBL, AQ is wholly unpopular in the Muslim world precisely because most Muslims think of them as criminals. This threat should be the core of any CIDOW data-seeding project.

Make al-Qaeda Answer Publicly for Killing Innocents, Particularly Children

There is virtually nothing left to be said about the AQ policy of killing innocent people. From the earliest days OBL made the jump from claiming not to kill innocents and justifying it with the Qur'an directly to authorizing the killing of innocents of all ages and creeds. As OBL said in so many different ways, "Yes, so we kill their innocents—this is valid both religiously and logically."[16]

However, in his continuing corruption of the Qur'an OBL often claims that "OK, it is forbidden, but not literally." For a strict constructionist this is hypocrisy of the highest order. OBL said in an interview with Al Jazeera:

> They say that the killing of innocents is wrong and invalid, and for the proof, they say that the Prophet forbade the killing of children and

women, and that is true. It is valid and has been laid down by the Prophet in an authentic tradition . . . but this forbidding of killing children and innocents is not set in stone, and there are other writings that uphold it.

However, OBL was being continually pressed on why this violation of the Qur'an was justified, and when pressed on how the Muslim world saw the deaths he came up with yet another justification that allowed the deaths in the New York City attack was accidental but acceptable:

As for the World Trade Center, the ones who were attacked and who died in it were part of a financial power. It wasn't a children's school! Neither was it a residence. And the general consensus is that most of the people who were in the towers were men that backed the biggest financial force in the world, which spreads mischief throughout the world. And those individuals shall stand before God, and rethink and redo their calculations. We treat others like they treat us. Those who kill our women and our innocent, we kill their women and innocent until they stop doing so.[17]

By 2006 bin Laden simplified matters on the thousands of innocent people his leader in Iraq, Abu Mussab al-Zarqawi, killed. In his eulogy, OBL claimed that the original Qur'anic justification was simplified down to a sin of guilt by association:

Abu Mussab had clear instructions to focus his fight on the occupiers, particularly the Americans, and to leave aside anyone who remains neutral . . . But for those who refused [neutrality] and stood to fight on the side of the crusaders against the Muslims, then he should kill them whoever they are, regardless of their sect or tribe. For supporting infidels against Muslims is a major sin.[18]

Bin Laden has a growing pool of former militants who now reject this tactic, including Sheikh Salman, who wrote an open letter called "The Ramadan Letter." This document was damning in its condemnation of mass murder. Salman wrote: "How many innocents, old men, children are killed in the name of al-Qaeda?"[19] Clearly AQ changes the definition of "innocents" and the justification for murdering them on a day-to-day basis, but Muslims resort to the ultimate authority on the matter: the Prophet Mohammed declared that anyone who kills another Muslim is considered himself to be *kufir*, a non-believer. Mohammed left a specific warning in the Qur'an: "Do not go back to kufr [being non-believers] after I am gone striking one another's necks (i.e., killing one another)."[20]

Make the Terrorists' Community and Families Fear for the Spiritual Safety of Recruits

One of the key methods AQ uses to keep its recruits from suffering a change of heart is to keep them in a state of Hijrah, or Emigration. In their ideology this is parlance for staying away from all things that are not part of the purification movement. Recall that in al-Wala' Wa al-Bara' the adherent must reject all aspects and people in life who are non-Muslim. If their family is considered not pure enough, they cut their ties or refrain from contact. This means limiting communications with family and former friends to those approved and who approve of the neo-Salafist ideology. It is a tool direct from the religious cult playbook.

In the Qur'an, Allah has much to say about fighting evil and those who carry out activities that do not fit within the folds of Islam. Most importantly, the Qur'an warns against the evil of men and the inspiration they find in their acts:

> They are not careless in fighting Iblis [the devil], striving to understand his plots and snares. They do not pay any attention to *waswasah* [whispers from the Satan] concerning *wudu'*, prayer and other acts of worship, because all of that comes from the Shaytan.[21]

The Qur'an has in place religiously based justice noted for the destination of those who commit OBL's type of suicide bomber murder and beheadings of other Muslims: "If a man kills a believer intentionally, his recompense is Hell to abide therein [forever], and the Wrath and the Curse of Allah are upon him, and a dreadful Penalty is prepared for him."[22]

More disturbing to Islam is that AQ closes the window to Dawa', the missionary work of calling non-believers to God and making them into practicing Muslims. The very activity of assuming that al-Wala' Wa al-Bara' rejects contact and friendship with all people who are not Muslims defeats the very purpose of God's command to further Dawa'. Interestingly, the only concession to Dawa' that neo-Salafists even mention is the single call they make to "convert" or die. This corrupt line of thinking is similar to the incorrect historical belief that Islam is a religion that converts people forcibly and by the sword. In fact, what this hypocritical call does is shut the window to allowing non-Muslims to even consider whether Islam is an alternative religion. In effect, it glorifies a counter-productive and stereotypical image of Islam that destroys the word of God and closes the rest of the world to hearing what Muslims believe is the highest command of Allah, spreading the "knowledge" of Islam. Qur'an 49:6 says:

> O, you who believe! If a *fasiq* [liar, evil person] comes to you with any news verify it, lest you should harm people in ignorance and afterwards you become regretful for what you have done.[23]

On this basis the truth that OBL claims to speak can only be said if he parses and cuts the Qur'an into an intolerant and militant reading of Islam. Each member of the Ummah is required by this verse to verify what is being said. If it is unverifiable or is found to come from a *fasiq* (liar), then it must be rejected and the truth known.

When OBL was confronted by the single highest religious authority in Islam, the Grand Mufti of al-Azhar, Sheikh Abdul Aziz al-Ashaikh, who said that the 9/11 attacks were "sacrilegious and had nothing to do with Islam," OBL demeaned him and disrespected him in a way that most Muslims would never support. OBL said:

> No official scholar's juridical decrees have any value as far as I am concerned. History is replete with such scholars who describe their own vested interests as just [although this is prohibited in Islam]. People like this also decree the Jewish occupation of Palestine and the presence of American forces around the houses in Saudi Arabia, whose sanctity should not be violated, as fair. These people are supporting the infidels for their own personal benefit. You [addressing the interviewer] tell me how you will react if Indian forces enter Pakistan. The Israeli forces are occupying our land and the American forces are sitting on our territory. We no longer have any choice but jihad.[24]

This rejection and personal attack on the Grand Mufti exemplified OBL's rejection of traditional Islam and instantly placed him within the pantheon of other rejectionists such as the Khawarij and the Qaramita. One scholar, when asked whether AQ and their methods were like the Khawarij, responded to the questioner:

> This group that has left the Muslims, rebelling against them—this is the result of disassociating oneself from the scholars. I mentioned the consequences of this during the last part of the [previous] lecture. They broke away from the scholars, broke away from the Muslim leaders, and the disbelievers and hypocrites put these ideologies into their heads. So, they have become outcasts in Muslim societies.
>
> They are Khawārij, no doubt. This act of theirs is the act of the Khawārij. Rather, they are even more violent and extreme than the [original] Khawārij. The [past] Khawārij did not used to destroy buildings and residents. The Khawārij used to show up face-to-face on the battlefield. They used to fight on the battlefield despite what they were upon of ignorance. But they did not used to collapse buildings on everyone inside them—women, children, the innocent, those at peace with Muslims, people with whom Muslims have a treaty, and other people guaranteed safety. The Khawārij used not to do this. This is worse and more violent than the actions of the [original] Khawārij. This is more like the actions of the Qarāmiṭah (a severely violent, misguided sect). They are more like the Qarāmiṭah because the actions of the Qarāmiṭah are secret, based on secrecy and underhandedness, and what these people today do is also based on secrecy. The former Khawārij—their actions were not kept hidden and secret; they would make themselves and their objectives known, publicly announcing them. So, these people are even worse than Khawārij.[25]

It will be up to the global community of Muslims to help foster the message that being in or associating with al-Qaeda is akin to losing Islam. Many Muslim scholars and leaders have called AQ apostate, and not only must this issue be discussed, but public offers must be made to bring individuals who have left out of false piety, pride, adventure, or the *waswasah* of OBL back into the fold of good Muslims.

A good example of this is the Saudi government's system of rehabilitation, where imams and theologians have meetings with the militant prisoners, emphasizing that the former terrorist must "get right" with God, for in the end it is His judgment that will be received by the offender. If the militant fears God above all (and that is the entire basis of the neo-Salafist motivation), then giving an alternative perspective on God's wrath is often enough to give him another opportunity to review what he believes and "come back to God."

In the end the hadiths in Sahih Bukari give us guidance on how Muslims fear for the safety of the terrorists' souls with justification from God Himself, as it is He who will decide in the end:

> Ubada bin As-Samat said:
>
> "I was among those Naqibs [selected leaders] who gave the Pledge of allegiance to Allah's Apostle. We gave the oath of allegiance, that we would not join partners in worship besides Allah, would not steal, would not commit illegal sexual intercourse, would not kill a life which Allah has forbidden, would not commit robbery, would not disobey [Allah and His Apostle], and if we fulfilled this pledge we would have Paradise, but if we committed any one of these [sins], then our case will be decided by Allah.[26]

Make People Remember They Can't Depend on Terrorists

For all of the preaching that the theorists and ideologues of AQ make, the major successes for the claims of the Victorious Denomination for the Muslims came at the hands of the Americans. When AQ was being formed in the post-Soviet jihad of Afghanistan it was AQ and the neo-Salafists who sought to bite the hand that fed them. When Kuwait, a country with surprising popular support for AQ, was invaded by Iraq it was America that formed a pan-Arab coalition and ejected Iraq at the cost of over two hundred lives. When Bosnian Muslims were undergoing a mini-genocide by the Bosnian Serbs (who were Christians) it was American air strikes that broke the back of the Serbian government. When Kosovar Muslims were undergoing ethnic cleansing it was NATO, led by the Americans, that flattened Serbia's military capability and won liberation for both Kosovo and later Macedonia, which was 33 percent Muslim. When Somali Muslims were starving in 1992 it was the U.S. military that arrived to feed and distribute food. In each of these instances neo-Salafist Takfiris played little or no part in the fighting and virtually none in the charity work. In fact, once they performed 9/11 they were responsible for all of the hardships that the Muslim world felt under George W. Bush's attacks.

In Algeria, Egypt, and Lebanon these groups resorted to massacring or

confronting the government through Baghy or Hiraba and contributed virtually nothing to the welfare of the people. One Algerian commentator
wrote this about the recent rift between AQ ideologues who are fighting in
the media: "I think that the message sent by Dr. [Sayyid Imam] Fadl will be
read by everyone with great attention, as it carries in itself a clear indication
to the Islamic groups that resort to violence, to the effect that you shouldn't
depend on 'us.' "[27]

In a BBC interview with Frank Gardner, another al-Qaeda rejectionist
mocked bin Laden about the way he seeks to invite disappointment in anyone whom he cannot rely on. Nu'man bin Othman said:

> He declared war. He didn't ask you, huh, you don't know about it, and
> after that he would like you to support him. And if you don't, he says,
> "Oh, you let me down. You failed me and you failed Islam." Why
> should I believe I have a duty or obligation towards al-Qaeda?[28]

Reframe al-Qaeda as Political Opportunists

Algerian journalist Nayla Berrahal of the newspaper *Echorouk* claims that al-
Qaeda in the Islamic Magreb (AQIM) has had difficulty buying into Algerian
society because of their support for any cause that gains them media attention,
particularly after the Israeli incursion into Gaza in December 2008. She claimed
AQ "is in a really difficult position since the start of the events in Gaza . . . due
to the reaction of the public." Algerians believe that AQ tried "to profit from the
situation to clean up its image following a series of suicide attacks and crimes
targeting civilians." More interestingly, for all of the bluster that twenty years
of operation AQ has claimed were done in the name of Palestine, not one operation, apart from the accidental miss of a rocket fired in Aqaba, Jordan, that
ended up hitting Israel a kilometer away, has been attributable to AQ. No volunteers or groups that are aligned with AQ operate within Palestine. This is a
fantastic level of hypocrisy for a group that claims that the liberation of Palestine is second only to the cleansing of Saudi Arabia of U.S. forces. Since U.S.
forces left Saudi Arabia in 2004, this claim has come off as an opportunistic
rhetorical flourish added to almost all AQ speeches. President Barack Obama,
speaking in Strasbourg, France, summed up their opportunism this way:

> It is going to be a very difficult challenge. Al Qaeda is still bent on
> carrying out terrorist activity. It is—don't fool yourselves—because
> some people say, well, you know, if we changed our policies with re-

spect to the Israeli-Palestinian conflict, or if we were more respectful towards the Muslim world, suddenly these organizations would stop threatening us. That's just not the case.[29]

Mustafa al-Ani, of the United Arab Emirates–based Gulf Research Center, argues that AQ is so far out of the game with their rhetoric on Palestine that they are losing strength and credibility:

They are losing credibility on their traditional battlefields . . . there is huge criticism in the Arab street and within Arab intellectual circles about al-Qaeda's attitude towards the Palestinian question, [critics say] they are not doing anything to attack Israel; at the same time they are criticizing Hezbollah and Hamas: who are fighting the Israelis.[30]

Encourage Positive Ideological *Fitna*

Since 2005 there has been a major ideological civil war, or *fitna*, occurring between past AQ followers that has rent the Takfiri world. The militants themselves have identified this as one of the most dangerous vulnerabilities to their cause. They react negatively to other militants who recant terror and often come out into the public domain to counteract their arguments, lest young recruits be negatively influenced by them. Many of these internal fissures have been identified by the two most influential organizations engaged in collecting data for counter-ideological warfare: the West Point Combating Terrorism Center (CTC) and the blog site Jihadica. Both of these take the reader deep into the heart of the fissures that are rending the neo-Salafist militant world. Given enough impetus and funding these micro-tears in the fabric of the Takfiri ideology could tear the ideology to shreds. Although it appears that the National Strategy for Combating Terrorism advocates identifying and stopping the spread of militant ideology, over the years, there appears to have been little, if any, organized effort to encourage the fighting among themselves. Jordan, Saudi Arabia, and Egypt appear to have harnessed the power of self-destruction among the former militants, but the United States has yet to truly set up organizations or execute policy that would make ideological mini-*fitnas* (civil wars among clashing personalities) transform into ideological mega-*fitnas* (civil wars between Islam and al-Qaeda). Properly performed, it could stave off the real inter-Islamic armed *fitna* AQ seeks.

Again, the tip of the spear in the American counter-ideological effort comes from two small but influential sources. These entities are so threatening that the neo-Salafist Takfiri world actually discusses their fears that they will gain influence and be a major force in breaking their ideology. The first is the Combating Terrorism Center at West Point.

Major initiatives started in 2005 by Jarret Brachman and William Mc-Cants (then under the command of Special Forces colonel Joseph Felter) made a small, underfunded center an intelligence powerhouse where military and civilian scholars are the tip of the spear in the counter-ideological battle against the militants. Their institute was designed to unravel the web that is the ideological road map of AQ. The CTC was one of the first to identify the vulnerabilities and weaknesses in the AQ ideology. Its magnum opus, *The Militant Ideology Atlas*,[31] is considered the best and only book of its kind. The massive document outlines all of the ideological discussions and personalities in the neo-Salafist militancy and their historical writings. It also maps out the network of the most influential writers and uses thousands of citations by the Takfiris' own writings and words to complete the analysis of who speaks loudest for the terror ideologues. This was followed by a manual called *Stealing Al-Qaida's Playbook*, where the CTC selected recommendations from al-Qaeda supporters and ideologues on how to best damage the group.

This effort wasn't done for academia. It was designed to be a road map to identify the global strategic communications and intelligence activities necessary to damage AQ. The CTC identified many of the most vulnerable and breakable links in AQ's ideology. The surprising part about this tremendous effort appears to be that despite the massive number crunching, there has yet to be in place an organized effort to use this information and damage these links. Many of the recommendations and ideas put forward by the CTC were incorporated into the Bush administration's 2006 National Strategy for Combating Terrorism and remain a vital part of the U.S. defense strategy. Its work has had great national-level attention, but it requires a global level of amplification to damage the AQ ideological effort on a broad scale.

William McCants maintains a highly praiseworthy blog called Jihadica,[32] which follows the minutiae of the AQ ideology wars to the point that an AQ-sponsored forum did a survey and identified it as ". . . the most important and dangerous of the sites in this group."[33] These are high honors for academics, but they have identified numerous key splits within the movements. Some of the most interesting conflicts include the following.

Egyptian Islamic Group Versus Egyptian Islamic Group

As early as 1997 militant groups such as the Islamic Group of Egypt had laid down arms and written their refutations of violence. The members of the Islamic Group wrote a multivolume set called the *Concept Correction Series (Silsilat Tashīh al-Mafāhīm)*. As these books are not published for the mass market, they have had little popular notice, but they are critical in that they have started mini-*fitnas* (civil wars) among those militants who still believe in violence and those who have abandoned it. Rehabilitation programs from Indonesia to Saudi Arabia have found that the best persons to help a group de-radicalize are former members themselves.

Hassan Hattab Versus al-Qaeda

Another reliable source of information on the *fitna* within the militant world was from those intelligence groups who were engaged with the militants from the first. While America was receiving the first minor blows from AQAP in the early 1990s, the Algerian government was embroiled in a major counter-insurgency. Salafist insurgents from two major religious revivalist groups, enflamed at winning major gains in Algeria's democratic election but being denied the seats by the government, took to Baghy. Their leadership chose a radical Salafist doctrine. Led by Armed Islamic Group (Groupe Islamique Armé), or GIA for short, and a sister group, the Islamic Salvation Army (AIS), the Salafist Group for Preaching and Combat (GSPC) was extremely small. Between 1992 and 1999 the GIA and AIS slaughtered over one hundred thousand Algerians. Their principal weapon was not the rifle but the knife. They sought to symbolically purify the nation in blood taken in the same way that a goat or camel is slaughtered at Ramadan.

The GSPC was a neo-Salafist splinter group of the GIA that broke off in 1998. The blood ran so deep that even its senior members started to see that the neo-Salafist Takfiris were simply in lust with mass murder. Facing a popular backlash from Algerian society, Hassan Hattab (aka Abu Hamza), at the urging of Osama bin Laden, took over neo-Salafist combat operations targeting principally the government soldiers. The GSPC changed methods to win over the few skeptical poor Algerians who had supported the Islamic movement before. Using the image of "Islamic Knights," Hattab made inroads where the GIA could not. The GSPC also limited the mass murders in order to regain ground lost by the GIA. In 2004 the GSPC declared "war on all foreigners and foreign interests in Algeria." It was then that Hattab left the organization to Abdelmalek Droukdel, who wanted to target and kill civilians as the GIA did.

On the fifth anniversary of September 11, in 2006, Dr. Ayman al-Zawahiri announced the "formal" alignment of AQ with the GSPC. They officially changed their name to al-Qaeda in the Islamic Magreb (AQIM). By 2007 the AQIM/GSPC, diminished greatly by the Algerian government's iron-fist policy toward insurgency, reaffirmed its religious ruling that innocent people must be killed in order to wage a new phase of the terrorist insurgency against the government. For Hassan Hattab, the founder of the GSPC, the smaller but arguably harder-line group, it was too much. He surrendered to Algerian authorities and renounced warfare forever.

In January 2009 Hassan Hattab, founder of the GSPC, issued a statement that the war had cost too much in blood. He called for the members of his group to lay down their arms and surrender to God. He called for an end to Baghy and to accept peace within Algerian society. He then condemned the attack being carried out in the name of Islam. Hattab asked: "What law or moral code could allow this? Is this really a jihad that would please God?" It was a shocker of a document.

Hattab was not finished; with his new role as repentant terrorist he called the same members to God using the very same verses he had used to justify terror. He claimed that terror did nothing for Islam and asked his brothers in arms to "obey God, halt your activities and return to society and your families; society is ready to welcome you and heal the wounds."

al-Zawahiri Versus Fadl

In 2007 a major ideological split occurred within the AQ movement. Sayyid Imam abd-al-Aziz al-Sharif, also known as Dr. Fadl, was a close associate and compatriot of AQ's second in command, Dr. Ayman al-Zawahiri. In the 1960s the two men went to school and practiced medicine together in Egypt. They both became believers in the Egyptian Islamic Brotherhood movement and went on to form the terrorist group known as the Egyptian Islamic Jihad. Al-Zawahiri was always seen as the public face of the EIJ, but it was Dr. Fadl who was the group's ideological and spiritual leader. Fadl's magnum opus, a book called The Essentials of Making Ready for Jihad (Al-'Unda fi I'dad Al-'Udda), was mandatory reading for jihadists throughout the world and was distributed in AQ training camps. Arrested in 2004 in Yemen, he repudiated terrorism and militant tactics in prison, where he wrote his later books.

In 2007 he wrote a book titled Rationalizing Jihad in Egypt and the World. In it he turned viciously on al-Qaeda and bin Laden and al-Zawahiri in particular. In the book Fadl excoriates them, claiming that all of the murders and the path since 9/11 were on the heads of al-Qaeda and that it was un-Islamic. Fadl ranted: "Nothing invokes the anger of God and His wrath like the unwarranted spilling of blood and wrecking of property."

These were direct shots at the heart of all AQ's arguments for terror. In addition, Fadl takes a flamethrower to the intent of the 9/11 attacks and questions their utility to Islam and the Muslim people:

> Ramming America has become the shortest road to fame and leadership among the Arabs and Muslims. But what good is it if you destroy one of your enemy's buildings, and he destroys one of your countries? What good is it if you kill one of his people, and he kills a thousand of yours?[34]

Fadl hit AQ with such ferocity that al-Zawahiri had to release several audiotapes and then respond more forcefully, with a two-hundred-page book called *Acquittal*. Al-Zawahiri was forced by his ex-associate to counter charges that al-Qaeda's ideology was a corruption of Islam, particularly the broad adoption of Takfir and killing innocent people. Cornered, al-Zawahiri reached for derisive sarcasm:

> Do they now have fax machines in Egyptian jail cells? I wonder if they're connected to the same line as the electric-shock machines.[35]

However, al-Zawahiri was forced to justify and defend positions that had until now never been questioned by former members. Fadl was having none of it, and his next book, called *Memo of Refutation of "Acquittal Book,"* kept up the exchange. The debate is entering its third year, and the effect on AQ has been nothing less than astounding. By the summer of 2008 the question of whether AQ could survive an ideological breakup was in the air. The result remains to be seen, but the groundwork to quickly make more fissures exists.

The Mullah Omar Versus the Takfiri Blogosphere

OBL refers to Mullah Omar, the founder and leader of the Afghanistan Taliban, as the first "Emir of the Islamic Republic of Afghanistan" and the "Commander of the Holy Warriors" and by the all-encompassing title of an Islamic Caliph "Commander of the Faithful." In the eyes of OBL, Mullah

Omar is the pinnacle of Islamic leadership in the NIC. Omar now commands the combined leadership council formed in 2003 and is said to operate in Quetta, Pakistan. He was considered one of the irreconcilable hard-liners who had been said to want to fight to the death.

However, in November 2008 Afghan President Hamid Karzai made an appeal to Omar to come to the negotiating table. Mullah Omar, responding to the potential of negotiating, issued a statement that read:

> We want to have legitimate relations with all countries of the world . . . We are not a threat to anyone. America believes that the Taliban is a threat to the whole world. And with this propaganda, America wants to use all other countries to advance their own interests.[36]

For the former leader of an "Islamic Emirate" that was recognized by Saudi Arabia, the UAE, and Pakistan, this is a diplomatic way of keeping one's options open. However, when Mullah Omar also mentioned solidarity with Iran, a predominantly Shia Muslim nation with which Afghanistan shares borders, the global supporters of OBL and AQ were outraged. Bloggers on public forums that openly supported OBL responded: "This is the worst statement I have ever read" and "The disaster of defending the [Iranian] regime is on par with the Crusaders in Afghanistan and Iraq."[37] Others wondered what had happened to Mullah Omar. The feud became so public that the Taliban's former ambassador to Pakistan, Mullah Salam Zaief, responded by dismissing AQ supporters:

> Nobody has the right to ignore the importance of stability in Afghanistan. They should at least not be making such irresponsible comments. [The al-Qaeda bloggers] were raising the question of the foreign-troop presence in Afghanistan. But now, I think Afghans have to tolerate the presence of foreign troops in the country because they have no other option.[38]

Though the mini-*fitnas* illustrated show that the militants have differing opinions, more important, they show where the fault lines within the movements lie and where the vulnerabilities could be exploited. This lends credence to the idea that an international campaign should be formed to make sure that the dissident and repentant voices are given a wide international platform and that the voices of those who see the truth about the neo-Salafist Takfiris be allowed to be heard without restraint and in media that are better suited to pushing their opinions down to the Muslim street.

Demand al-Qaeda Pay Its Blood Debts to Muslims and Non-Muslims

Bin Laden owes many people, their families, and, in particular, their children a blood debt that only he can repay. AQ is responsible for all deaths it has caused since its terror war began in 1988. They have killed or caused to be killed more than one hundred thousand people. How much would AQ owe the Muslim world if they were forced to pay Diyyah, or the blood debts proscribed in the Qur'an for wrongful deaths?

But let us look at our short list of those we were introduced to in the second chapter: Al-Qaeda owes a blood debt to the two women beheaded in the Pakistan tribal belt by the terrorist group Tarik-e-Taliban after they were accused of a wide range of illicit activities—from spying to prostitution. Al-Qaeda owes a blood debt to the thousands of Algerians who awoke at night and found armed militants cutting the throats of everyone alive. Al-Qaeda owes a blood debt to Iraqi Muslims mass-murdered by the thousands by al-Qaeda in Iraq. Al-Qaeda owes a blood debt to the thousands who died in Bali, London, Madrid, Mumbai, and Riyadh and all over Iraq.

If we were to calculate the average blood debt payment for families killed by the American army in Iraq at $7,500 per death, then AQ would owe an approximate blood debt of $1.5 billion to families in the Muslim world.

Muslims will say, "On the other hand, where is the justice for those innocent civilians killed in American air strikes or artillery attacks in Iraq, Afghanistan, and Somalia or torture in the Abu Ghraieb prison? Who shall pay their debt? Did these people not have a right to be held safe from harm in their lives?"

These questions must be addressed. In 2004 the U.S. government started a program of payments of blood debts to the families of innocent people they have killed and to repay for the property destroyed, in accordance with Islamic law and custom. So, unlike AQ, America is living up to its obligations.

The only obstacle in this part of the strategy is that America is not paying out Diyyah or compensation money for those we have killed in Afghanistan fast enough. Commanders are aware this is draining support from our mission. The United Nations claims that in 2008, 2,118 civilians were killed, and the BBC reports that 77 percent of people polled describe the results of our attacks as "unacceptable."

In a report by the Campaign for Innocent Victims in Conflict (CIVIC) called "Losing the People: The Costs and Consequences of Civilian Suffering in Afghanistan," Afghans interviewed wanted medical support first and then assistance toward financial recovery after losing a loved one. For America, despite our recent economic worries, investment in this is a drop in the bucket when compared to the costs of the ill will of AQ and Taliban recruiting officers. Erica Gaston states that in the best case "families who have lost a loved one would receive immediate medical relief from coalition forces; monetary payments soon after from coalition forces or from Kabul; community support from coalition forces and Provisional Reconstruction Teams; and monthly payments from various Afghan government funds."[39] The biggest problem is that people do not know how or are afraid to come to the coalition military. They are often "turned away at the gate." This has to stop.

However, the Muslim world has never heard OBL or any of his takfiris offer diyyah for those they have killed or caused to be killed. He offers only insincere excuses that he started his aggressions to fight an imaginary American "occupation" of Saudi Arabia, the food embargo of Iraq, and the corruption in Islam. Until 2002 he never mentioned Palestine or Iraq as a major reason to attack America, but the 2003 invasion of Iraq and the multiple Palestinian Intifadas and even the Shiite resistance to the Israeli invasion of Lebanon in 2006 (at a time when his deputies in Iraq were mass-murdering the Shiites in a sectarian war) quickly became part of his propaganda mantra. One part of his campaign was that Muslims who were killed were not collateral damage, but religious martyrs.

Errant or indiscriminate force on the part of America will only contribute to perpetuating cycles of violence in tribal and religious communities that see vengeance as a matter of individual and collective honor. The obligation to offer diyyah is not only the responsibility of the West. Al-Qaeda and their allies, too, must adhere to these traditions and be held to the same standard on the public stage.

When ninety people were killed in Afghanistan by accident in August 2008, Brigadier General Michael Dolan went to the families of those killed and offered his condolences and compensation for the incident. Has bin Laden done this for the children he has killed? Does he still insist that any Muslim with Americans or near Americans or who could be near Americans is *kufir* and deserves death? Never once has there been an apology for any Muslim killed by bin Laden or his men. He is more than capable of killing Muslims, but he leaves it to God to assign blame. Is there a greater hypocrisy?

Use the Same Viral Media Techniques They Do

In 2006 a British-based AQ supporter named MC Sheikh Terra made a video of a song, "Dirty Kuffar," where the ski-masked singer in a military jacket holds a Qur'an and a pistol and sings about killing non-believers, flashing images of the Iraqi flag and the black flag of al-Qaeda, interspersed with the word "Jihad," negative images of King Fahd, George Bush, Musharraf, and past leaders, calling each a "dirty Kuffar." It includes live video of IED and sniper attacks on U.S. forces in Iraq and Afghanistan flashing over. The lyrics are meant to be offensive and inflammatory:

> *dirty Kuffar*
> *wherever you are*
> *driving your car,*
> *disobeying Allah*
> *running around the world like the grand Pubah,*
> *we're gonna be taking over like we took over the Shah*
> *from Kandahar to Ramallah*
> *we comin', star;*
> *peace to Hamas and the Hezbollah,*
> *OBL [Osama bin Laden] crew be like a like a shiny star,*
> *like the way we destroyed them two tower ha-ha*

The video ends with live shots of the 9/11 hijackers crashing planes into the WTC. In Palestine there is a popular music video, "Who Is the Terrorist?," which combines good music and provocative lyrics with images of oppression that are effective at both transmitting its message and exciting people who may not understand the situation into action. These negative examples of harnessing of viral media are popular. More to the point, they are powerful and intense.

These videos have hundreds of thousands of views and have been shared countless numbers of times, throughout the Internet. However, as we have learned with the introduction of social media such as YouTube, MySpace, Facebook, and Twitter, and RSS feeds of news related to terrorism, these systems are responsible for global movements and awareness from things as mundane as dogs stealing bones from grocery stores to transmitting live video streams from terrorism incidents that bypass the global media. AQ relies on this system, and simply put, it can be taken away from them or at the least swamped in counter-ideological messages.

These same videos can be harnessed to overpower the militant message. Their own actions and claims can be reversed using better imagery, more popular personalities, and the power of swarming any dispatch they put out with a powerful, globally coordinated message. In Saudi Arabia they have singers who sing about true Islam and reject the extremist views and belittle militancy.

With the financial and media star power of the West, paid efforts to overwhelm the militants' viral media with our own could easily be made. Stars with global followings should be paid their usual rates to create and produce clear CIDOW messaging as a public service. Muslim Qur'an singers, regional and local stars should not be excluded. In Saudi Arabia, soccer games are extremely popular and the government takes pains to use that venue as a public service platform. During the games respected imams make pitches to the game audience to remember that terrorism and violence are un-Islamic and that violators will be judged by God in Paradise hereafter. The world should know what the message is, and it should be present in the face of AQ supporters.

Organize Counter-Extremist Message Swarming
A "swarm" is when an online location or medium is struck by thousands of like-minded posts or activities all at once. Given the challenge and a respectful counter-message script delivered to the public, a CIDOW organization could request that the public use the talking points provided and respond to any pro-militant immediately. This swarming strategy could generate literally tens of thousands of viral YouTube videos flooding the sites where videos are posted by the militants. In addition, militant media would most likely be ridiculed to the point that they were "shouted down" by the public. Given the task, most Web sites would collapse under the weight of the effort. A public swarming would also reveal that the message of the militants is minuscule compared to the power of the rest of the world. For every supporter who wants to blog, open a forum, or post in support of AQ and the neo-Salafist Takfiris there should be a million people who should be encouraged to dissent.

The same can be effected for message boards. Law enforcement can authorize same-language groups and individuals to help counter militant messages with a wide array of counter-messaging. These messages should be crafted within the master frame and swarmed, that is, delivered by the hundreds of thousands whenever any material or opinions supportive of the terrorists are posted. For each forum or blog post there should be a thousand responses with the proper counter-ideological message. However, this effort should be internationalized and operated by governments. We cannot be like the amateur vigilante "counter-terrorists" who have sprung up over the last eight years attacking Islam and everything Muslim with racial diatribes.

Should the government be in the business of shutting down Web sites with material that could be said to verbally support terrorists? It's a thorny First Amendment issue, but to best effect the mission of destroying AQ's online support, capability disruption needs to become an international law enforcement issue. Material and technical support can be given using increased funding for this purpose. Actions taken in cyberspace are called offensive counter-ideological warfare actions, or CIDOW disruption. Disruption can be as simple as removing the site from a server, blocking external access from a site, or swarming the site with CIDOW messaging.

The Washington Post recently noted that some terror supporters use hosting servers in the United States, because of the ease of setup and the relative long length of time it takes to find them.[40] Sites on hosts within our jurisdiction should have associated links redirected to the FBI Web site. After a few thousand instances of this nature, AQ supporters will become justifiably paranoid.

Swarming should be done with the knowledge that we want the militants to know their messages are no longer going to be allowed to stay in cyberspace unchallenged.

Although CIDOW messaging should be restricted to militant sites and servers that use or transmit militant sites, some servers may be used surreptitiously for supporting militant ideology and those that need an instant disruption action, but this should be done in such a way as to make it clear that a specific site is being targeted for a specific reason. Note that many people using the Internet will set up false sites just for the entertainment of watching auto-bot programs conduct CIDOW, but that should be expected from the opposition as well.

The message that needs to go out to the Web is that validated sites belonging to or supporting terror or their supporters will be monitored and may be blocked. This may force the militants to revert back to other, slower technologies of communicating, but that is also part of the plan to eliminate their base of support and messaging.

Help Stand Up and Support De-radicalization Programs and Plans

Arguably the most successful CIDOW is being performed by four nations without any major material support from the West. Saudi Arabia, Yemen, Indonesia, and Iraq have rehabilitation and reconciliation or ideological counseling programs in place that aim to perform on an individual scale what this book proposes on a global scale: de-radicalizing individuals away from armed militancy and violence. This issue has been discussed in many forums and has even been considered for application in the United States and the United Kingdom. The Iraqi program (and a fledgling Jordanian one) was crafted with the assistance of American psychological and behavioral sciences consultants.

In Saudi Arabia, after the massive five-year push toward destabilization and insurgency by AQAP, the Saudi interior ministry realized that their own Salafist ideology was a component of the problem. The Muwahiddun theology was not to blame so much as the corruptions and heretical innovations by AQ that made Saudi orthodoxy seem like raging liberalism to the terrorists. The basis of the Saudi program was to bring about theological and cognitive changes in those militants who were captured and show them the correct path via vigorous religious discussion and debate. Sequestered in a special facility, they have meetings, prayer sessions, and debates with imams and theologians who have the authority and scholarship to reveal that AQ was completely off the mark and if the militant does not return to true Islam he, too, could be lost to Satan. The Saudi Interior Ministry's director for ideological security, Abdul Rahman al-Hadlag, said:

> Changing mind-sets is not easy, and it takes a long time . . . We have to monitor mosques and the Internet, because the extremists use these places to recruit people. Sometimes they even use afterschool activities. Sleeper cells exist.[41]

The Saudi security forces, known for their unyielding brutality, act in compassion and understanding with the prisoners. Every effort is made to convert them back to mainstream Islam and let them speak out against the corruption by AQ. The rate of recidivism is a concern but a highly inconsequential one. There are those in the West who believe that one terrorist faking his way through the system and returning to the field of combat is equal to a total failure of any such program. No doubt some have not been completely turned, but the Saudis note an 80 percent success rate in converting these men from militancy. Errors most likely have occurred, but considering that the Saudis have removed hundreds of others, many of whom would have piloted suicide bombs in Saudi Arabia, Afghanistan, or Iraq, this is nothing short of impressive. Although they get benefits that others would have to work for, such as public welfare payments, cars, housing, and dowries for marriage (which the Saudis believe stabilizes them), they also are carefully monitored. The Saudi system has received praise from high-level advocates, including Senator John Kerry:

> The centerpiece of the new strategy was a groundbreaking counter-indoctrination program. While the real hard-liners, irreconcilables and terrorist leaders remained in high-security prisons, others were treated as responsible for their actions, yes, but also as members of a cult, to be deprogrammed and, where possible, reintegrated into society. Instead of being tortured, detainees are visited by imams who explained why violent jihadist theology was a perversion of Islam.[42]

The Saudi program has graduated more than 270 men and processed over 117 who were returned to the Kingdom from the Guantánamo Bay prison camp.

In the vacuum after 9/11, the emboldened Takfiri organizations answered the call to conduct operations in support of the effort to destabilize their national and regional authorities. However, the Takfiris suffered major defeats and some ideological rollbacks after lashing out. In Asia, after the militant al-Jamma' al-Islamiyya attacked Australian tourists in Bali, Indonesia, the popular support of the extremists nose-dived. The Indonesians soon carried out a de-radicalization campaign that marginalized the extremists to the point of complete destruction.

Indonesia has captured over four hundred hard-line militants, the largest number of any democracy. However, imprisoning them was not the best option. The Indonesian approach saw each terrorist as an individual and converted them back to society using other reformed members of the terrorist group. As in the Saudi system the terrorists are provided with social support, including a financial subsidy for their families. This removes the allure of the prisoner returning to paid terror work.

Another aspect that is critical for neo-Salafists is to psychologically return them from the state of Hijrah, the ideological state of avoiding all who are not Muslim enough to be neo-Salafiast Takfiris. This is done through socialization, not unlike cult deprogramming. The subject is returned to reality as opposed to the fantasy world of the Takfiri raider.

Yemen established a program in 2002 that has been hailed as one of the first programs to recognize and treat radicalized Yemenis. Some, such as the

9/11 plotter Ramzi bin al-Shibh and others, carried out numerous attacks for AQ, including suicide bombings on tankers, warships, embassies, and groups of tourists. The Yemenis created the Committee for Dialogue to persuade militants that their variant of Islam was incorrect. It was developed by Judge Hamoud al-Hittar and works like the Saudi program, which copied the Yemeni model. The Yemenis emphasize a system called PRAT: "Prevention, Rehabilitation, and Aftercare."[43] Yemen has the largest number of remaining captives in the Guantanamo Bay prison (almost 240), and until 2009 their return to a program that met American satisfaction was a major sticking point in closing the camp.

Do No Harm and Do Know Harm

The 247 "collateral" deaths of civilians at Deh Bala and other locations such as Wech Baghtu and Kandahar in Afghanistan and Fallujah and Makr al-Deeb near al-Qaim in Iraq marked the low level of humanity the War on Terrorism assigns to civilians. In the parlance of the enemy, "collateral damage" equates with new al-Qaeda recruits. The terrorist propaganda system, which we have found to be robust and diverse, can more rapidly make charges and propagate the accuracy of the aftereffects of civilian deaths, while well-meaning but invariably wrong American Public Affairs Teams and civil affairs officers flail about. It takes days for American forces to get to airstrike locations while it takes hours for Al Jazeera stringers to broadcast massacres internationally.

The most important question to be asked here is, how can the counter-insurgent, civil affairs, or intelligence officer in the field step in and gain the cooperation of the local people after an incident such as this? Every incident where indiscriminate or mistaken fire kills is a counter-insurgency win for the Taliban and the AQ allies.

American actions in Pakistan face the same charges when they make precision strikes using the Predator or Reaper unmanned aerial vehicles, or drones. Although these attacks are generally quite precise, they tend to happen in areas where militants we seek are with or near families who live communally. Most of the time the very militants sought are killed, but we often never have the ground intelligence assets (unlike Al Jazeera) to confirm the results and casualties of the attack. Invariably, as with the air strikes from aircraft, we assume that everyone involved is a terrorist. Not everyone agrees. Pakistan's foreign minister, Shah Mehmood Qureshi, said:

They [drone strikes] are counterproductive . . . My view is they are causing collateral damage, my view is that they are alienating people, my view is that they are working to the advantage of the extremists. We [Pakistan and the United States] have agreed to disagree on this.[44]

The current war kills hundreds of civilians who are critical to our effort to stop the spread of fanatic militants and creates a cottage industry where the Taliban recruits the survivors for the insurgency in order to satisfy a blood vengeance. Many Americans who view the war in Afghanistan and Iraq through the lens of infallibility often dismiss the deaths of foreign civilians as unfortunate accidents that occur when well-meaning U.S. forces try to "get the bad guys." Invariably they ask, "What purpose does it serve to assign blame? The damage has been done. Al-Qaeda is worse." It is errors and attitudes such as these that will push the civilian Middle Eastern populations further into the arms of the Taliban and AQ.

II. RECOMMENDATION: DON'T NEGLECT THE IMPORTANCE OF KILLING THE AQSL

AS EMIR AL Mujahideen ("Prince" or Commander of the Jihadists) for the global Takfiri insurgency, OBL has the dual role of combat commander in global terrorist operations as well as chief advisor to regional insurgency operations in both Pakistan and Afghanistan. His stature and ability to stop world opinion in an instant places him in a position not unlike that of his disciple Abu Mussab al-Zarqawi in Iraq. In an audiotape delivered to a convention of Deobandi scholars he stated, "Teach them that jihad for the sake of God can only be done by a group that listens and obeys a single commander, through which God unites them from their differences and disarray."[45]

One of the first acts of the Barack Obama presidency was the signing of the executive order to capture or kill bin Laden and the AQSL. Should OBL die, today or any day, his role in forcing his ideology worldwide through terror could quickly topple the very mission for which he fought. Despite referring to Mullah Omar as the Emir of the Islamic Emirate of Afghanistan, OBL is the embodiment of the concept of being a "Fighting Islamic Scholar" and establishing the NIC. He cannot be easily replaced, and though his spirit could live on, a new Emir of greater stature is not in the offing any time soon. The 1988 charter of AQ states that the Emir must be a jihadist fighter who is personally characterized with unswerving religious devotion "like an Imam" with the qualities of "Islam, Maturity, Freedom, Masculinity, Intelligence."[46] Osama bin Laden currently fills this role, and should he die, no one else could inspire until they performed a terror mission that makes 9/11 pale in comparison.

OBL is not holed up in Pakistan solely because he enjoys the standing he has in the FATA communities and Pakistan in general. It fulfills his religious belief that for having austerity and abandonment of his earthly life he will be better rewarded in Paradise. Soon after he fled to Tora Bora, I stood in the very room that OBL had lived in at his Jalālābād compound. Apart from his Krinkov submachine gun, a prayer carpet, a thin bed, and a wood stand for his Qur'an there was little more that he appears to have wanted or needed. OBL lives by the creed from the al-Bukahri hadith that says:

> The people said, "O Allah's Messenger! Sallallahu-alaihi wasallam shall we acquaint the people with the good news?" He said, "Paradise has one hundred grades which Allah has reserved for the Mujahideen who fight in his cause, and the distance between the Heaven and the Earth. So when you ask Allah [for something], ask for Al Firdous which is the middle [best] and the highest part of Paradise. And above it [Al Firdous Paradise] is the throne of the Benificent [i.e., Allah] and from it gushes forth the rivers of Paradise."[47]

OBL expects his rewards in Paradise and literally abandons all comfort in order to meet this literal translation of the Qur'an.[48]

AQ maintains its Afghanistan-Pakistan border refuge as a global political and strategic militancy headquarters. This core group of ideologues, al-Zawahiri, Mullah Omar, and al-Libi, who operate with and near OBL himself, are the critical Center of Gravity. Kill them and the ideology starts to die with them as they become memories and not activists.

In the al-Qaeda Senior Leadership (AQSL) under the two senior members sit the seven to ten members of the AQ Command Council (aka Ruling Council) and the political committee that "points [the commander] to meet his operational goals and his politics . . ."[49] This council is made up of OBL and al-Zawahiri and also includes members of the Taliban, TeT, or any other organization in direct or indirect communication with AQ. The AQ Military Committee serves as the command and liaison arm of the organization. The first generation was run by Shubi Abu Sitta, also known as Mohammed Atef or by his nickname Abu Hafs al-Masri. Abu Sitta, a former Egyptian police officer who joined in Afghanistan after meeting OBL in the anti-Soviet war, led the AQ internal security mission and the mobile training team that went to Somalia in 1993 to assist militants that opposed the UN and American humanitarian mission there. In 1996 he assumed command of the Military Committee after the original commander, Abu Ubaida al-Banshiri, accidentally drowned in Lake Victoria in Uganda. Atef was killed in an American bombing of Kabul on November 16, 2001, and AQ international military operations were thrown into disarray until Khalid Sheik Mohammed, an old hand with almost a decade of terrorist operations under his belt, took command. His capture in 2003 led to AQ shifting from direct planning and involvement of international operations to relying on the self-starting terror operations. However, AQSL has always maintained their role as final corporate arbiter in all external operations so that the propaganda machine is ready to fully exploit the mission's results. Killing the senior leadership, particularly bin Laden, would force a dramatic reevaluation of their strategic goals.

The failure of the Bush administration to appreciate the strategic important of killing bin Laden and to underestimate the strength of his personal impact on a global terror movement is almost as great an error as Bush's inexplicable invasion of Iraq. Leaving aside the arguments about the best way to do it, what if bin Laden is eventually killed? For OBL it is no matter. In 2003 he predicted that his hour would come:

> Before I end, I incite myself and my believing brothers to jihad by the words: "And most surely this year I will lead my steed and hurl it and my soul at one of the targets. So, O my Lord, if my demise has come, then let it not be upon a bier draped with green mantles . . . But let my grave be an eagle's belly, its resting place in the sky's atmosphere perched among eagles. And I become a martyr, dwelling amongst a band, attacked in a level mountain pass of the earth.[50]

OBL is pragmatic enough to factor in defeats and setbacks. Where he miscalculates is in estimating his own importance, particularly since his force of personality is all that is motivating the members of AQ. To create the NIC, the Takfiris must harness the ability to create, exploit, and empathize with populist anger from the date seller on the Muslim street up to the Gulf states' billionaire admirers, where the Takfiri militants speak loudest. The biggest megaphone they have is the occasional audiotape of bin Laden. When he speaks, the whole world listens. In claiming that they seek revolutionary change for the betterment of Islam they require more and more ruthlessness from the West to validate their worldview. Absent this justification, their words fall flat as more and more identify with the victims of their attacks, particularly when they are Muslims. To harness that anger the militants need a clear and decisive leader. If the Takfiris were actually working for the benefit of Islam it would be quickly apparent and could theoretically have an upward effect on public opinion; however, the militants are sworn not to work toward any goal that does not include establishing the ummah under the New Islamic Caliphate and excommunication, then death, to all Muslims who do not comply. Unfortunately for the militants, the heart and soul of their organization will leave them upon OBL's death unless the next leader can surpass the twenty-year record of the man from Jeddah. To top the "marvel" that was 9/11 and make America jump will require something more potent than hijacked aircraft—it will require a WMD and its immediate application in such a way as to make 9/11 look comforting to the victims.

There is little that will stop the leadership of AQ from continuing their insurgency until they achieve their goals or acquire the weapons to make their political dreams come true. This poem, recited by OBL on videotape after the 9/11 attacks' success, illustrates the depth of the personal commitment and madness we must defeat:

> I witness that against the sharp blade
> They always faced difficulties and stood together . . .
> When the darkness comes upon us and we are bit by a
> Sharp tooth, I say . . .
> "Our homes are flooded with blood and the tyrant
> Is freely wandering in our homes" . . .
> And from the battlefield vanished
> The brightness of swords and the horses . . .
> And over weeping sounds now
> We hear the beats of drums and rhythm . . .
> They are storming his forts
> And shouting: "We will not stop our raids
> Until you free our lands" . . . [51]

For all of his lyricism and poetry, OBL is the tip of the spear and once he is broken the organization will become highly susceptible to a major counter-ideological campaign. Should he remain alive, the links between Islam and his corrupt interpretation should be shown the light of day. Once that is shown, the Ummah will shun him and his adherents like they shun Satan.

10.

CIRCUIT BREAKER Strategy:
The Total Shutdown of al-Qaeda

. . . attaining one hundred victories in one hundred battles
is not the pinnacle of excellence. Subjugating the enemy's army
without fighting is the true pinnacle of excellence.
—SUN TZU

THE METRIC OF what is a success in the war against the al-Qaeda organization has been a remarkably changing bar. Most people would be satisfied if the organization were to disappear off the face of the earth. That is an admirable goal and fully achievable. The entire premise of this missive has been that the ideology of AQ is the sole pillar left to them. Absent the admiration and logistical support, however small it is in comparison to our mammoth network of butter, bullets, and bombs, AQ requires the acceptance of the people in the remote districts of Afghanistan and Pakistan to keep their refuge. This needs to end. If it is done correctly, the organization itself will dwindle down to the few "irreconcilables" who will have to be hunted and killed.

But with the popular support of AQ, the Taliban, the well-armed Tarik-e-Taliban Pakistan, al-Shabaab in Somalia, and AQ franchises in Iraq, Lebanon, Europe, North Africa, and the Arabian Peninsula the problem remains a difficult nut to crack.

We need al-Qaeda-inspired insurgencies to come to a quick end, as it did in Iraq. There has been too much emphasis in American combat strategy on killing or capturing the individual cells, instead of breaking the sinews of the neo-Salafist Takfiris' ideology. American war policy has been focusing on capturing and killing an individual termite instead of fumigating the entire house.

The terrorist hunters who need to dismantle al-Qaeda networks have tried every TV-oriented approach to countering them, from sniping, to drones, to laser-guided bombs dropped from B-2 bombers flying twenty-four hours a day from Missouri. We should not be focusing on just the "Jack Bauer" or "James Bond" aspects of hunting the individual cells.

The adoption of massive military force to deal with this asymmetric threat, the evisceration of street-level intelligence because of the war in Iraq, and a near-visceral fear of embracing the cultural respect for the Muslim people have yielded the most important battlefield to al-Qaeda, the battlefield of the mind. A Gallup poll of the Middle East notes: "The people of these Islamic cultures say that the West pays little attention to their situation, does not attempt to help these countries, and makes few attempts to communicate or to create cross-cultural bridges."[1] If our strategic communications and influence operations since 9/11 have been any reflection of that statement, then the War on Terrorism will remain precisely what it is today, a war without end.

It is time to employ the national bullhorn, shouting to the rafters, hourly, that America rejects loudly and forcefully the opinion that we seek to divide and humiliate Islam. It is time to convene conferences and debates, like the CNN International Doha Debates, where Muslims who are concerned and who want to be reassured can come out and speak to a real American (preferably one who speaks their language) and talk themselves out of AQ's ideological grip.

In 2008 I was invited to speak on the Islam Channel, a London-based satellite channel where I discussed the errors of the Bush administration resorting to torture. During my discussion I expressed my regret and disapproval. I also stressed that Americans actually respect Muslims and we seek common ground. The moderator was stunned. He told me that I was the first American with government service who spoke Arabic to ever visit them. In today's arena of militant risk there should be a U.S. spokesperson hired to be at the disposal of the Islam Channel and others like it every day. We cannot defeat AQ in the battle of ideas unless we are on the battlefield.

It Pays to Be a Winner—
a National Security Policy That Could Work

MATT ARMSTRONG, AN expert on public diplomacy, defines the American strategic communications needs on his blog, Mountain Runner:

Public diplomacy, back when it was simply called public affairs . . . is
the full spectrum psychological struggle of the early Cold War and not
the hearts and minds campaigns of Beers and Hughes. Public diplomacy must be re-framed as direct or indirect engagement of foreign
audiences to further America's national security.[2]

The prevention and combating of terrorism is a particularly pressing
need for U.S. security. We are in a fight where we need to tackle the enemy
and damage him as quickly as possible. The neglect of real public diplomacy
in the ideological war has become a selling point in al-Qaeda recruitment.
There is virtually no opposing viewpoint to their radicalization regime.

We cannot continue to keep trying to kill or capture a few individuals
while accidentally massacring thousands of civilians and pushing innocent
people through stereotyped human dragnets that alienate a billion people
and make the other 5 billion question our sanity. Farhana Ali, a specialist on
terrorism at the Rand Corporation, believes "the policy of capture and kill
has been ineffective . . . In the short term, it's effective . . . but in the long
term, new groups emerge."[3]

America needs to fight smarter instead of trying harder and throwing dollars into an endless hole. A change in course on this front is critical. The
counter-terrorism effort should be rooted in what Armstrong calls the full spectrum mission, for a wide variety of reasons. The most important is that it is an
insurance policy for the protection of the world, our citizens, and our soldiers.

Operationally America's Diplomatic, Intelligence, Military, and Economic
(DIME) forces need the benefits it could provide us. America's DIME assets
need:

• Cooperation on the streets of the nations we occupy or assist.
• To change the perception of mistrust to trust by our own deeds.
• To demonstrate our goodwill rather than force goodwill at the end of a
  gun or by threat of force.
• To separate terrorists from Islam.

We must change our vocabulary and learn the word "tolerance." There is
always opposition to something new. Many will find a proposal to go after
the minds of the Muslim world trivial and may complain it will limit resources
needed for the soldiers in the field. To those who cannot support a well-
grounded principle of diplomacy, I say support the shooters in this equation.

Our intelligence assets and military forces need the information gleaned from our goodwill and honesty. Our homeland security agencies, including Immigration, Customs Enforcement, the Border Patrol, and the Secret Service, need all of the long-range intelligence and cooperation from allied countries. The FBI needs investigative cooperation from our allies. These agencies and others are critical in our fight against the extremists.

By ignoring the enemy's ideology, we allow them to recruit freely. Once recruited, people radicalize into terrorists.

CIRCUIT BREAKER:
Striking Hard to End al-Qaeda

THE DEMISE OF the world's most capable terrorist group has been denied for over twenty years. If we take the steps proposed here to break the links to Islam, al-Qaeda can be damaged to the point of incapacitation in less than twenty-four months.

The heart of a new U.S. counter-terrorism strategy should consolidate the diplomatic, intelligence, military, and economic resources of every aspect of the U.S. government into a single concentrated strategic communications and operations campaign called CIRCUIT BREAKER.

CIRCUIT BREAKER is an aggressive global counter-ideological warfare strategy combined with diplomacy, intelligence, and precise use of combat power. Unlike current operations, CIRCUIT BREAKER first targets the ideology and then uses counter-ideology programs such as amnesty, repatriation, and rehabilitation for those who wish to leave militancy.

For the irreconcilables the mission to capture or kill them goes on.

If we invert the Hard Power–Soft Power formula and use every aspect of American resolve to emphasize the corruption of AQ and restore America as the beacon of hope for the world, then the information and support we have been denied will flow once again. Victory could come with dramatic speed if we successfully remove the population base of support from AQ.

If believable and truthful images of our goal are projected in a manner to reach the street level across the globe, only then will America have any meaningful impact on the opinions of the support base of AQ and their allies. The world needs to know precisely what we are doing and why we are doing it. We seek a cooperative alignment where our strong values can be deemed acceptable while we stress tolerance and work toward abolishing xenophobia in our own country.

We cannot allow into our dialogue harmful terms such as "Radical Islam," "Islamic Extremism," and "Islamic Fundamentalism" or ignorant insults such as "Islamofascism." When speaking about AQ, we must brand them a criminal cult with no validity in Islam.

BRINGING ALL ASPECTS OF AMERICAN
POWER DOWN ON THE LINK

THE CIRCUIT BREAKER campaign relies on every aspect of international governmental power being brought to bear on one single focus: breaking the link between Islam and al-Qaeda. Whether it is farm credits, radio broadcasts, or law enforcement cooperation, the entire might of the American communications and financial power will be focused on removing the radical ideology of AQ from the Muslim world. Unlike the Bush doctrine, this policy is principally based on communications and cooperation, not military force.

CIRCUIT BREAKER is designed to be a high-concentration, sustained push to incite such a global ideological backlash against al-Qaeda and other religious militant groups acting throughout the Muslim world that it will be as positively well known as the phrase "War on Terrorism" was negatively known.

The CIRCUIT BREAKER plan is not without risks, but they are limited by the level of transparency and honesty in our communications. We have no intention of forming an Orwellian "Ministry of Truth"—eight years of that was more than enough to cure us of trying to manipulate facts. It is a strategy to use what we already know in a coherent fashion to damage and defeat our enemy. It is a coalition of like entities facilitated by financial and ideological support from a coalition of governments.

There will be no need to infringe on civil liberties. CIRCUIT BREAKER is not a data-mining project and has no need to conduct surveillance or target the American public. It will totally focus, with intense laserlike precision, on the tenuous claims by AQ and neo-Salafists, on their legitimacy at every level.

CIRCUIT BREAKER IS CRITICAL
TO THE MILITARY AND INTELLIGENCE MISSION

THE MILITARY HAS refocused much of its global core combat skills at engaging in what is known as counter-insurgency (COIN). COIN is the "military, paramilitary, political, economic, psychological, and civic actions taken by a government to defeat insurgency."[4]

However, the Department of Defense is now engaged in a theater-wide

Irregular Warfare (IW) campaign that has both COIN and general-purpose forces. IW "encompasses operations in which the joint force conducts protracted regional and global campaigns against state and non-state adversaries to subvert, coerce, attrite, and exhaust adversaries rather than defeat them through direct conventional military confrontation." The core aspect of irregular operations emphasizes "winning heart and minds" by gaining the support of the population promoting the local friendly government and "eroding adversary control, influence, and support."[5] In an attempt to achieve its contribution to the strategic rationale for continued operations IW has become a hybrid of civil-military operations in the absence of sustained civilian and non-governmental agency support. The most salient component of IW is that in this form of conflict the civilian population and their support is the focus of nearly all operations. People come first.

There are at present many organizations performing information and influence warfare activities for the U.S. armed forces. Some are oriented to battlefield and intelligence activities, others the collection of data and data mining. The army's 1st Information Operations Command (Land) was organized in 1995. It maintains the Information Dominance Center, an entity that was created by the U.S. Army's Intelligence and Security Command (INSCOM) at Fort Belvoir, Virginia. This program created and sponsored the "Able Danger" project, which helped collect the first quantities of data on AQ. The navy has a Center for Information Dominance at NAS Corry Station in Pensacola, Florida, and the U.S. Air Force at its Information Warfare Battlelab in San Antonio, Texas. The psychological operations capability of the U.S. armed forces is also a component of the current information warfare effort.

Specialized battlefield and strategic psychological operations (PSYOP) assets exist at the USA Civil Affairs and Psychological Operations Command (USACAPOC). Although there is a broad capability to conduct influence operations targeting the local populace and support civil affairs and Provisional Reconstruction Teams activities, the PSYOP units are fully involved with bringing some measure of success to the Iraq and Afghan battlefields.

Each of these entities and agencies creates its own themes and meets tasked objectives for the Strategic Influence mission as ordered. They are experts in their fields and have performed admirably, in particular the U.S. Army PSYOP teams; they could almost be credited for convincing the five hundred thousand Iraqi army soldiers not to show up for the invasion of Iraq in 2003.

However, as instruments of national power we should eschew having numerous intelligence and influence organizations operating on individual missions that do not help the coalition focus on the most important of goals: breaking the link between AQ and the entire Muslim world.

This mission requires centralized planning, management, and oversight. Once the master plan is formulated, then organizations from the DIME assets to our allies can coordinate under one body to meet the goals of the National Command Authority. The mission of CIRCUIT BREAKER is to ease the burden of all IW stressors on the commanders, soldiers, and intelligence officers in the field simply by removing AQ's base of support.

TAKE FIVE BIG STEPS

MANY OF THE components of CIRCUIT BREAKER have been proposed, investigated, and even endorsed by former members of al-Qaeda and militant ideologues as the right way to hurt them. Yet no coherent national or global strategy was effected. Here are five quick steps we can take to implement the program:

1. **Appoint a new counter-ideology warfare director and give him an office:** The mission to attack AQ counter-ideologically requires an intelligence war fighter with the academic and management credentials who can harness the energy of the DIME assets assigned to the task. Saudi Arabia has a commander of counter-ideological warfare; so must we. We must establish a temporary government organization to coordinate America's informational influence operations on a global scale and bring the counter-ideological messaging down to the street level. A National Counter-Ideology Strategy Agency (NCISA) would develop and order the propagation of the U.S. government's strategic communications, apart from public diplomacy. With the elimination of the Under Secretary of State for Public Diplomacy and Public Affairs a position damaged by scandal, the functions of the NCISA will help both the Department of Defense and Department of State in developing a comprehensive, unified anti-ideology message and strategy.

2. **Create a special CIDOW Task Force from existing assets:** A mission-specific counter-ideology operations and warfare entity under the NCISA should be formed in a rapid fashion, no more than ninety days. The organi-

zation, which could be called the Joint Counter-Ideology Executive (JCIE), should be formed from whatever assets the U.S. government, academia, and allies can bring to bear. A global information dissemination mission could commence within 180 days of start.

3. **Commission the private sector:** Private public relations, media and influence companies, research centers, marketing agencies, and academics should be tendered contracts to sponsor communicating the American message to the world. Some specialized companies that have shown success in military and intelligence support will work with the NCISA to help craft master messaging for the civil affairs component of service operations. All awardees will be tasked to produce media that give al-Qaeda no chance to successfully refute the messaging in either the real world or cyberspace. The drumbeat of commercials, blog ads, viral video, music videos, and public service announcements will work hand in hand with concrete government, diplomatic, and academic activities to show that America, for all of its faults, means well and is here to assist in ending the spread of bin Ladenism.

4. **Launch CIRCUIT BREAKER:** CIRCUIT BREAKER is a full-scale public strategic communications operation. With the exception of the traditional military and intelligence operations, the program will be known to the public and will orient itself in such a way as to earn the public's support. AQ may be able to claim that the program is funded and supported by the West, but in fact it is global and the main thrusts will come from the Muslim world. This will remove the stigma of being considered a "secret" program run by a few individuals from a back room. The public who believe in the message of hope and rejection of AQ will be asked to participate. Once the polls solidify into a clear negative for AQ, then they will be reframed as a failed organization with a corrupt mission and evil goal.

ITIRAD (PRONOUNCED "IT-TEE-RAAD") is the acronym that represents the operational components of CIRCUIT BREAKER. It is compromised of six steps that spell the Arabic word "opposition." Virtually all of the components of the project have been laid out in previous chapters, but the major principles are:

- *Incite the debate.* The Muslim world should be encouraged and empowered to take a clear stand in protecting the true meaning of the Qur'an. The issue should be brought right out to the world media, that the

Muslim world and the West stand together and are willing to debate and, if necessary, shout down the terrorists in any forum.

- *Terror cult.* AQ is best described as a global religious death cult. A clear distinction between the one and a half billion peaceful Muslims and the comparatively small number of the cultist supporters of al-Qaeda should be stressed and reemphasized to the world. AQ is a cult led by a charismatic leader fostering a corruption of a mainstream religion for political gain on earth. OBL has sullied the true words and meanings of traditional Islam. This assertion can be made by both the Western and Muslim world allies.

- *Inform the Islamic street.* Virtually all aspects of the American information campaign to inform the Islamic world of our activities and gain cooperation and support have been a horrible failure. A new diplomatic, academic, and private effort, based on good faith, goodwill, and common goals in defeating militant fanaticism, must be inspired to start from within the Muslim world with global financial and political assistance.

- *Reframe terrorism.* Terrorism needs to be placed back in its proper classification as a tactic used by lawless entities, and can be dealt with more effectively with counter-intelligence and law enforcement and a small amount of military force. The "War on Terrorism" has officially ended and a "war on al-Qaeda" needs to be declared until the terrorists are rejected by the Muslim world.

- *Aggressive counter ideological warfare.* A new CIDOW director will take the lead in creating the policies and operations necessary to inspire a global movement against al-Qaeda. Outside of counter-insurgency countries (Afghanistan and Iraq), large-scale military operations emphasizing kinetic warfare are best reserved for emergencies and play a supporting role in meeting the diplomatic goals of the United States and support activities outside the scope of the intelligence community.

- *Dominate the entire information spectrum.* Al-Qaeda currently has better ability to spread their claims in the emerging world than the entirety of the U.S. armed forces and State Department. The global community, led by the American diplomatic, military, and intelligence apparatus, needs to retool and finance a sharply honed system for offensive information distribution to the emerging world.

5. **Strike while hot.** When all of the pieces of CIRCUIT BREAKER are in place they will strike together and apply sustained pressure through mes-

sage dominance until it is clear to all that the ideology of AQ is going to be broken, not just challenged. We will not break the will to fight the irreconcilables, but we will remove the rest of the world from their bench.

America and its assets will not engage AQ in a debate on Islam; we will state our case on their illegitimacy. Islam has rejected their justifications of having an Islamic base and we will assist in the dissemination of that opinion. If anything, we want to convince the Muslim world that AQ is a cult and not associated with Islam.

The international components of the campaign could be assembled swiftly if integrity, professionalism, and a respectful mind-set about the reality of the task ahead are foremost parts of planning. Finding the correct mix of information that fits one's public or propagandistic narrative in the media cycle will exact a challenge. We can start with the templates the Muslim world has used successfully in countering AQ for the last six years.

Will the Muslim World Listen to Us?

IT HAS BEEN argued that Muslims won't accept a message from America or may be reticent about its truthfulness. America is a nation with between 5–6 million Muslims. We have more than enough multilingual representatives. Just because the AQ enemy is considered Muslim does not mean America should have no voice. America has a moral justification and a righteous call for justice that trumps any sensitivity toward religion.

We cannot separate ourselves from the struggle simply because a large part of our nation is Christian. America is a nation built on values that have merit and that the world wants to hear those. We need the combined forces of all parties to combat this problem. We will help enable the voices in Islam to present their message, but that will not mean we do not have a message ourselves.

Take Back America:
Change Anti-U.S. Perceptions

CIRCUIT BREAKER WILL provide for an opportunity to spread the message that a new era for reconciliation and cooperation with the Muslim world has arrived. America and its values are no threat to Islam or to its culture. Our enemy is the cult of al-Qaeda and its spiritual followers. This is a message the world needs to hear daily, loudly, and clearly. In the war of ideas, al-Qaeda and its viral messengers need to be shouted down.

America needs to re-engage using CIRCUIT BREAKER as its principal weapon. With AQ ideologically under attack and flailing to defend themselves, the mission can free up the military's ability to hunt and neutralize this group, once and for all.

Pushing the American Story Down to the al-Qaeda Street

AMERICA'S RE-EMBRACE OF its fair-broker nature could be publicized in a massive effort via television, the Internet, radio broadcasts, podcasts, and live streaming to the world through a newly supplemented Voice of America (VOA). VOA should be expanded and broadcast 24/7/365 beyond its current forty-four languages to over one hundred, micro-targeting even the smallest listenership. Its mission will be to push the American vision deeper into the emerging world's national and regional languages and seek common ground and respect for the American perspective. It will be ordered to establish rigorous rules for journalistic ethics and objectivity on par with the BBC. Its new mandate is to become the single most reliable source of news in the world and a conduit for the world's opinion.

The Single Best Tool
in the American Arsenal Are Three Video

THE UNITED STATES has had the best tool to win the war against al-Qaeda in its possession all along. The U.S. Department of State runs a video in its waiting rooms called *I Am an American*. The video is an extended version of the public-service commercial produced by the Ad Council. Just ten days after the 9/11 attacks the Ad Council launched the video campaign using thirty-second and sixty-second spots of American citizens, of all different races, creeds, and ethnic origins. The ad is simple and stunning in its ability to send a simple yet powerful message: the terrorists did not hit a country, they struck a people, and the people are not the image the terrorists portray.

Karen Hughes, the State Department Under Secretary for Public Diplomacy and Public Affairs, may not have been the best person to manage changing the image of the United States (a task made impossible by the actions of her boss, George W. Bush), but she did create one of the single most potent weapons in the American arsenal. In conjunction with the Disney company, the Department of State produced a seven-minute video called *Welcome: Portraits of America*. Hughes got it right when she said, "This video conveys a clear message of welcome and quietly communicates our greatest strength, the great spirit and diversity of our people."[6]

The final piece of messaging was a video developed by a non-profit called Business for Diplomatic Action. Their Web site states that they "enlist the U.S. business community in actions to improve the standing of America in the world with the goal of once again seeing America admired as a global leader and respected as a courier of progress and prosperity for all people."[7]

This is a worthy goal and Business for Diplomatic Action has been operating under the public radar for years, sponsoring conferences and creating dialogue that needs to become the model of the efforts CIRCUIT BREAKER hopes to harness. It is completely transparent and difficult to counteract. Bridge building and outreach to the rest of the world is what is missing from the President's counter-terrorism options.

The Business for Diplomatic Action's video, called *I Am America*, is now shown in embassy waiting rooms around the world. I have personally witnessed people from all parts of the globe watching this video in rapt fascination, nudging each other when Americans of a similar cultural background are showcased saying, "I am America." Like the other two videos, it is powerful. America should back organizations like these in a big way.

These videos eclipse any activity that has been undertaken to date. Combined, they are the most powerful tools in the American arsenal. The only drawback has been that to see them one must go to a Customs and Border Patrol entry point or an embassy waiting room or watch them on YouTube.

The best part about these media masterpieces is that they are not seen as propaganda in the classic sense. They are honest, well-focused presentations of the real America. In fact, there is no real need to make up or create fantastic images about AQ or America. Both sides of this battle are so clearly definable that engaging in a truth campaign is more than acceptable. Truth damages AQ more than it does America in any matter, and the facts support our mission. Conservative columnist Max Boot states:

I agree we shouldn't engage in "blatant propaganda." If it's too blatant it's self defeating. But what's wrong with skillful, not-so-blatant propaganda? Not only is there nothing wrong with it, it is an essential task at which we are now failing. We cannot afford unilateral disarmament in the battle of ideas.[8]

Yes, these videos may be subject to cruel ridicule on the Web with amateur take-offs, but the people who see them understand that there is a difference between what they are being told and what they see. Once we have taken back the popularity of the American individual, then the message, coupled with deeds of the current administration, will filter up in popularity as well.

Media Domination: Buy It; Own It; Disseminate It 24/7/365

THE UNITED STATES has the greatest media machine in the world and al-Qaeda knows it. Often the militants blame their lack of communication on the domination of America in the global media. Despite the misgivings and conspiracy theory, the American public broadcast system has considerable reach. However, there is no need to use those assets within the United States. We seek to reach all other global media with the message against AQ.

The CIRCUIT BREAKER program should pay market prices for media spots in virtually every third-world country to the point of total information dominance. When the television in Peshawar comes on, the United States should have a presence for at least five minutes of every hour. The message needs to be pushed to the street, and satellite television, radio, a Web presence, and local broadcast television should be our mediums. No need to distribute matchbooks with OBL's photo on them (an effort effected by the FBI in the 1990s) when newspaper advertisements, magazine spreads, and every other visual and audio medium in the world could propagate the message—whether it be our values or countering the AQ media machine. CIRCUIT BREAKER seeks to be there "firstest with the mostest."

New Framing: Counter-Terrorist with Global Justice

AMNESTY INTERNATIONAL HAS an outstanding motto and narrative for fighting the War on Terrorism. Their "Counter Terror with Justice" campaign is an excellent use of the core idea that America seeks to project.

The information war against al-Qaeda needs to be completely reworked into a strategic, multiagency narrative that restores honor and credibility to America's word and banishes the legacy of the Bush administration's failures. More important, it needs to restore America's image and damage al-Qaeda where they can least afford it, among the people.

We must work to remove that popular support, but not one Civil Affairs Team or humanitarian project at a time. We must make a massive ideological, political, and humanitarian push to meet all of the needed objectives nearly simultaneously, first in the Afghanistan-Pakistan region, then throughout the rest of the Islamic world.

Get New Spokespeople

ONE OF THE biggest problems over the last few years has been American spokespersons.

The President is Public Diplomat in Chief, but President Obama is more than that; he is a skilled orator who has the ability to make people believe his words. The best tool in our quiver, next to the great character of the American people themselves, is President Obama.

Matt Armstrong, a specialist in strategic communications, demurs, as he believes the problem is a matter of a lack of synchronization between the White House and Defense and State departments. We must limit or eliminate our combat commanders' getting on Al Jazeera to explain just how great our combat operations are for the Arab world. We must realize that our military forces are seen outside of the United States as a killing machine, no matter how many civil affairs programs we run. The words of the man with the gun will always be suspect. We can mitigate this by making our government spokespeople come from the public diplomacy arena and take our combat commanders off camera.

Our public communicators must take the challenge that was offered by Islam Channel, Al Arabiya, and Al Jazeera and go speak directly to the Muslim world, on their terms, answering their questions at any time of day or night. This will have rapid good results, and over time the wounds of distrust will heal.

Mr. Armstrong is right when he notes that the biggest megaphone today may be in the hands of the secretary of defense rather than the president simply because bombs are louder than our current ideological campaign, which is non-existent.

Build Democracy

IN ADDITION, DEMOCRATIC support to political parties must not be limited but expanded using non-governmental organization (NGOs) and political support agencies. Support for Islamic political groups has polled to be strong, and the United States must support Islamic participation in democratic elections. AQ fears democratic-based Islamic movements greatly and targets democracy in virtually all communications. How can democracy be incompatible with Islam when the Prophet Mohammed allowed his first successor for Caliph to be chosen democratically? When America is disrespected globally, bin Laden wins a strategic victory. If America is respected and a fair arbiter of democracy in the eyes of his potential recruiting base, then AQ loses.

Encourage Interfaith Dialogue and Commonality

COUNTERING EXTREMIST IDEOLOGY need not be just a Muslim activity. More to the point, it benefits all religions and peoples, even secular and agnostic ones, to explore the voices of other faiths and devotions. AQ has made it patently clear that they detest the very idea that Muslims have communications with non-Muslims. This is a component of the al-Wala' Wa al-Bara' philosophy—to hate all that is not their interpretation of Islam.

Sheikh al-Habib Ali al-Jifri, the founder of the Tabah Foundation, a center for tolerance and understanding in the traditional Muslim world, notes how dialogue can assist in the moderating effect on all religions:

> We're now studying how we can look at places like Indonesia and the African continent and identify the fundamentalist churches and imams that preach there . . . Continuing to be angry won't work . . . Nor is the solution exclusively with the Muslims. The leaders of other religions in the Muslim world must be engaged as well.[9]

The Tabah Foundation sponsors a program called *Kalimat Siwaa*, or a Common Word. It is an initiative to deliver a message of understanding. All of the Tabah's foundation staff are Muslim scholars. Sheikh Jifri notes:

> . . . the West has done so much more to advance the goals we're working toward in the Common Word . . . In Europe, individuals who are

divisive or incite hatred are looked upon as fanatical, but this is not so in our part of the world.[10]

To be sure, there are other more orthodox leading Muslims and members of the ulema that advocate al-Wala Wa al-Bara', such as Sheikh Abdulaziz al Rayyis of Saudi Arabia. But even he proposes moderation and dialogue. In the middle of his most impassioned speeches, Sheikh Rayyis foils the neo-Salafist concept of hiding behind al-Wala' Wa al-Bara', particularly when proponents espouse killing and speaking to other faiths:

> There is a difference between inviting to dialogue and inviting the unionization of the religions. If from the fact that dialog be they Jew or Christian (if the said Muslim is endowed with knowledge, convincing arguments and proofs), it is, in the said manner that Allah might be majestic be he, has advocated in his book by saying "call to the way of your Lord by wisdom and good exhortations—likewise debate them in a manner that is best."[11]

Propagate the Terrorists' Fitna

WE MUST PUSH AQ out of their comfort zone ideologically using all of the CIDOW options. AQ is a very sensitive organization when it comes to how they are perceived by their target audience. Accusations, based on facts and using persons who have rejected AQ, will incite a continuing backlash. Infighting will expose the organization to internal fissure, defections, and rapid withdrawal of public support even in areas where they dominate ideologically.

As has been noted before, the greatest weakness of AQ's religious militant ideology is any analytical dissection of their motives and political goals. AQ operates in an extremely shallow environment, and the deeper the analysis the more frightened they become. By assisting the Muslim world to challenge and publicly, repeatedly, and loudly reject the ideological basis of AQ, we will force the terrorists to defend themselves in such a way as to be detrimental to their community standing and freedom of operations.

CIRCUIT BREAKER will identify the core supporting organizations and personalities. They will be challenged as well, not by one person asking a question but by millions of questioners asking about their legitimacy and calling them back to traditional Islam.

The Metrics: Public Reaction
to al-Qaeda Presence

THE METRIC WE seek is the reaction of the neo-Salafist militants to the loss
of their public support base under withering communications dominance
during the CIRCUIT BREAKER period. In the short run they will most
likely try to be dismissive, but as the campaign pressures increase and push
down into their base of support they may lash out with violence. This, too,
will become a component of the strategy, as any negative activities they
perform will be rolled into the campaign quickly and immediately publicized, to their detriment. The goal is to dominate far faster than they can
respond.

Public buy-in will be reflected in polls and through civil watchdog groups
like Jihadica. Initially, AQ will ridicule and be dismissive. Like Abu Yahya al-
Libi when he bragged how we could best damage his organization, they do
not care about us or what we do (because they think we are not fast enough
to defeat them) but about their constituency. We must watch carefully the
terrorists' reactions to the messaging campaign and adjust it as AQ loses support.

AQ should be forced to come out into the open and "go public" to explain
exactly why they are not what America says. We should ensure that they never
have another easy go of it until they are destroyed. A clear sign of success is the
day that Osama bin Laden and his senior staff must issue videos or statements
directly responding to the messaging from CIRCUIT BREAKER.

It has been argued that Muslims won't accept a message from America or
may be reticent about its truthfulness. We cannot separate ourselves from
the struggle simply because a large part of our nation is Christian. America is
a nation with between 5–6 million Muslims who have not been called upon
to be the spokespeople of America. That must change.

America has a moral justification and a righteous call for justice. America
is a nation built on values that have merit and that the world wants to hear.
Just because the enemy is Muslim does not mean America should have no
voice. We need the combined forces of all parties to combat this problem. We
will help enable the voices in Islam to present their message, but that will not
mean we do not message ourselves.

We must keep the pressure on AQ not just through an appeal to freedom
and democracy but also by taking the messages of a peaceful traditional Islam, which embraces tolerance. We will use all of the tools of strategic com-

munications and a singular anti-AQ message. We will then hammer it, hammer it, hammer it into the global psyche that AQ is an illegitimate cult that must not be assisted and must be rejected. We must apply universal pressure. Not just American pressure or Saudi pressure or Christian pressure or even Muslim pressure, it will be a moral pressure from all sides that will continue until AQ breaks under the strain.

The time has come to reorient our diplomatic, intelligence, military, and economic agencies and those of like-minded allies to counter the ideology of hatred both *harder* and *smarter*. President Obama will have to be up to the task to reverse the backward slide or we will continue to assist bin Laden in accumulating victories.

Al-Qaeda is bankrupt both morally and ideologically. The missing component in the debate on their extremism is the broad-scale discussion of the truth of al-Qaeda's goals for Islam. Once publicly rejected, AQ members should be given the opportunity to repent and return to the fold for rehabilitation.

Target: Twenty-four Months to Break al-Qaeda

RECALL THAT THE al-Qaeda in Iraq organization saw their complete devolution occur in less than one year because their sponsors, the Sunnah insurgents, suddenly saw them as a greater threat than the U.S. Army. Al-Qaeda forced marriages into Sunnah families, attempted to impose Sharia law and their extremist interpretation of Islam, and tried to carve out a piece of their community as the Islamic State of Iraq. It was too much for the former regime loyalists who had become insurgents to endure, and they turned on al-Qaeda, first with their own weapons and then by inviting the Americans to help get rid of AQ.

To OBL, the events of 2008 in Iraq were not a matter of great importance. His star is rising in Afghanistan and Pakistan. AQ senior leadership and their new Pakistan force are reconstituting in the sanctuary of western Pakistan. Aligned with both the Afghan and Pakistani Taliban, AQ is gaining political allies in hopes of destabilizing that nation and working with its allies to secure nuclear weapons. Yet the killing portion of the game is simple but cannot effect a victory without defeat of the ideology, which buoys their motivation for combat. To paraphrase Mao, as every potential terrorist is like a fish in the ocean, the ideological buy-in of a religious justification for bin

Laden's Jihad by the Islamic world is the water. In this instance the ocean must be drained.

We can defeat al-Qaeda in two years or we will lose over the next decade. If CIRCUIT BREAKER is applied across the entirety of the strategic communications spectrum, particularly in supporting the battlefield nations of the Muslim world, AQ will be so disrupted that its entire mission will be at a crossroads. Supporters will be forced to choose to continue to operate with the Muslim world crashing down upon them or isolate their field operatives worldwide to the point that they cannot operate without being captured. Given the right resources and expertise, we can make the entire Islamic world turn on al-Qaeda in the exact same manner that they experienced in Iraq.

Let us tackle the source of the problem but not forget who started this fight. Had the September 11 attacks not occurred and the window to the dark recesses of the souls of wicked men not been opened, we would never have found ourselves where we are today. This conflict must end and it can no longer be led by guns. The leaders in the struggle exist and have always been with us. Often they were ignored or drowned out in our own ignorance. It takes men and women like Dr. Khaled Abo El Fadl who succinctly brought to light the evil of AQ with his typical eloquence:

> I am fighting for the soul and identity of Islam itself. There's no question that the extremists and puritans want to be the only representatives of Islam. They want to be the ones with the 800-number to God, who can tell you what God wants and what Islam is and that's the beginning and the end.[12]

Epilogue:
The Real Face of 9/11

IT WAS A clear morning with a crystal blue sky. A twenty-three-year-old American graduate of Queens College was on his way to work. A former high school football player, he held a job as a research assistant at Rockefeller University. He wanted to be a doctor and spent the day at the university. At night he worked part-time as an Emergency Medical Technician (EMT). He also was a New York City Police cadet. About the time he would have been on the number 7 train the first aircraft smashed into the World Trade Center. He did not return home that night.

Worried, his uncle went to his office and found that he had never shown up for work. He had no reason to be near the towers that day, but his parents knew he could have seen the attack from the train traveling from Queens to Manhattan. It would have been in his nature to rush right over to help. He was the all-American boy.

Some weeks after his disappearance, the FBI was said to have questions for this man. After all, he was an American of Pakistani origin and seemed to fit the profile of the nineteen hijackers. In addition, the neighbors started to talk about the coincidence of his disappearance and the attacks. One day, law enforcement officers showed up and asked about him and the sudden disappearance of the chemistry major. However, no one who knew him doubted what had happened. The boy had somehow seen the attack and had gone to help. Still, the talk continued about the missing student and terrorism.

Mohammad Salman Hamadani, known as Sal, the all-American boy with a dog named Ulysses and a motorcycle with the license plate "Yung Jedi," was found six months later in the debris of the World Trade Center by a recovery team. He was found buried under the debris of the North Tower with his EMT trauma kit next to him. Though he had been suspected of being involved in the plot, he had, in fact, gone to the site and died doing what he could for the victims.

God had chosen the moment, the place, and the time for him to enter Paradise. The Prophet Mohammed said:

> The best of the Shuhada' [martyrs] are those who fight in the first rank, and do not turn their faces away until they are killed. They will have the pleasure of occupying the highest dwellings in Paradise. Your Lord will smile at them, and whenever your Lord smiles upon any of his slaves, that person will not be brought to account.

Mohammad Salman Hamadani fought in the first rank and like a real martyr, not like the cowards who slaughtered thousands—he gave his life so that others could live. Through his inspiring story, the real face of the Muslim world was shown by his bravery on 9/11. He showed that neither love nor humanity was defeated on September 11 or March 11 or July 7 or November 26 or the anniversary of so many other deaths from this one incident.

With the true face of a Muslim who was heroic and compassionate at the same time, the goal of the al-Qaeda terrorists, to destroy love of life, hope, and true love of God, failed. Each of these acts of terror by criminals and cultists is designed to destroy the human spirit. Each one has had the opposite effect. They have galvanized the surviving victims, their families, their nation, and the world to see terrorism for what it truly is: cowards using fear to influence other human beings. . . . In the end the terrorists influence nothing.

So let us start the great debate on an international, interfaith scale. We now must begin the discussion about Osama bin Laden, his philosophy, his ideology, and the fate of the souls of his followers. Particularly in Islam, the question to be asked is if these are true men of God, wayward children to be brought back into the fold, or followers of the Satanic soul of one man. Let the debate begin.

Notes

1: FROM TRAGEDY TO TRIUMPH

1. David McCullough, *John Adams* (New York: Simon and Schuster, 2001).
2. Frederick W. Kagan, "Spend Whatever It Takes on the War on Terror," *Los Angeles Times*, Monday, October 15, 2007, http://www.aei.org/publications/filter.all,pubID.26956/pub_detail.asp.
3. Steve Clemons, *The Daily Show*, on GAO Critique of Bush Anti-Terror War, "We Could Have Gotten Here by Doing Nothing," April 24, 2008, http://www.huffingtonpost.com/steve-clemons/daily-show-on-gao-critiqu_b_98457.html.
4. "Pakistan Is a Top 'Failed State,'" BBC, May 2, 2006, http://news.bbc.co.uk/2/hi/south_asia/4964934.stm.
5. Bruce Blair, "The Ultimate Hatred Is Nuclear," *New York Times*, October 21, 2001.
6. General David Petraeus, "The Future of the Alliance and the Mission in Afghanistan," February 8, 2009, http://smallwarsjournal.com/blog/2009/02/the-future-of-the-alliance-and/.
7. Senator Barack Obama, "Obama Unveils Comprehensive Strategy to Fight Global Terrorism Delivers Address on National Security, Woodrow Wilson Center," http://www.wilsoncenter.org/events/docs/obamaspo807.pdf.
8. Osama bin Laden, audiotape to Al Jazeera, CNN, November 2, 2004, http://edition.cnn.com/2004/WORLD/meast/11/01/binladen.tape/.
9. U.S. Department of Defense, *Quadrennial Roles and Missions Review Report*, http://www.defenselink.mil/news/Jan2009/QRMFinalReport_v26Jan.pdf.
10. Richard Wike, "Karen Hughes' Uphill Battle, Pew Global Attitudes Project," http://pewresearch.org/pubs/627/karen-hughes.
11. Assaf Moghadam, "The Salafi-Jihad as a Religious Ideology," *West Point CTC Sentinel* 1, no. 3 (February 2008).
12. Tim Winter (aka Dr. Abdal Hakim Murad), "Bin Laden's Violence Is a Heresy Against Islam," Council of American-Islamic Relations (CAIR), http://www.cair.com/AmericanMuslims/AntiTerrorism/BinLadensviolenceisaheresyagainstIslam.aspx.
13. The Islam Project, "Frontline: Muslims," Carnegie Foundation, http://www.islamproject.org/muslims/muslims.htm.

2: CRUSHED IN THE SHADOWS

1. Adil Zarif, "Why Death Is Not a Tragedy Anymore," *Pashtun Post*, http://www.pashtunpost.com/news.php?news=137&category=0.

2. Sahih Sunnah Abi Dawud.

3. Larry McShane, *New York Daily News*, http://www.nydailynews.com/news/2009/03/10/ 2009-03-10_guantanamo_bay_prisoners_justify_sept_11.html.

4. Jeff Israely, "Pope Tackles Faith and Terrorism," *Time*, September 13 2006, http://www. time.com/time/world/article/0,8599,1534640,00.html.

5. Fareed Zakaria, "He Kept Us Safe But . . . ," *Newsweek*, http://www.washingtonpost .com/wp-dyn/content/story/2009/01/19/ST2009011900824.html.

6. John McKinnon, "Bush to Highlight Success in War on Terrorism," *Wall Street Journal*, October 29, 2008, http://blogs.wsj.com/washwire/2008/10/29/bush-to-highlight-success-in war against terrorism/.

7. George W. Bush, transcript of "Remarks by the President to United States Troops at Wiesbaden Army Airfield," February 23, 2005, the White House, Office of the Press Secretary, http://germany.usembassy.gov/germany/bush_troops.html.

8. Brent Budowsky, "John McCain on Russia: Angry, Bellicose, Belligerent and Extreme," August 14, 2008, http://www.opednews.com/articles/John-McCain-on-Russia-Ang-by-Brent-Budowsky-080814-298.html.

9. Fareed Zakaria, "He Kept Us Safe, But . . . ," *Newsweek*, January 19, 2009, http://www .washingtonpost.com/wp-dyn/content/story/2009/01/19/ST2009011900824.html

10. U.S. Army statistics on combat dead of the Iraqi insurgents have not been accurately kept. The preponderance of insurgents were Iraqi former Ba'athists, who were occasionally called al-Qaeda by politicians. These statistics do not include the several thousand Iraqi resistance fighters and soldiers killed who were not al-Qaeda members.

11. Dr. Mohammed Ali Al-Hashimi, *The Ideal Islamic Society* (Riyadh: International Islamic Publishing House, 2007), 101.

12. 'Abdullah al-Athari, *Islamic Beliefs—a Brief Introduction to the Aqidah of the Ahl as Sunnah wal Jama'ah* (Riyadh: International Islamic Publishing House, 2004).

13. "Letter Exposes New Leader in al-Qa'ida High Command," September 29, 2006, Combating Terrorism Center at West Point, http://www.ctc.usma.edu/harmony/CTC-AtiyahLetter.pdf (downloaded on December 1, 2006).

3: COMPANIONS OF THE FIRE: THE CORRUPTED FRAMEWORK OF AL-QAEDA'S IDEOLOGY

1. Osama bin Laden, interview with al Jazeera, December 1998, in Bruce Lawrence, *Messages to the World: The Statements of Osama bin Laden* (London: Verso Press, 2005), p. 82.

2. Osama bin Laden, interview with Jamal Ismail, in Al Jazeera documentary, *Al-Qaeda: Destruction of the Base*, June 10, 1999.

3. Peter L. Bergen, *The Osama bin Laden I Know* (New York: Free Press, 2006).

4. Shaykh Seraj Kendricks, "Kharajites and Their Impact on Contemporary Islam," http:// www.sunnah.org/aqida/kharijites1.htm.

5. Helen Chapin Metz, ed., *Iraq: A Country Study* (Washington, DC: GPO for the Library of Congress, 1988), http://countrystudies.us/iraq/15.htm.

6. Kendricks, "Kharajites and Their Impact on Contemporary Islam."

7. Ian Richard Netton, ed., *Arabia and the Gulf: From Traditional Society to Modern States* (Beckenham, Kent, UK, Croom Helm Ltd., 1986) p. 23.

8. Ibid. p. 24.

9. Malcolm C. Peck, *The United Arab Emirates* (Boulder Colorado : Westview Press, 1986), p. 25.

10. Hugh N. Kennedy, *Armies of the Caliphs* (New York: Routledge, 2001), p. 163.

11. Carl F. Petry, ed., *The Cambridge History of Egypt: Islamic Egypt, 640–1517*, vol. 1 (Cambridge, UK: Cambridge University Press, 1999), p. 106.

12. "Qaramatians of Bahrain," First Ismaili Electronic Library and Database, http://ismaili. net/histoire/history05/history510.html.

13. M. A. Shabaan, *Islamic History* (Cambridge, UK: Cambridge University Press).

14. Yaroslav Trofimov, *The Siege of Mecca* (London: Penguin, 2007), p. 250.

15. 'Abdullah al-Athari, *Islamic Beliefs—a Brief Introduction to the Aqidah of the Ahl as Sunnah wal Jama'ah* (Riyadh: International Islamic Publishing House, 2004).

16. Khaled Abou El Fadl, *The Great Theft* (New York: HarperCollins, 2007), p. 75.

17. al-Athari, *Islamic Beliefs*, p. 64.

18. Christopher Henzel, "The Origins of al-Qaeda's Ideology: Implications for U.S. Strategy," *Parameters: U.S. Army War College Quarterly*, Spring 2005, pp. 66–80.

19. Ibid.

20. David Aaron, *In Their Own Words: Voices of Jihad* (Rand 2008), p. 51.

21. Sheihk Abdulaziz al Rayyis, audiotape of "Al-Wala' Wal al-Bara'."

22. Osama bin Laden, Interview with Taysir Alluni, Al Jazeera, October 21, 2001, in Bruce Lawrence, *Messages to the World*, p. 123.

23. Joas Wagemakers, "Abu Muhammad al-Maqdisi: A Counter-Terrorism Asset?" *West Point CTC Sentinel* 1, no. 6 (May 2008).

24. al Rayyis, "Al-Wala' Wa al-Bara'."

25. Bernard P. Lewis, "Jihad vs. Crusade," *Wall Street Journal*, September 27, 2001, http://www.opinionjournal.com/extra/?id=95001224.

26. Ahmed Y. Hassan, "Gunpowder Composition for Rockets and Cannon in Arabic Military Treatises in Thirteenth and Fourteenth Centuries," *International Committee for the History of Science and Technology Journal*, Vol. 9 (2003) found at http://www.history-science-technology .com/Articles/articles%202.htm.

27. Muhammad 'Abdus Salam Faraj, *Jihad: The Absent Obligation*, p. 28.

28. Ibid., p. 28.

29. U.S. Department of Justice, "UK/BM-5 Translation of the Al Qaeda Manual," http://www.usdoj.gov/ag/manualpart1_1.pdf.

30. William McCants and Jarret Brachman, *The Militant Ideology Atlas* (West Point, NY: Combating Terrorism Center, U.S. Military Academy, 2005).

31. Shaykh Muhammad Al-Akili, *Biography of Ibn al-Qayyim al-Jawziyya, Natural Healing with the Medicine of the Prophet* (Philadelphia: Pearl Publishing House, 2008).

32. Six points from Sira, Majmu'at at-Tawhid. http://www.worldofislam.info/ebooks/Al%20 Wala%20wal%20Bara%20part%202.pdf

33. Ibrahim Kalin, biography of Sayyid Jamal al-Din Muhammad b. Safdar al-Afghani, Center for Islam and Science, http://www.cis-ca.org/voices/a/afghni.htm.

34. McCants and Brachman, *The Militant Ideology Atlas*, p. 338.

35. Richard P. Mitchell, *Society of the Muslim Brothers* (Philadelphia: Oxford University Press, 1969), p. 232.

36. McCants and Brachman, *The Militant Ideology Atlas*, p. 335.

37. El Fadl, *The Great Theft*, p. 81.

38. Sayyid Qutb, *The America I Have Seen: In the Scale of Human Values* (Lahore: Kashf ul Shubat Publications, 2007).

39. Gilles Kepel, *Muslim Extremism in Egypt: The Prophet and the Pharaoh* (London: Saqi Books, 1985), p. 101.

40. Salafiyah Press, "References to the Doctrines of Sayyid Qutb in the Western Press," www.thenoblequran.com/sps/downloads/pdf/GRV070025.pdf.

41. Malcolm W. Nance, *The Terrorist Recognition Handbook*, 2nd ed. (New York: CRC Press, 2008).

42. Andrew McGregor, "Jihad and the Rifle Alone: 'Abdullah 'Azzam and the Islamist Revolution," *Journal of Conflict Studies* 23, no. 2 (Fall 2003).

43. Abdullah Azzam, "Notes on Jihad, Jihad Quotes," http://salafiyyah-jadeedah.tripod.com/Qital/Notes_on_Jihad.htm.
44. McCants and Brachman, *The Militant Ideology Atlas*, p. 353.
45. Evan Kohlman, *Al-Qaeda's Jihad in Europe* (Berg, NY: 2004).
46. McCants and Brachman, *The Militant Ideology Atlas*, p. 353.
47. Trevor Stanley, "Muhammad Abd al-Salam Faraj: Founder of Jama'at Al-Jihad, the Group That Killed Anwar Sadat," *Perspectives on World History and Current Events*, 2005, http://www.pwhce.org/faraj.html (downloaded on April 9, 2009).
48. Not to be confused with Salafist terror cells that have named themselves after this conceptual nomenclature. They include suicide bomber cells that attacked in Egypt (The Victorious Denomination, Al-Ta'ifa al-Mansoura) and in Iraq (The Army of the Victorious Sect, Jaysh Al-Tai'fa al-Mansoura).
49. Saleh al-Oufi, "Sout-ul-Jihaad Interviews Saleh al-Oufi, Voice of the Jihad," June 25, 2004, http://talk.islamicnetwork.com/showthread.php?t=485.

4: THE POLITICAL OBJECTIVES OF BIN LADENISM

1. Samuel P. Huntington, *The Clash of Civilizations and the Remaking of World Order* (New York: Simon and Schuster, 1998).
2. Osama bin Laden, interview with Taysir Alluni, Al Jazeera, October 21, 2001, in Bruce Lawrence, *Messages to the World: The Statements of Osama bin Laden* (London: Verso Press, 2005), p. 118.
3. Sayyid Qutb, *In the Shade of the Quran*, vol. 1 (Fi Dhilal al-Qur'an), http://d.scribd.com/docs/1b9w7zwopatbuqu52tew.pdf.
4. Steve Coll, *Ghost Wars* (New York: Penguin Press, 2004), p. 229.
5. Osama bin Laden, interview with Al Jazeera, in Lawrence, *Messages to the World*, p. 73.
6. Khalil Gebara, "The End of Egyptian Islamic Jihad?" *Terrorism Monitor* 3, no. 3 (February 9, 2005), http://www.jamestown.org/single/?no_cache=1&tx_ttnews%5Btt_news%5D=27523.
7. Ibid.
8. U.S. Army Combating Terrorism Center, "Translation of Captured Documents Al Qaeda Organization, AFGP-2002-000080," West Point, New York, 2002.
9. Osama bin Laden, interview with Al Jazeera, December 1998, in Lawrence, *Messages to the World*, p. 91.
10. Lawrence, *Messages to the World*.
11. Alec Gallup, Gallup Poll of the Islamic World, February 26, 2002, p. 11.
12. Frank Newport, Gallup Poll of the Islamic World, February 26, 2002, p. 5.
13. Ibid. p. 3.
14. Osama bin Laden, interview with Peter Arnett, CNN transcript, March 1997.
15. Ibn Taymaiyya, *Collection of Fatwas (Majmu' al-Fatawa)*, vol. 28. (Antiquarian document.)
16. Octavia Nasr and Pam Benson, "Purported Bin Laden Message: Iraq Is 'Perfect Base' for Jihad," CNN, March 20, 2008, http://edition.cnn.com/2008/WORLD/meast/03/20/binladen.message/index.html.
17. Osama bin Laden, interview with Taysir Alluni, Al Jazeera, October 21, 2001, in Lawrence, *Messages to the World*, p. 107.
18. Stephen Kull, "Public Opinion in the Islamic World on Terrorism, Al Qaeda, and U.S. Policies," *World Public Opinion*, February 25, 2009.
19. Ibid.
20. Osama bin Laden, interview with Al Jazeera, November 3, 2001, in Lawrence, *Messages to the World*, p. 136.

21. Sayyid Qutb, *The America I Have Seen: In the Scale of Human Values* (Lahore: Kashf ul Shubat Publications, 2007).
22. Newport, Gallup Poll of the Islamic World, p. 5.
23. Lawrence, *Messages to the World.*
24. Osama bin Laden, videotaped statement to Taysir Alluni, Al Jazeera, October 7, 2001, in Lawrence, *Messages to the World*, p. 104.
25. U.S. Department of Justice, "UK/BM-5 Translation of the al Qaeda Manual," http://www .usdoj.gov/ag/manualpart1_1.pdf.
26. Kull, "Public Opinion in the Islamic World on Terrorism, Al Qaeda, and U.S. Policies."
27. Muhammad 'Abdus Salam Faraj, *Jihad: The Absent Obligation*, (Brimingham, UK: Almaktabah al-Ansaar, 2000) p. 44.
28. Kull, "Public Opinion in the Islamic World on Terrorism, Al Qaeda, and U.S. Policies."
29. Qur'an 16:126.
30. Anne Stenersen, "The Internet: A Virtual Training Camp," Norwegian Defence Research Establishment, October 26–28, 2008.
31. MEMRI, "Bin Laden Lieutenant Admits to September 11 and Explains al-Qa'ida's Combat Doctrine," Special Counterterrorism Dispatch no. 344, February 10, 2002.
32. Dr. Gail Luft, "Breaking Oil's Monopoly in the Transportation Sector," July 22, 2008, Senate Committee on Homeland Security and Security Affairs, http://hsgac.senate.gov/ public/_files/072208Luft.pdf.
33. Ibid.
34. Osama bin Laden, audiotape to Al Jazeera, CNN, November 2, 2004, http://edition.cnn .com/2004/WORLD/meast/11/01/binladen.tape/.
35. B. Raman, *Mulla Omar to Lead Jihadi Intifada—What Happened to Bin Laden?* International Terrorism Monitor, Paper no. 187, South Asia Analysis Group, February 13, 2007, http:// www.southasiaanalysis.org/%5Cpapers22%5Cpaper2134.html.

5: THE CULT OF DEATH

1. Hadith al-Baqara, p. 190.
2. The Islam Project, "Frontline: Muslims," Carnegie Foundation, http://www.islampro ject.org/muslims/muslims.htm.
3. Bernard P. Lewis, "Jihad vs. Crusade," *Wall Street Journal*, September 27, 2001, http:// www.opinionjournal.com/extra/?id=95001224.
4. Ibid.
5. Abdullah Azzam, "Two Types of Jihad," Harakat al-Mujahideen Web site, www.harkat ulmujahideen.org/jihad/t-jihad.htm.
6. "Interview with Mujahid Usamah Bin Ladin," *Nida'ul Islam*, 15th issue (October–November 1996).
7. "Fighting in the Jihad and Visiting the Battlefronts," 1997, www.azzambrigades.com.
8. Ibid.
9. Ibid.
10. Hadiths Sinun al-Tirmidh and Ibn Majah.
11. Bruce Lawrence, *Messages to the World: The Statements of Osama bin Laden* (London: Verso Press, 2005), p. 97.
12. Muhammad 'Abdus Salam Faraj, *Jihad: The Absent Obligation*, p. 79.
13. Osama bin Laden, interview with Taysir Alluni, Al Jazeera, October 21, 2001, in Lawrence, *Messages to the World*, p. 118.
14. Qur'an 8:17.

15. David Aaron, *In Their Own Words: Voices of Jihad* (Santa Monica, CA: Rand Corporation, 2008), p. 107.

16. "The True Meaning of Shaheed, Harakat al-Mujahideen, www.harkatulmujahideen. org/jihad/t-shahed.htm, January 14, 1999.

17. "Abu Ruqaiyah," *Nida'ul Islam*, 16th issue (December–January 1996–1997), http://www. islam.org.au.

18. Hadiths Sahih Bukhari and Sahih Muslim.

19. "Abu Ruqaiyah, *Nida'ul Islam*."

20. U.S. Department of Justice, "UK/BM-5 Translation of the al Qaeda Manual," http://www .usdoj.gov/ag/manualpart1_1.pdf.

21. Mujahid Usamah bin Ladin, "Powder Keg in the Middle East," *Nida'ul Islam*, 15th issue (October–November 1996).

22. Qur'an 7:40.

23. "UK/BM-5 Translation of the al Qaeda Manual."

24. Ibid.

25. Sir Andrew Tumbull and John Gieve, Memorandum: Relations with the Muslim Community, British Home Office, April 6, 2004.

26. "UK/BM-5 Translation of the al Qaeda Manual."

27. Interview with Professor Khaled Abou al Fadle, *Frontline*: "Faith and Doubt at Ground Zero," Public Broadcasting System, transcript found at http://www.pbs.org/wgbh/pages/ frontline/shows/faith/interviews/elfadl.html

28. Owais Tohid, "Injured Islamic Militant Tells of U.S. Missile Attack," AFP, August 22, 1998.

29. Osama bin Laden, interview with Peter Arnett, CNN transcript, March 1997.

30. Aaron, *In Their Own Words*, pp. 21–22.

31. Dr. Umar Al-Ashqar, *The Final Day: Paradise and Hell in the Light of the Quran and Sunnah* (Riyadh: International Islamic Publishing House, 2004).

32. Qur'an 39: 53.

33. "Singer Killed at Attack on Algerian Nightclub," *Telegraph*, June 19, 2001, http://www.tele graph.co.uk/news/worldnews/asia/1379322/Singer-killed-in-attack-at-Algerian-night-club.html.

34. Charisse Jones, "The Agonizing Road for Kids of September 11," *USA Today*, October 19, 2001, http://www.usatoday.com/news/sept11/2001/10/19/kids-usatcov.htm.

35. Associated Press, "Female Suicide Bomber Kills 40 in Iraq," *Wall Street Journal*, http:// online.wsj.com/article/SB123452319916382281.html.

6: AFGHANISTAN-PAKISTAN:
THE NEW TAKFIRI EMIRATE OF OSAMA BIN LADEN

1. Prophet Mohammed to Zaid bin Khalid, Hadith Sahih Bukhari.

2. "Interview with Mujahid Usamah bin Ladin," *Nida'ul Islam*, 15th issue (October–November 1996).

3. Osama bin Laden, written statement to Al Jazeera, September 24, 2001, in Bruce Lawrence, *Messages to the World: The Statements of Osama bin Laden* (London: Verso Press, 2005), p. 101.

4. Octavia Nasr and Pam Benson, "Purported bin Laden Message: Iraq Is 'Perfect Base' for Jihad," CNN, March 20, 2008, http://edition.cnn.com/2008/WORLD/meast/03/20/bin laden.message/index.html

5. Ayman al-Zawahiri, letter to Abu Mussab al-Zarqawi, 2005.

6. Ron Moreau, Sami Yousafzai, and Michael Hirsh, "The Rise of Jihadistan," *Newsweek*, October 2, 2006.

7. Ron Suskind, *The One Percent Doctrine* (New York: Simon and Schuster, 2006), p. 27.

8. U.S. Department of the Treasury, Terrorism and Financial Intelligence Unit, list of charities designated as supporters of terrorist organizations designated under Executive Order 13224, December 20, 2001, http://www.treas.gov/offices/enforcement/key-issues/protecting/charities_execorder_13224-p.shtml#u.

9. Suskind, *The One Percent Doctrine*, p. 70.

10. Office of the Director of National Intelligence, *Unclassified Report to Congress on the Acquisition of Technology Relating to Weapons of Mass Destruction and Advanced Conventional Munitions*, May 2006.

11. Mike Boettcher and Ingrid Arnesen, "Al Qaeda Documents Outline Serious Weapons Program," CNN, January 25, 2002, http://www.isis-online.org/publications/terrorism/cnnstory.html.

12. Osama bin Laden, interview with Al Jazeera, December 1998, in Lawrence, *Messages to the World: The Statements of Osama bin Laden*, p. 72.

13. Ibid.

14. Reuven Paz, "Yes to WMD, the First Islamist Fatwah on the Use of Weapons of Mass Destruction," [Project for the Research of Islamist Movements], *PRISM Special Dispatches* 1, no. 1 (May 2003).

15. "Pakistan Nuclear Weapons Program, Federation of American Scientists," http://www.fas.org/nuke/guide/pakistan/nuke/.

16. Khaled Abou El Fadl, *The Great Theft* (New York: HarperCollins, 2007), p. 76.

17. Osama bin Laden, interview with Taysir Alluni, Al Jazeera, October 21, 2001, in Lawrence, *Messages to the World*, p. 128.

18. U.S. Department of Justice, "UK/BM-5 Translation of the al Qaeda Manual," http://www.usdoj.gov/ag/manualparti_1.pdf.

19. Bernard Lewis, 2007 Irving Kristol Award, American Enterprise Institute, March 20, 2007, http://www.aei.org/publications/pubID.25815,filter.all/pub_detail.asp.

20. Ibid.

21. Osama bin Laden, interview with Al Jazeera, December 1998, in Lawrence, *Messages to the World*, p. 78.

7: RALLYING TO THE DEFENSE OF ISLAM

1. Abdullah Azzam, "Notes on Jihad, Jihad Quotes," http://salafiyyah-jadeedah.tripod.com/Qital/Notes_on_Jihad.htm.

2. Saeed Haider, "Attacks Leave Many Unanswered Questions," *Arab News*, June 2, 2004, http://www.arabnews.com/?page=1&section=0&article=46135&d=2&m=6&y=2004&pix=kingdom.jpg&category=Kingdom.

3. David Aaron, *In Their Own Words: Voices of Jihad* (Santa Monica, CA: Rand Corporation, 2008), p. 28.

4. Ibid.

5. Steve Coll, *Ghost Wars* (New York: Penguin Press, 2004), p. 229.

6. "Saudi Arabia: A New Crackdown on Mujahideen," *Global Muslim News*, April 21, 1998, www.azzambriagdes.com.

7. Osama bin Laden, interview with Peter Arnett, CNN transcript, March 1997.

8. al-Qurtubi, *Ahkaam al-Qur'an* 8/94. (Antiquarian document.)

9. Philip Shenon, "Saudis Rebuffed United States Efforts to Interrogate 1995 Bombers," *New York Times*, June 28, 1996, http://www.nytimes.com/1996/06/28/world/bombing-saudi-arabia-security-saudis-rebuffed-us-efforts-interrogate-1995.html.

10. "Defense Department Briefing: Bombing Incident, Dhahran, Saudi Arabia, 25 June, 1996," http://www.globalsecurity.org/intell/library/news/1996/x062696_x0625bom.html.

11. Mujahid Osamah bin Ladin, "Powder Keg in the Middle East," *Nida'ul Islam*, 15th issue (October–November 1996), www.islam.org.au.

12. "Interview with Mujahid Usamah bin Ladin," *Nida'ul Islam*, 15th issue (October–November 1996).

13. Ibid.

14. "Saudi Authorities Blame Alcohol Traders for Bombing," *Guardian*, September 30, 2002, http://www.guardian.co.uk/world/2002/sep/30/saudiarabia.

15. Susan Taylor Martin, "Target: Westerners," the *Saint Petersburg Times*, July 22, 2002, http://www.sptimes.com/2002/webspecials02/saudiarabia/day2/story1.shtml.

16. "American Killed in Suicide Blast," CBS News, http://www.cbsnews.com/stories/2001/10/06/world/main313823.shtml.

17. "Sout-ul-Jihaad Interviews Saleh Al-Oufi," *Voice of the Jihad*, June 25, 2004, http://talk.islamicnetwork.com/showthread.php?t=485.

18. Aaron, *In Their Own Words*, p. 85.

19. "Calls to Intensify Fighting During Ramadan—'the Month of Jihad,'" MEMRI Special Dispatch no. 804, *Sawt al-Jihad*, October 22, 2004.

20. "Interview with Mujahid Usamah bin Ladin."

21. Ibid.

22. "Sout-ul-Jihaad Interviews Saleh al-Oufi."

23. Roger Harrison and Javid Hassan, "Al-Qaeda Chief in Kingdom Killed," *Arab News*, August 18, 2005.

24. "Global Poll Finds That Religion and Culture Are Not to Blame for Tensions Between Islam and the West," BBC World Opinion Poll, 2007.

25. Ibid.

26. Ibid.

27. Interview with Prof. Khaled Abou al Fadl, "Faith and Doubt at Ground Zero," *Frontline*, Public Broadcasting System, transcript found at http://www.pbs.org/wgbh/pages/frontline/shows/faith/interviews/elfadl.html.

28. 'Abdullah al-Athari, *Islamic Beliefs—A Brief Introduction to the Aqidah of the Ahl as Sunnah wal Jama'ah* (Riyadh: International Islamic Publishing House, 2004), p. 193.

29. Fatwa of Sheikh Ibn Taymaiyya, Majmoo'ul Fataawaa (20/164). (Antiquarian document.)

30. Tim Winter (aka Dr. Abdal Hakim Murad), "Bin Laden's Violence Is a Heresy Against Islam," Council of American-Islamic Relations (CAIR), http://www.cair.com/AmericanMuslims/AntiTerrorism/BinLadensviolenceisaheresyagainstIslam.aspx.

31. Miriam al-Hakeem, "Bin Laden Is the Preacher of Evil, Says Saudi Scholar," *Gulf News*, July 10, 2008, http://www.gulfnews.com/news/gulf/saudi_arabia/10227813.html.

32. Council on American Islamic Relations, "Response to September 11, 2001, Attacks," March 28, 2007.

33. Osama bin Laden, interview with Al Jazeera, December 1998, in Bruce Lawrence, *Messages to the World: The Statements of Osama bin Laden* (London: Verso Press, 2005), p. 80.

34. Ibid.

35. Bernard P. Lewis, "License to Kill, Usama bin Laden's Declaration of Jihad," *Foreign Affairs*, November 1998, p. 14.

36. Council on American Islamic Relations, "Response to September 11, 2001, Attacks," March 28, 2007, p. 15.

37. Paolo Pontoniere, "Al Qaeda—Call It a Cult," *Asia Week*, November 22, 2001.

38. Osama bin Laden, interview with Al Jazeera, November 3, 2001, in Lawrence, *Messages to the World*, p. 136.

39. Isambard Wilkinson, "Taliban Blocks UN Polio Treatment in Pakistan," *Telegraph*, March 26, 2009.

40. "Taliban Order NGOs to Leave Swat," *Daily Times*, March 23, 2009, http://www.daily times.com.pk/default.asp?page=2009\03\23\story_23-3-2009_pg1_8.

41. Sheikh Ṣāliḥ al-Fawzān in answer to question asked on answering extremism, http:// www.answering-extremism.com/ae/reader.aspx?file=ae_saf_2.pdf&CFID=8629105& CFTOKEN=25768314.

42. Abdullah Azzam, Last Will and Testament, April 20, 1986.

43. Qur'an Surah At-Taubah, verse 5.

44. Qur'an 4: 29–30.

45. "In Speech on Terrorism, Kerry Responds to Sec. Gates' National Defense Strategy Assessment," July 31, 2008, http://kerry.senate.gov/cfm/record.cfm?id=301602.

46. Osama bin Laden, interview with Al Jazeera, December 1998, in Lawrence, *Messages to the World*, 103.

8: REFRAMING AMERICA, REFRAMING AL-QAEDA

1. Interview with Prof. Khaled Abou El Fadl, "Faith and Doubt at Ground Zero," *Frontline*, Public Broadcasting System, transcript found at http://www.pbs.org/wgbh/pages/front line/shows/faith/interviews/elfadl.html.

2. Osama bin Laden, interview with Al Jazeera, November 3, 2001, in Bruce Lawrence, *Messages to the World: The Statements of Osama bin Laden* (London: Verso Press, 2005), p. 135.

3. Stephen Kull, "Public Opinion in the Islamic World on Terrorism, Al Qaeda, and U.S. Policies," *World Public Opinion*, February 25, 2009.

4. Osama bin Laden, letter posted on the Internet, October 6, 2002, in Lawrence, *Messages to the World*, p. 170.

5. Osama bin Laden, interview with Taysir Alluni, Al Jazeera, October 21, 2001, in Lawrence, *Messages to the World*, p. 107.

6. "Al-Qaeda Issues Pakistan Threat," BBC, July 11, 2007, http://news.bbc.co.uk/2/hi/south _asia/6293914.stm.

7. Mujahid Usamah Bin Ladin, "Powder Keg in the Middle East," *Nida'ul Islam*, 15th issue (October–November 1996).

8. "Al-Qaeda Tape Rejects Annapolis," BBC, December 31 2007, http://news.bbc.co.uk/2/ hi/middle_east/7144515.stm.

9. Kull, "Public Opinion in the Islamic World on Terrorism, Al Qaeda, and U.S. Policies."

10. Ibid.

11. David A. Snow et al., "Frame Alignment Processes, Micromobilization, and Movement Participation," *American Sociological Review* 51 (1986).

12. Joas Wagemakers, "Framing the Threat to Islam: Al-Qala' Wa al-Bara' in Salafi Discourse," *Arab Studies Quarterly* 30, no. 4 (Fall 2008).

13. President Barack Obama, transcript: "Crossroads in Turkey," April 6, 2009, White House, Washington, D.C.

14. John Simpson, "Battling the al-Qaeda Franchise," BBC, October 3, 2005, http://news.bbc. co.uk/2/hi/asia-pacific/4304516.stm.

15. Malcolm W. Nance, *The Terrorists of Iraq* (Charleston, SC: Book Surge, 2007).

16. Ibid.

9: BREAK THE LINKS TO ISLAM:
WAGING COUNTER-IDEOLOGICAL WARFARE

1. Osama bin Laden, interview with Taysir Alluni, Al Jazeera, October 21, 2001, Bruce Lawrence, *Messages to the World: The Statements of Osama bin Laden* (London: Verso Press, 2005), p. 128.
2. National Security Council, The National Strategy for Combating Terrorism, 2006.
3. National Counterterrorism Center, www.nctc.gov.
4. James Dao and Eric Schmitt, "Pentagon Readies Efforts to Sway Sentiments Abroad," *New York Times*, February 19, 2002.
5. Vincent Vitto, *Report of the Defense Science Board Task Force on Strategic Communications*, September 2004.
6. Senate Committee on Homeland Security and Government Affairs, "Confronting the Terrorist Threat to the Homeland: Six Years After 9/11," http://www.dni.gov/testimonies/20070910_transcript.pdf.
7. Ibid.
8. Thom Shanker, "Pentagon Closes Office Accused of Issuing Propaganda Under Bush," April 15, 2009, *New York Times*, http://www.nytimes.com/2009/04/16/us/politics/16policy.html?_r=1&ref=politics.
9. John Brown, "Out to Pasture," *Guardian*, November 2, 2007.
10. General Accounting Office, *U.S. Public Diplomacy: Actions Needed to Improve Strategic Use and Coordination of Research*, GAO-07-904, July 18, 2007.
11. Ibid.
12. James K. Glassman, "America Knows That Bullets Alone Will Not Win This War," *Independent*, September 16, 2008, http://www.independent.co.uk/opinion/commentators/james-k-glassman-america-knows-that-bullets-alone-will-not-win-this-war-932016.html.
13. President Barack Obama, interview with Al Arabiya Arab TV network, January 26, 2009, http://www.huffingtonpost.com/2009/01/26/obama-al-arabiya-intervie_n_161127.html.
14. Adel Al-Jubeir, "Press Conference on National Campaign Against Terrorism and Extremism, Embassy of Saudi Arabia, Washington D.C., March 7, 2005," http://www.saudiembassy.net/2005News/News/NewsDetail.asp?cIndex=5108.
15. Roger Harrison and Javid Hassan, "Al-Qaeda Chief in Kingdom Killed," *Arab News*, August 18, 2005.
16. Osama bin Laden, interview with Taysir Alluni, in Lawrence, *Messages to the World*, p. 118.
17. Ibid.
18. "Bin Laden Praises al-Zarqawi," AP, June 30, 2006, http://www.msnbc.msn.com/id/13600778/.
19. Sultan al-Qassemi, "Al Qaeda Is Its Own Worst Enemy," *National*, September 13, 2008.
20. Hadiths Bukhari and Muslim.
21. 'Abdullah al-Athari, *Islamic Beliefs—A Brief Introduction to the Aqidah of the Ahl as Sunnah wal Jama'ah* (Riyadh: International Islamic Publishing House, 2004), p. 215.
22. Qur'an 4: 93.
23. Qur'an Surah al-Hujurât 49, verse 6.
24. Osama bin Laden interview with *al-Ausaf* newspaper, November 12, 2001, in Lawrence, *Messages to the World*, p. 141.
25. Sheik Ṣāliḥ al-Fawzān, reply to question asked on "Answering Extremism," http://www.answering-extremism.com/ae/reader.aspx?file=ae_saf_2.pdf&CFID=8629105&CFTOKEN=25768314.
26. Sahih Bukhari, vol. 9, book 83, "Blood Money (Ad-Diyat)," no. 12.

27. Mawassi Lahcen, Jamel Arfaoui, and Said Jameh, "Maghreb Reacts to Latest Book by al-Qaeda Mastermind Dr. Fadl," *al-Maghrebia*, March 13, 2009.
28. "Bin Laden PR Push Seen to Reflect Islamist Rivalry," Reuters, May 20, 2008.
29. President Barack Obama, transcript, "Remarks of President Obama at Strasbourg Town Hall," Talking Points Memo, April 4, 2009, http://www.talkingpointsmemo.com/news/2009/04/transcript_remarks_by_president_obama_at_strasbour.php.
30. "Bin Laden PR Push Seen to Reflect Islamist Rivalry."
31. William McCants and Jarrett Brachman, *The Militant Ideology Atlas* (West Point, NY: Combating Terrorism Center, U.S. Military Academy, 2005).
32. www.jihadica.com.
33. Abdul Hameed Bakier, "Watching the Watchers," *Terrorism Focus* 5, no. 33 (September 18, 2008), http://www.jamestown.org/programs/gta/single/?tx_ttnews[tt_news]=5159&tx_ttnews[backPid]=246&no_cache=1.
34. Iqbal Latif, "Sayyid Imam al-Sharif (Dr Fadl) Takes Islam Out of the Alqaeda Equation Leaving Only Criminality Behind," *Newsvine*, February 22, 2009, http://iqballatif.newsvine.com/_news/2009/02/22/2464940-sayyid-imam-al-sharif-dr-fadl-takes-islam-out-of-the-alqaeda-equation-leaving-only-criminality-behind.
35. Lawrence Wright, "The Heretic," *Guardian*, July 13, 2008, http://www.guardian.co.uk/world/2008/jul/13/heretic.alqaida.part.one.
36. Ron Synovitz, "Afghanistan: Al-Qaeda Bloggers' Sparring with Taliban Could Signal Key Differences," Radio Free Europe/*Liberty*, March 12, 2008.
37. Ibid.
38. Ibid.
39. Woodrow Wilson Center for International Scholars, "Civilian Casualties in Afghanistan: Compensation, Aid, and Relief Efforts," February 18, 2009, http://www.wilsoncenter.org/index.cfm?topic_id=1462&fuseaction=topics.event_summary&event_id=502605.
40. Joby Warrick and Candace Rondeaux, "Extremist Web Sites Are Using United States Hosts," *Washington Post*, April 9, 2009, http://www.washingtonpost.com/wp-dyn/content/article/2009/04/08/AR2009040804378.html.
41. Robert F. Worth, "Saudis Retool to Root Out Terrorist Risk," *New York Times*, March 31, 2009, http://www.nytimes.com/2009/03/22/world/middleeast/22saudi.html.
42. "In Speech on Terrorism, Kerry Responds to Sec. Gates' National Defense Strategy Assessment," July 31, 2008, http://kerry.senate.gov/cfm/record.cfm?id=301602.
43. *Beyond Terrorism: Deradicalization and Disengagement from Violent Extremism* (New York: International Peace Institute Publications), p. 6.
44. Jonathan S. Landay, "Do U.S. Drones Kill Pakistani Extremists or Recruit Them?" McLachy Newspapers, April 7, 2009.
45. Osama bin Laden, audiotape to International Conference of Deobandis, April 9, 2001, in Lawrence, *Messages to the World*, p. 97.
46. U.S. Army Combating Terrorism Center, "Translation of captured documents of al-Qaeda organization," AFGP-2002-000080, West Point, New York, 2002.
47. Sahih Bukhari, vol. 1, p. 391.
48. Abu Huraira Radhiallahuanhu, narrator, "The Grade of the Mujahideen," December 9, 1998, http://hafsallah.multiply.com/notes/item/78.
49. Ibid.
50. Sean O'Neill, "New bin Laden Recording Predicts al-Qaeda Leader's Own Death," *Telegraph*, February 13, 2003, http://www.telegraph.co.uk/news/uknews/1421954/New-bin-Laden-recording-predicts-al-Qaeda-leaders-own-death.html.
51. Osama bin Laden, transcript of December 13, 2001, videotape, translated by George Michael and Dr. Kassem M. Wahba, http://www.defenselink.mil/news/Dec2001/d20011213ubl.pdf.

10: CIRCUIT BREAKER STRATEGY: THE TOTAL SHUTDOWN OF AL-QAEDA

1. Frank Newport, Gallup Poll of the Islamic World, February 26, 2002, p. 5.
2. Matt Armstrong, "The False Hope of the President's Public Diplomacy," Mountain Runner Blog, http://mountainrunner.us/2009/04/false_hope.html.
3. Eben Kaplan, "The Rise of al-Qaedaism," Council on Foreign Relations, http://www.cfr.org/publication/11033#8.
4. U.S. Department of the Army, Counterinsurgency, United States Army Field Manual FM 3-34, December 2006
5. U.S. Department of Defense, *Quadrennial Roles and Missions Review Report*, http://www.defenselink.mil/news/Jan2009/QRMFinalReport_v26Jan.pdf.
6. Karen Hughes, "Transcript: The Situation Room," CNN, October 22, 2007.
7. Business for Diplomatic Action, http://www.businessfordiplomaticaction.org/who/index.html.
8. Max Boot, "The Future of Information Operations," *Commentary*, April 16, 2009, http://www.commentarymagazine.com/blogs/index.php/boot/62462#comment-3620631.
9. Rasha Elass, "Anger Hinders Muslim Progress: Scholar," *National*, Abu Dhabi, November 17, 2008, http://www.acommonword.com/en/a–common-word-in-the-news/14-general-news/136-anger-hinders-muslim-progress-scholar.html.
10. Ibid.
11. Sheikh Abdulaziz al Rayyis, transcription from audio recording of "Al-Wala' Wa al-Bara'," part 2.
12. Interview with Professor Khaled Abou al Fadl, "Faith and Doubt at Ground Zero," *Frontline*, Public Broadcasting System, transcript found at http://www.pbs.org/wgbh/pages/frontline/shows/faith/interviews/elfadl.html.

Acknowledgements

This book could not have been made possible without the help of my family and friends. Special thanks goes out to my sister, a devoted Muslima and American patriot who knows more about the human motivation of bin Laden's cultist terrorists than all of the world's intelligence agencies. For seven long years my family never stopped giving me unlimited support to ensure that any solution to bring al-Qaeda to justice involves adhering to the core values of American democracy and Islam's peacefulness. Further thanks go out to my agent, Ryan Fischer-Harbage, and editor, Marc Resnick, both of whom worked tirelessly to put my beliefs and knowledge into print. My friends "Koch of Kuwait," Ali Hassan, Linda, Stina, the counter-insurgency warriors at the *Small War's Journal* and the contributors of the counter-ideology Web site *Jihadica* all gave valuable insights into developing the tools of a global counter-ideology strategy to break al-Qaeda.

Index

Iran, Islamic Republic of, 50, 63
Iraq
  AQI in, 44, 49, 52, 80–81, 110, 151–53, 174–75, 204, 211, 271
  collateral damage in, 29, 30, 134, 136–37, 194–95, 200,
    241–42, 248–49
  due legal process in, 53
  embargo on, 186, 242
  Hussein in, 45, 49, 50, 52
  Islamic Emirate of, 9, 151–52, 212
  Kurds in, 49
  oil in, 123, 200, 204
  U. S. invasion of, 19, 22, 47, 50, 51, 52–53, 110, 126, 150,
    151, 211
  U. S. strategic communications about, 28–29, 198–99,
    220–21
Iraqi Intelligence Service/Special Forces, 2, 9
Iraqi Ministry of the Interior, 2
Iraqi Sunnah Insurgents, 2, 9, 55, 64
irja (tolerance), 7, 190, 256
IRTPA. *See* Intelligence Reform and Terrorism
  Prevention Act
Islam
  AQ corruption of, 6, 34–36, 42, 52, 53, 56–67, 87, 103,
    126, 132, 179, 183, 228
  AQ link to, 10, 27, 35, 59, 164, 193, 206, 209, 213, 226–49
  AQ/OBL as threat to, 144, 205, 208–9
  Baghy for, 35, 233–34, 237–38
  Barelvis of, 54
  Bid'ah in, 34, 38–39, 58, 131–32, 179, 181
  Christianity and, 27, 41, 42, 52, 53, 64, 68, 82–84, 97,
    101, 103, 105, 109, 161–64, 199, 203, 208
  as conservative/traditional, 27, 33, 42, 54–55, 66, 181,
    218
  cults within, 3, 6, 8, 11, 39, 54–57, 65–66, 69, 101, 134,
    185–88, 189, 193, 227, 262
  diversity of, 54
  empowerment of, 36, 161, 192
  expansion of, 41
  history of, 70–76
  Ibadis of, 54, 69, 74
  image of, 2, 53–54
  irja by, 7, 190, 256
  Mahdi for, 72, 73, 76
  missionary work by, 27, 230–31
  Mongols/Khanates and, 84–86, 97, 109, 161, 181
  murder of innocents and, 5, 15–18, 65–67, 94, 95, 133–34,
    192–93, 229–30, 241–42
  of OBL, 6, 65–66
  Salafism and, 5, 23, 32, 36, 63, 75–80, 96–98, 101, 104,
    106–7, 114–16, 127–32, 151, 161, 173, 178, 181–82, 237–38,
    254
  scholars of, 54, 87–96
  suicide and, 2, 3, 5, 7, 18–19, 23, 47, 53, 57, 63, 110, 119, 125,
    132, 137, 139, 140, 141, 143–44, 151, 162, 173–74, 187, 193,
    204, 241
  Sunnah/Shiite split in, 54, 71–73, 184
  Takfir for, 9, 24, 26, 34–35, 44, 72, 78–79, 81, 92, 93,
    97–98, 99, 104, 106–8, 114, 117, 119, 126, 130, 132–34,
    136, 138, 157, 164, 169–70, 179, 188–91, 207, 233–34,
    251–52
  Taliban and, 37, 39, 116, 149, 154, 189, 239–40, 249, 250
  ulema of, 54, 58, 106
  Ummah for, 7, 102, 105, 112–13, 124, 129–30, 140, 171,
    178, 181, 182, 193, 252
  values of, 112–13
  Wahabism of, 54, 57, 77, 142–43, 189
  al-Wala' Wa al-Bara' for, 34, 79–81, 98, 117, 132, 144, 179,
    185, 190, 205, 230, 269
  Witness/Shahada for, 3, 33, 114, 128

Islam Channel, 255, 267
Islambouli, Khaled, 95–96, 147
Islamic Caliphate. *See* New Islamic Caliphate
Islamic Courts Union, 19
Islamic Emirate of Afghanistan, 20, 38, 116, 148, 153–54,
  249
Islamic Emirate of Iraq, 151, 212
Islamic Group, 94, 132, 237
Islamic Jihad Bureau, 147
Islamic Jihad Organization (IJO), 5, 63
Islamic Religious Research Center, 183
Islamic Salvation Army (AIS), 237
Israel / the enemy, 111, 114–15, 161, 218
ITIRAD, 261–62
IWB. *See* Information Warfare Battlelab

Jahiliyyah, 91–92, 93
al-Jamma' al-Islamiyya, 18, 47, 247
Al Jazeera (television), 100, 105, 116, 168, 193, 228–29, 248,
  267
JCIE. *See* Joint Counter-Ideology Executive
al-Jifri, Aheikh al-Habib Ali, 268–69
Jihad: The Absent Obligation (Faraj), 85–86
Jihad Group, 90, 95–96
Johnson, Paul, 175–76
Joint Counter-Ideology Executive (JCIE), 260–61
Al-Jubeir, Adel, 227
Jusbah-E-Jihad ("Emotion of Jihad Intoxication"),
  141

Kagan, Frederick W., 22
Kahuta nuclear research facility.
  See A. Q. Khan Research Laboratories
Kalin, Ibrahim, 89–90
Karmal, Babrak, 145
Karzai, Hamid, 240
Kenya, bombing in, 6, 66, 127
Kerry, John, 192, 247
Khabbab, Abu, 158–59
Khan, Abdul Qadeer, 160
Khan, Genghis, 84, 181
Khan, Mohammad Daoud, 145
Khan, Muslim, 187
Khanates/Mongols, 84–86, 97, 109, 161, 181
al-Khattab, Umar ibn, 70
Khawarij (outsider), 3, 54, 71–73, 101, 133, 164, 181, 184, 188,
  231–32
al-Khawarij, Ibadi sect of, 54, 69, 74
Khobar Towers, massacre at, 6, 167, 171–72, 173, 175
Kingdom of Saudi Arabia. *See* Saudi Arabia, Kingdom of
Kitab al-Tawhid (Abd al-Wahab), 96
KSA. *See* Saudi Arabia, Kingdom of
Kuwait, invasion of, 147–48, 169, 233

Laheedan, Saleh Al, 182–83
Land of the Two Holy Shrines. *See* Saudi Arabia,
  Kingdom of
Lashkar-e-Jangvi, 48
Lashkar-e-Taiba, 48
Lebanon, 5, 19, 48, 50, 63
"The Letter of Demands," 169
Leventhal, Todd, 223
Lewis, Bernard P., 83, 128, 162–63, 184
al-Libi, Abu Yahya, 9, 97, 226, 250, 270
Lieberman, Avigdor, 50
Lieberman, Joseph, 222
Lincoln Group, 221
"Lion of Panjshir." *See* Masoud, Ahmed Shah
Long War. *See* bin Laden, Osama; War on Terrorism